Hayek's Political Theory, Epistemology, and Economics

Hayek thought that all economic behavior (and by implication other human behavior) is based on fallible interpretations of what information is important and of its implications for the future. This epistemological idea animated not only his heterodox economic thought, but his ideal of the rule of law; his road-to-serfdom thesis; and his critique of the notion of social justice. However, the epistemological idea is a protean one that Hayek did not always handle carefully. This volume presents one of the most sophisticated critical reflections on Hayek ever assembled between two covers.

This book was originally published as a special issue of *Critical Review*.

Jeffrey Friedman, a visiting scholar in the Department of Government, University of Texas at Austin, USA, received an MA in History from the University of California, Berkeley, USA, and an MA and Ph.D. in Political Science from Yale University, USA. He is the editor of *Critical Review: A Journal of Politics and Society*.

Hayek's Political Theory, Epistemology, and Economics

Edited by
Jeffrey Friedman

Routledge
Taylor & Francis Group

LONDON AND NEW YORK

First published 2015
by Routledge

2 Park Square, Milton Park, Abingdon, Oxfordshire OX14 4RN
711 Third Avenue, New York, NY 10017

Routledge is an imprint of the Taylor & Francis Group, an informa business

First issued in paperback 2018

British Library Cataloguing in Publication Data
A catalogue record for this book is available from the British Library

ISBN 13: 978-1-138-82251-1 (hbk)
ISBN 13: 978-1-138-37953-4 (pbk)

Typeset in Bembo
by RefineCatch Limited, Bungay, Suffolk

Publisher's Note
The publisher accepts responsibility for any inconsistencies that may have
arisen during the conversion of this book from journal articles to book chapters,
namely the possible inclusion of journal terminology.

Disclaimer
Every effort has been made to contact copyright holders for their permission to
reprint material in this book. The publishers would be grateful to hear from any
copyright holder who is not here acknowledged and will undertake to rectify
any errors or omissions in future editions of this book.

This special issue of *Critical Review* was made possible through the support of
a grant from the John Templeton Foundation. The opinions expressed in this
publication are those of the authors and do not necessarily reflect the views of
the John Templeton Foundation.

Contents

CONTENTS

Citation Information

The chapters in this book were originally published in *Critical Review*, volume 25, issue 3-4 (November 2013). When citing this material, please use the original page numbering for each article, as follows:

Please direct any queries you may have about the citations to
clsuk.permissions@cengage.com

Notes on Contributors

Peter J. Boettke is University Professor in the Departments of Economics and Philosophy, George Mason University, Virginia, USA.

Jeffrey Friedman is a visiting scholar in the Department of Government, University of Texas at Austin, USA and the founder and editor of *Critical Review*.

Andrew Gamble is Professor in the Department of Politics and International Studies at the University of Cambridge, UK, and the author of *Hayek: The Iron Cage of Liberty* (1996).

François Godard is a doctoral student in comparative politics at the University of Geneva, Switzerland.

Daniel Kuehn is a doctoral student in the Department of Economics, American University, Washington D.C., USA.

Paul Lewis is Reader in Economics and Public Policy at King's College London, UK and currently Visiting Scholar at the Mercatus Center at George Mason University, Virginia, USA.

Andrew Lister is Associate Professor in the Department of Political Studies at Queen's University, Kingston, Canada.

Kyle W. O'Donnell is a PhD student in the Department of Economics, George Mason University, Virginia, USA and a visiting PhD student in the Department of Economics, New York University, USA.

Alan Ryan is Professor of Politics at Princeton University, New Jersey, USA and is the author of *The Making of Modern Liberalism* (2012).

Michael Strong is co-founder of the Flow Movement and works on the Conscious Capitalism project.

Karen I. Vaughn is Professor of Economics at George Mason University, Virginia, USA, and the author of Austrian Economics in America: The Migration of a Tradition (1994).

Jeffrey Friedman

HAYEK'S TWO EPISTEMOLOGIES AND THE PARADOXES OF HIS THOUGHT

ABSTRACT: *Hayek developed two contradictory epistemologies. The epistemology for which he is famous attributed dispersed knowledge to economic actors and credited the price system for aggregating and communicating this knowledge. The other epistemology attributed to human and non-human organisms alike the error-prone interpretation of stimuli, which could never truly be said to be "knowledge." Several of the paradoxes of Hayek's economic and political thought that are explored in this symposium can be explained by the triumph of the first epistemology over the second, including his historical interpretation of socialism as a planning mentality; his tendentious definitions of "liberty" and "justice"; and his opposition to economic redistribution even as he endorsed all manner of economic and social regulations.*

This is the third theme issue of *Critical Review* on F. A. Hayek. Introducing the second issue, in 1997,[1] I wrote that the first one, published in 1989,[2] had appeared "at the apogee of Hayek's political influence," when his ideas inspired many of the leaders of the Eastern European governments that had just come to power. By 1997, though, "Hayek's political influence" had been exposed, I wrote, as "ephemeral" (Friedman 1997, 1). That was premature. With the rise of the Tea Party and the assistance of

Glenn Beck, Hayek's *The Road to Serfdom* has become a best seller again. However, François Godard's contribution to this issue (Godard 2013) shows that Hayek's renewed popularity among libertarian conservatives is based on a misconception: that Hayek was an advocate of small government. In truth, he supported a vast range of government activities and did not seem to favor even a "limited" government: As long as government acted on the basis of general rules, Hayek would have had it provide a host of services and regulate a host of private activities. What Hayek opposed was "socialism." His definition of that term was shaped by what it had meant during the "socialist-calculation debate" in which he participated in the 1930s. At issue had been the possibility of centrally directing an entire economy according to a single plan.[3] In arguing against the feasibility of this type of socialism, Hayek maintained that the central planners would face insuperable epistemic barriers. But as he elaborated his epistemological position during the course of his career, he committed himself to the view that the "knowledge problem" facing central planners was solved, under capitalism, by the price system. It only stood to reason, then, that as long as government activities did not interfere with the price system (and took the form of general rules), Hayek had no fundamental objection to them.

Hayek's epistemological focus—emphosized here by Peter J. Boettke and Kyle W. O'Donnell (2013), Michael Strong (2013), Karen I. Vaughn (2013), and especially Paul Lewis (2013)—explains the ongoing interest of this journal in his work. As far as I know, no other major figure in any social science, including even Herbert Simon, was as preoccupied by questions of knowledge as Hayek was. In this respect, Hayek was exemplary and offers lessons for political theorists. Yet he was not entirely successful in answering the epistemological questions he asked, and his failures may explain some of the blind alleys to which his political theory led—dissected below by Andrew Gamble (2013), Andrew Lister (2013), and Alan Ryan (2013).

In this introduction I will pull together the successes and the failures by describing two contradictory strands of Hayekian epistemology. A relatively unknown strand, which is found in Hayek's completely apolitical *The Sensory Order*, is fallibilist and interpretivist. The more famous and politically charged strand, found in his paper on "The Use of Knowledge in Society" and in many later essays and books, leaves little room either for fallibility or interpretation, since it attributes "knowledge" to the participants in a capitalist order, albeit knowledge that is locally dispersed. This knowledge, reflected in prices, is supposed to be inaccessible to central planners, making a prosperous socialist economy impracticable.

Hayek's Interpretivist Epistemology

Hayek did not set out to be an economist. In 1920, while his future mentor, Ludwig von Mises, was launching the socialist-calculation debate (Mises 1920), Hayek was a law student who had, however, turned to the study of psychology and was writing a paper on neurobiology. This paper grew into *The Sensory Order*, published in 1952. Hayek later said: "The insights I gained—and I can't say now when—both from the first stage in 1920 or later," when he was writing the book in the 1940s, "were probably the most exciting events that ever happened to me, which shaped my thinking. But it works both ways. What I'd done in economics helped me to do this biological work as much as the opposite" (Kresge and Wenar 1994, 153).

The Sensory Order uses a fairly straightforward associationist psychology to describe learning at the neurological level. But from this Lockean foundation (with admixtures of Weber and ultimately Kant),[4] Hayek seeks to establish that facts—even primal facts such as sensations, not to mention perceptions—never speak for themselves. His "theory of the formation of sensory qualities," therefore, "is no more than an extension and systematic development of the widely held view that every sensation contains elements of interpretation" (Hayek 1952b, 42).

Hayek argues that we cannot sense "facts" that we are not pre-equipped to sense. The necessary equipment often consists not only of our sense organs and other neurology but, in addition, the central nervous system's registry of previous encounters with our (ultimately unknowable) environment. The stimuli produced by such experiences, when interpreted by the central nervous system, prepare an organism to notice similar experiences in the future.

The interpretive question is what qualifies, in the judgment (as it were) of the central nervous system, as a "similar" experience. Clearly this type of interpretation does not mean the exercise of "judgment" that is inspired or arbitrary. Indeed, in Hayek's account the organism (including the human organism) contributes nothing that might be thought of as "creative," in the ordinary sense of the word, to its ongoing interpretation of the environment. Instead, Hayek's psychological system, which he rightly calls a "theory of the determination of mental qualities" (Hayek 1952b, 53), attributes an organism's interpretation of sensations to the propensity of its central nervous system to make "linkages" among various stimuli that happen to be experienced at the same time (ibid., 107). A classification of contiguous stimuli as being associated with each other is an "interpretation." There is no spontaneity to it; it is strictly determined by the conjunction of stimuli with the neurological ability to associate them with each other.

Thus, "'sensation' and 'perception' ... constitute merely different stages in an even more comprehensive range of processes, all of which can be interpreted as acts of classification (or evaluation) performed by the central nervous system" (Hayek 1952b, 77). "The connexions formed by the linkages between different impulses," Hayek continues, "will evidently reproduce ... a sort of record of past associations of any particular stimulus with other stimuli which have acted upon the organism at the same time" (ibid., 107). As this record builds, it is abstracted into "signals reaching the higher and more comprehensive centres [that] will often not represent individual stimuli, but may stand for classes or groups of such stimuli formed at lower levels" (ibid., 109). Thus, "not merely a part but the whole of sensory qualities" is ultimately "an 'interpretation' based on the experience of the individual or the race" (ibid., 42). And "the principle used to explain these phenomena applies also to the so-called 'higher' mental process such as the formation of abstract concepts and conceptual thought" (ibid., 78). So a full name for Hayek's theory might be "the mechanical determination of perceptions and ideas by the associative interpretations created by previous experiences."

Although Hayek seemed reluctant to say so,[5] one aspect of his theory of interpretation relies as much on Darwin as Locke or Kant. The ability to sense certain stimuli and not others, the ability to associate contiguous stimuli, the ability to remember the associations, abstract from them, and engage thereby in conceptual thought; all, in Hayek's account, are adaptive for an organism in a particular environment, because they contribute to the ability to form somewhat reliable expectations about the environment. The "correct anticipation of future events in the environment ... implies that there exists inside the [neurological] structure a system of relationships between events caused by external circumstances which is in some measure structurally equivalent to the system of relationships which exists between those external events" (Hayek 1952b, 129). The factors that contribute to a neurological ability to "model" the organism's external environment in certain respects (those that are targeted by the organism's sensory array) must, one assumes, be explicable only as an outcome of natural selection, since organisms that tended not to have this ability would not long have survived.

A theory that explains generic organisms' ability to model the external environment by means of neurological association may seem an unpromising foundation for a theory of interpretation that can explain human behavior. But the deterministic part of Hayek's theory offers the advantage of explaining perceptions and thus (especially in conscious organisms) actions without relying on non-explanations such as irrationality or free will. In particular, Hayek's determinism dispenses with appeals to will, choice, or arbitrary judgment to explain the *differing* interpretations produced by different individuals; and it provides an alternative to irrationalist explanations for the *errors* inhering in various interpretations. (As we shall see, Hayek by no means suggests that the ability of an amoeba or a human being to model its environment is infallible.) In addition, the Darwinian side of the theory allows Hayek to make due allowance for the subjective element in interpretation without denying the existence of objective reality or suggesting that it—rather than our perception of it—is "constructed."

In Hayek's view, different individuals' differing interpretations, far from resulting from arbitrary or underdetermined acts of will,[6] are the necessary products of each organism's inevitably different experiences. Individuals' different conceptual maps will be

> determined by factors which are sufficiently similar to make those maps … similar to each other. But they will not be identical. Complete identity of the maps would presuppose not only an identical history of the different individuals but also complete identity of their anatomical structure. (Hayek 1952b, 110)

This makes it understandable that different people can look at the same facts and reach different conclusions: In the past, they have looked at slightly different sets of facts, and this cumulative experience forms the lens through which present facts are interpreted.

In turn, the adaptive aspect of Hayek's approach to interpretation can explain erroneous interpretations without invoking irrationality (as is so often done by social scientists, especially economists). Hayek's explanation for error juxtaposes the wider objective world against expectations that we form on the basis of *local* objective conditions (as reflected by the stimuli we notice). "The kinds of physical stimuli which will act on a particular organism, and the relative frequency of the simultaneous occurrence of the different stimuli, will correspond not to conditions in the world at large, but to conditions in the particular environment in which the organism has existed" (Hayek 1952, 108). Therefore, the "reproduction of those relations ... will not necessarily be representative" of objective conditions in the world at large. Moreover, as we automatically classify primal classifications into ever-more-abstract categories, "the order which the linkages will gradually create in the central nervous system will ... constitute not only a very imperfect but in some respects even a definitely erroneous reproduction of the relations which exist between the corresponding stimuli" (ibid.), because we are abstracting away what we interpret to be irrelevant details. Thus, Hayek's account of learning describes the correction of our subjective interpretations by further experience with the objective environment. "The experience that the classification based on the past linkages does not always work, i.e., does not always lead to valid predictions" of the future associations of stimuli from the environment, "forces us to revise that classification" (ibid., 168).

In accounting for differing and erroneous interpretations historically or biographically—as necessary consequences of the past experiences of fallible creatures with limited experience—Hayek grounds interpretive charity as not merely a kindness, but as a necessary precondition for understanding interpretations that are different from one's own, which one therefore views as erroneous. In principle, all differences of opinion can be traced to different experiences and the interpretations these experiences necessitate. Even consciously held interpretations—such as hypotheses about which facets of a given political or economic situation are important and require analysis—simply reiterate what our (inevitably somewhat idiosyncratic) experience tells us is likely to be important in this situation, given that we classify it as similar to certain earlier situations.

Thus, in trying to understand an interpretation different from one's own, the only procedure that might make headway is to infer what experiences have made the other person's interpretation seem to her to be (literally) compelling. In practice, this procedure will be possible only to a limited degree, since we do not possess extra-sensory perception and cannot know or infer more than a small fraction of the many influences that have led someone to believe what she does. But we can be sure that everyone has what they view as good reasons for their beliefs, even when these beliefs seem, to us, to be obviously mistaken.

A recognition of this fact would go far toward dispelling many pseudo-problems in political science, such as the "paradox" of voting in a large electorate (where one's chance of determining the outcome is minuscule). Faced with a voter who defies these odds by voting, we ought first to ask whether she ever gave the slightest thought to the odds that we (political scientists) think are so crucial. By virtue of the fact that she voted, our initial hypothesis should be that she was ignorant of the odds, such that her reasons for preferring one candidate over another suffice to explain why she voted; or that she was aware of the odds but felt a civic obligation to vote; or that she voted both from ignorance of the odds and from a sense of civic duty. (Survey data confirm that most American voters are oblivious of the odds against their vote mattering and that they also feel a civic duty to vote.)[7]

However, these advantages of Hayek's deterministic and historical approach to interpretation must be set next to a lacuna: the absence of *cultural* "stimuli" from his schema. Hayek was, after all, trying to explain the sensory order, not the political or (as we shall see) even the economic order. The only stimuli come from the organism's direct interactions with its natural environment. But this incompleteness in the theory is readily enough corrected. We simply have to add other people's interpretations to the list of stimuli that may constitute an individual's experience. For organisms such as ourselves, these stimuli, transmitted through various cultural media, are likely to far outweigh the influence of physical stimuli emanating from our immediate surroundings.

Hayek's Non-Interpretivist Epistemology

From this bare summary of the main argument of *The Sensory Order*, it may be understandable why, for more than personal reasons, Hayek leapt to Mises's defense during the later stages of the calculation debate (Hayek 1935b and 1940). Market socialists such as Fred Taylor (1929), Henry Dickinson (1933), Abba P. Lerner (1934), and Oskar Lange (1936) had proposed that as long as consumer-goods prices are allowed to respond to supply and demand, central planners can decide how to allocate the means of production (which, under capitalism, are allocated by the sales of capital goods by and to private parties). If Hayek was thinking analogically, he might have seen market socialism as akin to the conscious mind trying to do away with its foundation: the manifold experiences of the nervous system in learning about the environment. How could the planners at the center of an economy know what is encoded in the experiential knowledge of the rest of the economy, which is constantly interacting with external realities that a rational planner would have to take into account?[8] At best, over time, a rational planner would receive from the social "nervous system" abstract interpretations that were to some extent misleading because they necessarily left out detail. But without actual neurons linking the planners to the planned, how would even these abstract signals be transmitted to the center?

Under capitalism, however, exchanges of private property may be analogized to neurologically transmitted *adaptive* impulses only in the limited sense that the buyer and seller are reacting to classifications of "environmental" stimuli *of some sort*. Even if this analogy could be made less vague, it would not sustain the conclusions that Hayek advanced in his most influential paper, "The Use of Knowledge in Society" (Hayek 1945), where he made an objection very similar to the one just outlined, but without drawing a biological analogy. In this paper, published in the *American Economic Review*, Hayek argued that the needed economic "knowledge" unproblematically exists; the only problem is that it is unavailable to central planners because it is dispersed among all the participants in an economy. It needs therefore to be "communicated" from each of us to the rest of us, and prices do the trick. Economic exchanges that affect prices allow the divided, dispersed knowledge of those on each side of the exchanges to be brought together in aggregated numerical form.

However, Hayek identified no means by which the capitalists on one side of each of these exchanges—who could be replaced, according to market socialists, by central planners—could *know* rather than merely *opine* about such crucial economic facts as the future consumer demand for a product and the best way to meet this demand. Such knowledge, or opinion, will determine capitalists' actions in bidding up the prices of the capital goods they think are needed to produce the consumer goods they think will be in demand. Whether consumers will want to buy the goods a given capitalist produces, and at the price for which he offers them, is a matter of interpretation. More precisely, it is a prediction about future consumer behavior based on an interpretation of present conditions, including the "meaning" of prevailing prices for future demand as well as for future supply. Even if the capitalists are compared to simple organisms interpreting a fixed physical environment, Hayek would soon show in *The Sensory Order* that such interpretation rarely if ever qualifies as "knowledge" because local conditions may not be representative of the larger environment; and because interpretations of local conditions may leave out crucial details even of the stimuli that the organism happens to have been equipped, by evolution and experience, to notice.

In addition, the stimuli being interpreted by capitalists are almost always cultural. A capitalist's predictions about future prices, including the future prices she can set for her own products without losing money, are not based on adaptive interactions with the sensory stimulus of consumer "demand" (a highly abstract concept, not a physical reality that emits stimuli we are equipped, by natural selection, to detect); nor by previous capitalists' adaptive economic interactions, encoded genetically in neurological architecture passed down to the capitalist over the course of human evolution. Instead, capitalists' predictions, hence their actions, and hence the effect of these actions on prices, will be based largely on sheer interpretation—interpretation *almost* all the way down.

While there is an objective bedrock of actual actions—sales—underlying current prices, the entrepreneur who uses, say, tin must interpret an increase in its price (Hayek's example) as indicating a temporary constriction in supply or a permanent rise in demand (or some combination) if she is even to begin to know what action she should take in response to it. Each interpretation of the price increase will suggest a very different action. But these interpretations will be based primarily on what one reads in newspapers about business conditions, what one hears elsewhere about them, what one has learned in school about macroeconomics, what one has read in specialist journals about the tin industry, and so on.

Elsewhere, Hayek (1952a, 63–64) asserts without argument that people's often-spurious "speculative" opinions are "entirely different" from the opinions on which their economic actions are based.[9] But the price generated by a sale, let alone by hundreds of millions of sales aggregated into one price, no more speaks for itself than does any other fact. Lacking any experience of prices, consumers, and markets that is not culturally mediated,[10] it is difficult to see how capitalists can avoid using speculative opinions of various kinds in trying to interpret the "meaning" for future prices of an array of current prices. Thus, the interpretive process that Hayek would come to point out is so error-prone in a naturally determined setting must surely be even more so—*ceteris paribus*—in a culturally determined one. (The *ceteris paribus* clause, here, stands in for *unless one produces a theory of how culturally transmitted interpretations of human behavior tend to be accurate*—a theory that has been produced neither by Hayek nor by anyone else.) Since one's interpretations lead to the actions through which one exerts an influence on prices, the "knowledge" conveyed by prices may well be spurious guides to future action.

A nice example of Hayek's failure to notice the dependence of prices on speculative opinion is provided by his business-cycle theory, discussed by Daniel Kuehn (2013) below. Hayek argues that if the central bank reduces interest rates below the level that would reign in an unhindered credit market, it causes a lengthening of the production process, involving the use of more capital goods, and that this elongated structure can be sustained only by continued monetary easing to keep interest rates low. But the degree to which businesses take advantage of low rates to lengthen the production process surely depends on whether their proprietors *agree with Hayek* that the low rates are merely creating an artificial boom that cannot sustain the products they would create if they took advantage of the low rates. If entrepreneurs were to agree with Hayek about this, they would not borrow at the low rates to fund lengthier production processes. To the extent that Hayek's theory might be applicable in a given case, it would have to be because entrepreneurs tended to interpret the implication of low interest rates differently than Hayek would.

Because Hayek failed to acknowledge the need to interpret prices, his discussion of economic epistemology in 1945 took precisely the opposite position on the utility of local experience from the position expressed seven years later in *The Sensory Order*. In 1945 the local "man on the spot" (Hayek 1945, 83–84) *knows* what to do about whatever he observes locally (such as the empty hold of a tramp steamer) (ibid., 80)—at least as long as he also has access to prices that transmit to him "knowledge" from other parts of the economy. He knows what to do because he combines the knowledge derived from prices with private "knowledge" about "people," "local conditions," and "special circumstances" (ibid.). Yet his forecast that his actions will be *profitable* depends on how well his interpretation of this local information captures realities in the wider economy, since those realities will determine the future price of the goods he will try to sell.

The capitalist, then, relies on speculative interpretations in two senses. First, as we have seen, the price "information" that is an input into his decisions depends, in part, on other capitalists' speculative opinions. Second, the capitalist himself must speculate about the implication of given prices for a putatively profitable action of his own. It does not seem to cross Hayek's mind that the man on the spot may therefore misinterpret the empty hold as a great opportunity to ship cargo, such as tin, that in reality will not pay off (e.g., because demand for it is declining despite the temporary increase in price caused by the collapse of a tin mine). Yet his action—buying tin to ship in the hold, then chartering the ship—will be as fully reflected in tomorrow's prices for tin and for ship rentals (and all the other prices that are affected by these prices) as would actions that were based on accurate interpretations.

Only if all producers' (and consumers') interpretations of prices and local experiences were entirely accurate could we justify calling what they are transmitting to each other through prices "knowledge" about anything except their own fallible theories. Apparently, then, in 1945 Hayek had not sufficiently developed the implications of his 1920 study of neurology to see that the interpretive nature of all putative knowledge undermines its reliability (*cet. par.*). In fact, in 1945, Hayek committed the very sin of which he had, in 1937, forcefully accused the mainstream of economics, as Boettke and O'Donnell (2013) point out below. Like the economics mainstream, Hayek wished away the epistemic issue by assuming that economic agents' subjective perceptions and expectations match objective realities. Indeed, in a clear reference to his opponents in the socialist-calculation debate, Hayek (1945, 77) began "The Use of Knowledge in Society" by criticizing economists who assume that "*if* we possess all the relevant information, *if* we can start out from a given system of preferences, and *if* we command complete knowledge of available means, the problem which remains is purely one of logic" (which can be solved by a central planner). Yet Hayek himself assumed in the same essay that "we" possess all the relevant information, albeit in dispersed form. This is an assumption that Hayek regularly repeated over the years and that, as we shall see, became the basis of his political theory.

In contrast, an interpretive solution to the knowledge problem posed by the socialist-calculation debate was prefigured by a phrase in Hayek's 1935 paper, "The Present State of the Debate," where he mentioned that central planners, like capitalist entrepreneurs, would have to deal with unpredictable future events about which the expectations "of different entrepreneurs will naturally differ" (Hayek 1935b, 234). If this is true, then at least some of the entrepreneurs' interpretations must be wrong, such that the effect of their actions on prices will be perverse.

Hayek (e.g., 1946 and 1968) would later say that competition among entrepreneurs is the solution to the problem of knowing how to act in the face of an unpredictable future. That is the problem facing entrepreneurs who disagree with each other; it is not the problem of communicating to each other what they already "know."[11] However, Hayek never explained that disagreement about appropriate action in the face of uncertainty was the key to the competitive solution. He might have said, but did not say, that in light of this disagreement, each competing enterprise can be seen as embodying a competing interpretation of which products and methods of production will turn out, in the future, to be the best way to provide consumers with something they are willing to buy (cf. Lavoie 1985, 123). Competition is, in this view, not a means of aggregating or harnessing local knowledge, nor is it a means of generating knowledge. It is instead a way of spreading society's bets among predictions that may all be wrong in one way or another because knowledge of the future is hard to come by. Since competition is made possible only by the plural ownership of capital goods—the defining feature of capitalism, for purposes of the calculation debate—capitalism itself can be seen as a way of spreading society's bets. The alternative would be to bet all societal resources on the interpretation held by the central planners.

Since Hayek never repudiated "The Use of Knowledge in Society," the received view of his contribution to the epistemology of economics has long been, as Strong notes below, the notion that prices merely communicate what is known already. Were *The Sensory Order* more widely read, however, it might be recognized that the only problem of knowledge that Hayek actually gives us reason to think is important is the problem of correcting errors in what we think we "know." An epistemologist need not take it for granted that knowledge unproblematically exists and is "used," as Hayek did in 1945. One can also start from the assumption that we are ignorant and ask whether what we take to be knowledge is genuinely reliable, as Hayek did in 1952.

The Incompatibility of "Coordination" with Hayek's Non-Interpretivist Epistemology

Hayek's failure to carry into economic theory the interpretive view he developed in *The Sensory Order* accounts for the problem wrestled with by Vaughn as well as by Boettke and O'Donnell: Hayek's conviction that the central problem of economics is accounting for "the" tendency toward coordination, or equilibrium, under capitalism (however troublesome Hayek increasingly found the equilibrium metaphor). It is true that a mere "tendency" toward coordination does not presuppose that prices fully reflect "knowledge," as Hayek had assumed in 1945, since the failure to reach full coordination must entail ignorance on the part of at least some economic actors. Yet in positing a tendency toward coordination, Hayek did assume a tendency toward full knowledge (or error correction). Thus, his assertion that economics should be an effort to *explain* this alleged tendency begs the epistemological question unless he identifies the learning or error-correcting mechanism that is supposed to underwrite the alleged tendency. Until this mechanism is specified, we are entitled to infer from the role of speculative interpretation in the determination of market prices that markets may well tend toward disequilibrium. This fact, as Lewis (2013) reminds us, stood behind Ludwig Lachmann's portrayal of the economy as "kaleidic" rather than as tending toward coordination.

Although Boettke and O'Donnell conclude that competition is the main mechanism that might account for a coordinating tendency, this could be true only if competition not only spread society's bets (by concurrently putting several different interpretations to work), but if society tended over time to put its chips on the best bets. This tendency, however, would presuppose some means of sorting good from bad interpretations. If there is to be no guidance in how to do this sorting from a central planner above, it must come from below. That is, the sorting mechanism must be the consumers who buy the goods and services produced by capitalists' interpretations of what they can sell.

If consumers are the source of a tendency toward coordination, their actions will help to ensure (although not guarantee) that the economic system is serving its function, conceived as the satisfaction of consumer wants. But if consumers are to fill this role, we need an explanation of how they can reliably sort good interpretations from bad ones. Hayek hinted at the rudiments of a psychological explanation in *The Sensory Order* and in his 1946 lecture on "The Theory of Competition," but he did not follow up on them. Since the hinted-at explanation of consumer choice would link up to an interpretivist understanding of competition, it may be worth detouring down this road that Hayek failed to take.

In "The Meaning of Competition," Hayek (1946, 97) allowed that in the real world, consumers have "inadequate knowledge of the available commodities or services." But he went on to assert that this fact "is made up for by [consumers'] experience with the persons or firms supplying them." In *The Sensory Order*, this idea is paralleled by Hayek's discussion of "the 'feed-back' principle." One's "sensory representation of the environment," he writes,

> will evoke a movement pattern generally aimed at the achievement of [a] goal. But at first the pattern of movement initiated will not be fully successful. The current sensory reports about what is happening will be checked against expectations, and the difference between the two will act as a further stimulus indicating the required corrections. (Hayek 1952b, 95)

Together, the two passages suggest that the psychological sorting mechanism may involve the use of trial and error by consumers. A consumer unhappy with a purchase based on her erroneous interpretation of what she wanted returns the product and tries another. Products that produce negative consumer reactions are those, in turn, that embody erroneous entrepreneurial interpretations of what consumers want to buy. Consumer dissatisfaction leads to losses for the firms that make these products. As loss-making firms are selected out, the system as a whole tends toward coordination.

This is a minimalist model of capitalism in that it has no need for the extravagant theoretical assumptions (such as perfect competition and perfect knowledge) on which economists typically base the equilibrium principle. Indeed, the minimalist model may seem to be so commonsensical that it requires no psychological foundation. But if consumers are to play their epistemic role in the model, an implicit psychology of *reliable* consumer experimentation must be at work. There is no reason not to make it explicit.

Like other animals, human beings have the evolved capacity to notice proximate sources of their own, personal discomfort, especially when the stimulus is tangible, immediate, and repeated. This is the basis of classic or Pavlovian conditioning, in which "the main general predictors are contiguity (including temporal order and temporal contiguity) and contingency (reliable succession)" (MacDonald and Hershberger 2005, 32). The automatic learning that can be produced by noticing contiguous causation "reflects the fact that causes are reliable predictors of their effects, that causes precede their effects, and that in general causes tend to occur in close temporal proximity to their effects" (ibid.). Consumers whose choices are determined by classical conditioning may reliably (although far from perfectly) select from among the competing speculative interpretations of consumer needs embodied in various consumer goods and services. They need only be able to experiment with these competing products by "exiting" from those that, they notice, produce unsatisfactory contiguous sensations.[12]

This basic psychology is consistent with *The Sensory Order* (although it goes beyond it). However, contrary to what Hayek says there, the experience of a frustrated expectation does not, on its own, "indicat[e] the required corrections" (Hayek 1952b, 95), either for an amoeba or a human being. All one "knows" after a failed experiment is that something went wrong. It is the ability to try alternative products that may allow one to hit upon a better result. Classical conditioning has to be coupled with the ability to try different products if it is to work. Of course, the same model can be applied to employment relationships, personal relationships, and many other examples of activity in the private sphere.[13]

Hayek's Traditionalism and His Non-Interpretivist Epistemology

Vaughn's contribution suggests that in the place of a theory of consumer psychology, Hayek came to believe that rule following, such as habitual and traditional behavior, might account for the posited tendency toward coordination. If so, then Hayek seems to have taken a wrong turn.

Rule following does not substitute for a theory of consumer psychology since, without such a theory, the rules followed by consumers may turn out to harm them. Moreover, it is hard to see why we would need competing entrepreneurial interpretations of what rule-following consumers will want. If consumers follow rules closely enough, a central planner might reliably predict, with experience, how to satisfy their wants.

Hayek's notion that traditional rules and habits embody tacit knowledge (Hayek 1967) does not help, because the central planner need not be able to articulate the rules consumers are following as long as their behavior is regularized by the rules. Moreover, Hayek's idea that rule following serves a tacit epistemic function entails some rule-sorting device that would retain rules that carry wisdom while discarding misguided rules. Natural selection, of course, is the ideal type of an unconscious sorting mechanism, but it is almost never the case that the habits followed by people—whether as individuals or groups[14]—in modern societies so radically affect their chances of surviving and then passing on their genes that natural selection can be sorting good habits from bad ones. Evolutionary processes of rule selection (e.g., cultural processes) that *lack* a sorting mechanism such as natural selection, however, may well produce perverse rather than helpful habits and traditions.

Hayek's Political Theory

Hayek's growing respect for inherited rules and institutions as "evolved," therefore, must be seen as one of many dead ends in his social and political theory, most of which are discussed here by Godard, Gamble, Lister, and Ryan.

Lister analyzes Hayek's odd campaign against the phrase *social justice*, a campaign that contradicts the egalitarian, utilitarian thrust of his economic theory and of *both* his interpretive and his dispersed-knowledge epistemologies. The economic-calculation debate had raised epistemic issues, after all, only because the question was whether central planners could know what they would need to know if they were to duplicate or outdo capitalism in providing for people's material needs and wants. The knowledge allegedly embodied by prices (and habits, and traditions)—like the reduction of error that might be brought about by competition among different interpretations—is no more an end in itself than is economic "coordination" or "equilibrium." If this knowledge, or error reduction, is so important that its institutional preconditions should be defended as desirable, as Hayek believed, then it must be because it is in some way beneficial.

Thus, he wrote that "the justification of any particular rule of law must be its usefulness" (Hayek 1960, 159). While he objected to the impossible epistemic requirements of act-utilitarianism, he endorsed "what has been called 'restricted' utilitarianism," that is, a utilitarianism applied to institutions and rules of action, not particular acts. "The end of the law ought to be the welfare of the people," he concluded (ibid.). Utilitarianism carries with it a commitment to the welfare of *all* the people inasmuch as this is practicable. Accordingly, as Lister points out, Hayek thought a society admirable to the degree that one would want to be a randomly chosen member of it—a criterion that differs from Rawls's difference principle in details, but not in the basic idea that a good society will be one that works to the benefit of all. If this is not a theory of social justice, Lister asks, what is?

For Rawls, of course, the grounds for improving the condition of the least advantaged was not their well being, but their freedom of action: Material resources are, in his theory of justice, "primary goods," i.e., means to a large range of ends that one might choose to pursue. Hayek, in contrast, rejected not only the idea that "justice" could characterize a distribution of goods, but the idea that "freedom" could be defined as one's range of opportunity, choice, or action. Gamble argues that Hayek's alternative, narrower definition of freedom—freedom from "coercion," which Hayek defined as the deliberate reduction of one's options by another—seems to serve little purpose but to ratify the outcomes of capitalism, regardless of their effect on individuals' range of choice, merely on the grounds that these outcomes are not deliberately intended by anyone. Similarly, Hayek's broadly egalitarian criterion of an admirable society contradicts his opposition to egalitarian income redistribution—which Lister shows is justified only by Hayek's narrow definition of "justice."

In his definitions both of justice and of freedom, Hayek insists that we ignore the harms *unintentionally* produced by social institutions—even though his claims for the allegedly epistemic properties of capitalism, the price system, habits, and traditions are claims for these institutions' unintended benefits. One must therefore ask why Hayek's political theory did not confine itself to identifying the epistemic advantages of the institutions that he favored, and to specifying the good consequences to be expected from these advantages. This would have spared him the need to rely on unconvincing redefinitions of terms that, in any event, contradicted both the utilitarianism and the egalitarianism that undergirded his defense of capitalism.

Hayek's Intellectual History of the Left

Unraveling the paradoxes of Hayek's political theory requires that we turn from *The Sensory Order* to the other book he published in 1952, *The Counter-Revolution of Science: Studies on the Abuse of Reason*. Here Hayek tried to trace the historical sources of what he had come to see as his intellectual antagonist: an "engineering type of mind" (Hayek 1952a, 25) or planning mentality, which he later rechristened "constructivist rationalism" (Hayek 1973, 17). This form of rationalism was associated, according to Hayek, not only with socialism but with a variety of pernicious doctrines in social-science methodology and social theory, such as positivism and "a 'pragmatic' interpretation of social institutions which treats all social structures which serve human purposes as the result of deliberate design," and "which denies the possibility of an orderly or purposeful arrangement in anything which is not thus constructed" (Hayek 1952a, 142). This attitude, in a nutshell, is what Hayek viewed as the root cause of socialism.

Ryan suggests that constructivist rationalism does not describe the mindset of such democratic socialists as John Dewey; Godard adds Marx and Rosa Luxembourg to the list. Elsewhere, Bruce Caldwell (2010, 40) adds Bakunin, Kropotkin, the Frankfurt School, and the New Left. The only socialists whom Hayek *is* describing accurately are, arguably, Auguste Comte and many of Hayek's contemporaries in early twentieth-century Britain, who were afire with the promises held out by central planning. But as Godard maintains, it is a grave mistake to conflate any "technology," such as central planning, with the emancipatory, egalitarian, democratic, and welfarist ideals of the left. Central planning was seen by many early twentieth-century socialists as an effective means to those ends. But the vogue for planning passed as quickly as it had arrived. Left-wing thought and sentiment long predated the planning fad and easily outlasted its demise. Godard contends that in consequence, *The Road to Serfdom* was obsolete almost as soon as it was published.

He also condemns Hayek's one-dimensionally economic analysis of societies along the planning/unplanned axis. The same narrow econo-mism may explain why Hayek could consistently confuse a dispensable means to left-wing ends with the ends themselves. Given the formative role played by his encounter with socialist economists who did defend central planning, it is understandable that he would try to get to the bottom of their mistake by tracing it to social-scientific doctrines originating in the previous century. However, if their error lay in tacitly presuming their own omniscience—as suggested by Hayek's condem-nation of their assumption that "we possess all the relevant information" (Hayek 1945, 77)—the roots of the error probably had more to do with the particular practices of modern economics than with any larger current in social science as a whole (Boettke 1997). Even now, after having "learned" the epistemic lessons taught by Hayek, economics suffers from an inability to deal credibly with human ignorance, a fact that Boettke and O'Donnell explore at length.[15] But this problem seems to afflict the other social sciences only to the extent that they have been influenced by economics.

In economics, the root problem may be the need to go beyond theorizing that predicts general patterns of behavior (given certain initial conditions) to predicting the precise effects of public policies. Caldwell (2004, 96) quotes Wesley Clair Mitchell, one of Dewey's students and an extremely influential American economist, on the discovery during World War I that prewar economic theory was next to useless in making policy:

> It seldom sufficed to say that a given action would have consequences of a certain kind, that would have been easy—and trifling. The important thing was to find out at least in what order of magnitude these consequences should be reckoned.

Explicitly, finding this out seemed to require undertaking quantitative research. But implicitly, it may have been necessary to impute something like omniscience to economic agents—and something even more like omniscience to the economists who model agents' behavior—since only agents whose knowledge is known to the modeler can behave predictably enough to fit into a quantitative model. While one can predict the behavior of an agent who knows all the "relevant" information (relevant according to the economist), or even of an agent who knows a, b, and c but not d, one cannot predict the behavior of an agent who may know any of these things or may not; who in any case may interpret them differently than does the modeler; and who may know things, or think that she knows things, that the modeler does not know.

Such an agent is suggested if we insert the organism described in *The Sensory Order* into a modern economy, where she would be the palimpsest of unobservable and partly unique experiential influences, including cultural influences that she interprets idiosyncratically because of the unique path of her prior cultural exposure. In principle, a determinist theory of psychology, such as Hayek's, may enable one to predict the behavior of such agents—if one knows the precise order in which all of their experiences occurred, and thus the interpretive lens each of them brought to each successive experience. Obviously, though, such knowledge is unattainable, and not just because of the unobservable nature of each person's experiences. More important is the fact that one would oneself have to have experienced the agent's experiences in precisely the same order and context as the agent had if one were to be able to duplicate the interpretative configuration to which the agent has now been led, which would be necessary if one's predictions of her future behavior were to be accurate. Yet we are often unable to predict how we ourselves will react to a new circumstance. Given the practical impossibility of predicting one's own behavior, reliable predictions of mass behavior seem highly improbable. Counterintuitively, then, interpretive determinism *in practice* leads to behavioral unpredictability. If that is the case, then Mitchell's problem will never be solved. Obviously, however, economists do not come anywhere close to thinking that this is the case. It would be invaluable to have a history of twentieth-century economics that explained why economists adopted models of behavior that implicitly solved this problem by assuming that agents' knowledge, hence their future behavior, can be known by the economic modeler. But that would be a very different history than the one Hayek presents in *The Counter-Revolution of Science*.

The "engineering" mentality is not particularly oriented toward prediction; instead, those who are supposed to be in its grip are said to believe that "no result of the action of many men can show order or serve a useful purpose unless it is the result of deliberate design" (Hayek 1952a, 142). Such a belief is retrospective, not predictive. In effect, Hayek is suggesting that socialists have looked at the history of capitalism, found no intentional design, and then concluded—on this basis alone—that capitalism *must* be useless. This theory of socialism almost certainly cannot be right, however, since the conviction that capitalism is merely useless would not account for the *hatred* of it that has characterized so many its critics. Moreover, for the theory to be right, we would need to hear socialists indicting capitalism on the general ground that it is unplanned, not on the grounds of the specific injustices and social problems that they attribute to it. Similarly, if planning is supposed to be the "constructivist" alternative to the unplanned capitalist order, it would hardly matter *who* did the planning. But socialists tended to insist that either workers or the people at large do it. This is not because workers or the people at large were credited with any peculiar skill at planning, but because they were thought to be peculiarly victimized by capitalist injustices and tormented by capitalist depredations. Setting things right was a matter of putting the right people in charge of society, not making society more deliberately organized. If anything, capitalism was all too deliberately organized—to benefit the capitalists. This was the thesis of Karl Polanyi's *The Great*

Transformation (1944), an immensely influential left-wing work of history that, to my knowledge, Hayek never mentions.

Instead of tracking any historical or logical socialist movement, Hayek's theory of constructivist rationalism sounds very much like one that might have been developed by an economist who had the experience of responding to specific charges against capitalism by pointing to the other side of the ledger, namely, its beneficial consequences. In rejoinder, the economist's socialist interlocutors might have said that such consequences seem unlikely given the unplanned design of capitalism. If my hypothesis is valid, Hayek's elaborate history of constructivist rationalism would explain, at best, an argumentative move made by socialists of a certain era in defense of their initial indictment of capitalism. The indictment itself, however, is grounded not in any general doctrine or mindset that holds the unplanned to be pointless, let alone undesirable, but rather in the links that people saw (and see) between capitalism and specific, serious human problems.

Spontaneous Order and Hayek's Political Theory

Even if Hayek's notion of constructivist rationalism represents a failure to understand his opponents' perspective, it may help us to understand his political theory. The theory's first and fullest iteration was presented in *The Constitution of Liberty* (1960), where Hayek produced the polar opposite of a doctrine holding that capitalism is useless because it is unplanned: a defense of capitalism based on his characterization of it as being a "spontaneous" rather than planned order—a product of human action but not of human design. The importance of characterizing capitalism as a spontaneous order clearly depended on the need to counter the imagined antagonist of capitalism, constructivist rationalism. Thus, Hayek (1960, 159) asserted that "much of the opposition to a system of freedom under general laws arises from the inability to conceive of an effective co-ordination of human activities without deliberate organization by a commanding intelligence."

By contrast, Hayek continued, "one of the achievements of economic theory has been to explain how such a mutual adjustment of the spontaneous activities of individuals is brought about by the market, provided that there is a known delimitation of the sphere of control of each individual" (Hayek 1960, 159). The economic theory to which Hayek referred was his own non-interpretive epistemology. A spontaneous social order, he wrote, "involving an adjustment to circumstances, knowledge of which is dispersed among a great many people, cannot be established by central direction" (ibid., 160). Thus, "the rationale of securing to each individual a known range within which he can decide on his actions is to enable him to make the fullest use of his knowledge, especially of his concrete and often unique knowledge of the particular circumstances of time and place" (ibid., 156).

Hayek's political use of the epistemology of dispersed knowledge has important consequences. To draw out these consequences, let me consider a counterfactual: some political implications of the alternative, interpretivist epistemology.

In the minimalist model of capitalism, capitalists are founts of interpretation, not repositories of local knowledge. In this model, any normatively desirable "tendency toward coordination" stems not from the aggregation of local knowledge, but from consumers' ability to try the products of capitalists' competing interpretations and keep the ones they find more satisfactory. The ability to buy competing products, however, depends not only on the legal right to buy them, but the financial means to do so. Therefore, the minimalist model might, in principle, justify income redistribution; otherwise, capitalism would violate the egalitarian premise that makes its putative epistemic advantage desirable. Neither Mises nor Hayek would have defended capitalism if they had thought that its epistemic advantages chiefly served the interests of the rich.

Had Hayek made better use of the interpretivist framework developed in *The Sensory Order*, then, he might not have gone to such illogical lengths to deny the legitimacy of the redistribution of wealth. At the same time, Hayek's interpretivist epistemology has negative implications for the economic regulations that—as Gamble, Godard, and Lister each point out—were freely endorsed by Hayek. It is difficult to think of any regulation that would not be acceptable under Hayek's definition of the rule of law, which prohibits only commands directed at particular outcomes or individuals. The attempt to achieve particular outcomes might seem to characterize all regulations, but Hayek (1960, 224) denies this, even while he explains that most regulations may not be "wise." One reason for their unwisdom is that "they will always limit the scope of experimentation and thereby obstruct what may be useful developments" (ibid.). Such phrases recall the fallibilist and experimental picture of concept formation that Hayek had produced in *The Sensory Order*, but

Hayek is explicitly excluding experimentalism and the correction of error from his political theory, which, he is explaining, allows regulation *despite* the fact that it *always* limits the scope of experimentation. Admirably, Hayek is separating his political theory from his convictions about the wisdom of types of public policy; all too often, political theory involves a rationalization of a theorist's policy preferences instead of a critical appraisal of them.

However, if Hayek had built into his political theory experimentalist conclusions drawn from his interpretivist epistemology, he could not very well have grounded the theory in the "knowledge" that was supposed to be aggregated and communicated in prices.[16] Given the path Hayek took, price controls are among the few types of government action, and the only type of regulation, that Hayek (1960, 227–28) disallows as a matter of political theory. An entirely different political theory might have been produced by Hayek's interpretivist epistemology. If prices convey opinion, not wisdom, then there is nothing special about them that demands an exemption from regulation that is not granted to other private-sphere activities. Instead, Hayek might have been expected to ask how the authors of regulations are any better qualified, epistemically, than central planners are. Like central planners, regulators are imposing on an entire economy a single interpretation of what needs to be done. If the interpretation is prone to error due to its abstraction from detail and its extrapolation of the planners' "local" experiences—including their cultural experiences, such as their theoretical training—across an unobservable society, then there is a serious risk that society is placing the wrong bet. Conversely, *if* regulators are epistemically qualified to place such bets, there is no epistemic argument against central planning except the one grounded, implausibly, in the non-speculative "knowledge" of the local man on the spot.

This is not to say that regulation and central planning are equivalent. One is piecemeal; the other comprehensive. Nor does regulation lead to central planning, as Hayek was thought to have said in *The Road to Serfdom*. My point is simply that while Hayek's actual political theory opposed income redistribution but favored regulation, a political theory based on his interpretivist epistemology might have done exactly the reverse.

The ultimate question, then, is *why* Hayek came to build his political theory around the local-knowledge epistemology presented in "The Use of Knowledge in Society" (1945), despite articulating his alternative, interpretivist epistemology seven years *later*, in *The Sensory Order* (1952). A full answer would require a monograph; I will close by merely suggesting two possibilities.

The first concerns timing. *The Sensory Order* was published in the same year as *The Counter-Revolution of Science*, but the latter consisted of essays that had appeared during the previous decade. Thus, even as Hayek was writing *The Sensory Order*, he was creating the constructivist-rationalism construct. This construct was so literalistic about "planning" that it did not analyze what planning entailed: the prediction of human behavior—also required by regulation. As we have seen, the impracticability of such prediction is an implication of the deterministic framework of *The Sensory Order*. Had Hayek restricted his attention to his actual antagonists in the socialist-calculation debate—economists who assumed perfect knowledge—rather than assimilating them to "socialism" *tout court*, he might have deployed this implication against them.

The second possibility is consistent with the first. Although *The Sensory Order* originated in a paper that predated Hayek's training in economics, the book itself was completed long afterwards. In the meantime, Hayek had adopted the catalogue of (speculative) policy opinions typical of the modern economist. He was bracketing a great deal when he excluded from his political theory his conclusions about the wisdom of particular types of government activity. This did not stop him from expressing these conclusions, however, in summary form. While the political theorist proscribes only violations of the rule of law, thereby allowing virtually any regulation to be enacted, "the economist," he wrote, "will remain suspicious" of regulation, holding "that there is a strong presumption against such measures because their over-all cost is almost always underestimated" (Hayek 1960, 224–25). *The Constitution of Liberty* is littered with policy conclusions of this sort. Such conclusions entail predictions of human behavior.

In attributing the "planning" mentality to "socialists," Hayek missed his target. It was much closer to home.

NOTES

1. *Critical Review* vol. 11, no. 1 (1997).
2. *Critical Review* vol. 3, no. 2 (1989).
3. A penetrating, blow-by-blow account of the calculation debate is found in Lavoie 1985.

4. Weber (1904) contributed the insight that all observation presupposes theory or interpretation; see Caldwell 2004, ch. 4, for the Weberian influence on Hayek. Weber's view, in turn, was neo-Kantian. For the Kantian influence on Hayek, see Gray 1984. On the limitations of this view in relation to *The Sensory Order*, see Caldwell 2004, 273.

5. See Caldwell 2004, 277–78.

6. Friedman 2013 maintains that conceptions of free will that disallow antecedent determination of the will by ideas (or, in Hayek's terms, by interpretations) rely inescapably on arbitrary determination instead.

7. "Survey data suggest that over 70 percent of voters believe that their individual votes 'really matter'" (Somin 2013, 74). And the Civic Participation Survey shows that 95 percent of voters rate "civic duty" as an important reason for having voted (Campbell 2006, 52).

8. Hayek (1952b, 185) closed *The Sensory Order* by contending that a mind can understand only systems less complex than itself. This impossibility theorem might have been directed against the ability of central planners to predict consumers' desires, but such an argument would have applied as much against capitalists as against central planners. Alternatively, Hayek may have seen the theorem as a knock-down argument against the "constructivist rationalism" that he attributed to socialists, rather than against the efficacy of socialism itself.

9. As we have seen, *The Sensory Order* suggests that *all* conscious opinions, or interpretations, are speculative in that they extrapolate from local conditions and eliminate what past classifications suggest is irrelevant detail. My use of "speculative" in the text, then, is not intended to insert an arbitrary element into the otherwise-deterministic epistemology I am advancing.

10. Even the concepts "consumers," "prices," and "markets" are, of course, culturally mediated, as are people's conception of prices as being determined by the intersection of fictional supply and demand curves.

11. E.g., Hayek 1946 and 1968.

12. This paragraph is adapted from Friedman 2006, 479, which also describes the need for operant conditioning if feedback is to work as a mechanism of reliable consumer choice. In Friedman forthcoming, ch. 8, I describe the limits of this mechanism as the contiguity of a product or service and its effects is diminished, and I compare the overall effects that can be expected in the exit-based private sphere with those in the political sphere, where almost no effects can be directly traced to their policy causes without the use of speculative opinion because cause and effect are almost always linked distally, not contiguously.

13. One might object that the explanation relies on such a primitive psychology that it cannot account for the undesirable effects on consumer choice of consumers' own speculative theories about what they want. However, experiential feedback can often overcome such opinions (e.g., those based on advertising). As Schumpeter (1950, 263) wrote, "The picture of the prettiest girl that ever lived will in the long run prove powerless to maintain the sales of a bad cigarette." We can assume that a consumer has some speculative reason to make an initial purchase. The speculation is the hypothesis that the purchase will achieve some objective. When feedback from the purchased good or service falsifies this hypothesis, the consumer can try something else. Unlike feedback from speculative predictions in politics and the social sciences, the feedback from experiments based on speculative consumer opinion can be directly experienced by the consumer (in some cases), providing a reliable test of her hypotheses.

However, Schumpeter's example suggests that this is not always the case. The contiguous feedback from a "good" (tasting) cigarette is positive, while the distal effects of smoking it can be disastrous. Classical conditioning works only when the effect is contiguous to the cause. See Friedman forthcoming, ch. 8.

14. Hayek became a proponent of group selection of rules, but such passages as the following reveal the distance between group selection and historical reality: "Most of the steps in the evolution of culture were made possible by some individuals breaking some traditional rules and practicing new forms of conduct— not because they understood them to be better, but because the groups that acted upon them prospered more than others and grew" (Hayek 1979, 161). Did the conquest of the West by Greek and then Christian ideas follow this pattern? Did capitalism spread because it enabled the population of Britain to outstrip that of Russia and China, or that of Europe to outstrip that of Africa? There is also the fact that the larger population made possible by following a given practice may be unhappier than a smaller population that the larger population crowds out or annihilates—for example, because the larger population lives closer to subsistence level or in more inhuman conditions. An instance of this might be the transition from hunting and gathering to agriculture, as depicted by Marshall Sahlins (1974).

15. Given Hayek's continued propagation of the dispersed-knowledge epistemology, however, even after he published *The Sensory Order*, it is hard not to assign some of the responsibility for this problem to him. The dispersed-knowledge view merely shifts the locus of omniscience from individual economic actors to the economy as a whole.

16. Notice that Hayek's argument against the wisdom of regulation is that it impedes the discovery of *new* knowledge, not the correction of old mistakes (Hayek 1960, 224).

REFERENCES

Boettke, Peter J. 1997. "Where Did Economics Go Wrong? Equilibrium as a Flight from Reality." *Critical Review* 11(1): 11–64.

Boettke, Peter J., and Kyle W. O'Donnell. 2013. "The Failed Appropriation of F. A. Hayek by Formalist Economics." *Critical Review* 25(3–4): 305–41.

Caldwell, Bruce A. 2004. *Hayek's Challenge: An Intellectual Biography of F. A. Hayek.* Chicago: University of Chicago Press.

Caldwell, Bruce A. 2010. Introduction to Hayek 1952a. In *Studies on the Abuse and Decline of Reason: Text and Documents.* Vol. 13 of *The Collected Works of F. A. Hayek.* Chicago: University of Chicago Press.

Campbell, David E. 2006. *Why We Vote.* Princeton: Princeton University Press.

Dickinson, Henry. 1933. "Price Formation in a Socialist Community." *Economic Journal* 43: 237–50.

Friedman, Jeffrey. 1997. "Hayek's Political Philosophy and His Economics." *Critical Review* 11(1): 1–10.

Friedman, Jeffrey. 2006. "Taking Ignorance Seriously." *Critical Review* 18(4): 469–532.

Friedman, Jeffrey. 2013. "Freedom Has No Intrinsic Value: Liberalism and Voluntarism." *Critical Review* 25(1): 38–85.

Friedman, Jeffrey. Forthcoming. *No Exit: The Problem with Democracy.*

Gamble, Andrew. "Hayek and Liberty." *Critical Review* 25(3–4): 342–63.

Godard, François. 2013. "*The Road to Serfdom*'s Economistic Worldview." *Critical Review* 25(3–4): 364–85.

Gray, John. 1984. *Hayek on Liberty.* Oxford: Basil Blackwell.

Hayek, F. A., ed. 1935a. *Collectivist Economic Planning.* London: Routledge.

Hayek, F. A. 1935b. "The Present State of the Debate." In Hayek 1935a.

Hayek, F. A. 1940. "The Competitive Solution." *Economica* 7: 125–49.

Hayek, F. A. 1944. *The Road to Serfdom.* Chicago: University of Chicago Press.

Hayek, F. A. 1945. "The Use of Knowledge in Society." *American Economic Review* 35(4): 519–30.

Hayek, F. A. 1946 [1948]. "The Meaning of Competition." In idem, *Individualism and Economic Order.* Chicago: University of Chicago Press.

Hayek, F. A. 1952a [1979]. *The Counter-Revolution of Science: Studies on the Abuse of Reason,* 2nd ed. Indianapolis: Liberty Press.

Hayek, F. A. 1952b. *The Sensory Order: An Inquiry into the Foundations of Theoretical Psychology.* Chicago: University of Chicago Press.

Hayek, F. A. 1960. *The Constitution of Liberty.* Chicago: University of Chicago Press.

Hayek, F. A. 1967. "Rules, Perception, and Intelligibility." In idem, *Studies in Philosophy, Politics, and Economics.* Chicago: University of Chicago Press.

Hayek, F. A. 1968 [1978]. "Competition as a Discovery Procedure." In idem, *New Studies in Philosophy, Politics, and the History of Ideas.* Chicago: University of Chicago Press.

Hayek, F. A. 1973. *Rules and Order.* Vol. 1 of *Law, Legislation and Liberty.* Chicago: University of Chicago Press.

Hayek, F. A. 1979. *The Political Order of a Free People.* Vol. 3 of *Law, Legislation and Liberty.* Chicago: University of Chicago Press.

Kresge, Stephen, and Leif Wenar, eds. 1994. *Hayek on Hayek: An Autobiographical Dialogue.* Chicago: University of Chicago Press.

Kuehn, Daniel. 2013. "Hayek's Business-Cycle Theory: Half Right." *Critical Review* 25(3–4): 497–529.

Lange, Oskar R. 1936 [1964]. "On the Economic Theory of Socialism." In Lippincott 1964.

Lavoie, Don. 1985. *Rivalry and Central Planning: The Socialist Calculation Debate Reconsidered.* Cambridge: Cambridge University Press.

Lerner, Abba P. 1934. "Economic Theory and Socialist Economy." *Review of Economic Studies* 2: 51–61.

Lewis, Paul. 2013. "Hayek, Social Theory, and the Contrastive Explanation of Social Order." *Critical Review* 25(3–4): 386–408.

Lippincott, Benjamin E., ed. 1964. *On the Economic Theory of Socialism.* New York: McGraw-Hill.

Lister, Andrew. "The 'Mirage' of Social Justice: Hayek Against (and For) Rawls." *Critical Review* 25(3–4): 409–44.

MacDonald, Kevin, and Scott L. Hershberger. 2005. "Theoretical Issues in the Study of Evolution and Development." In *Evolutionary Perspectives on Human*

Development, ed. Robert Lee Burgess and Kevin MacDonald. Thousand Oaks, Calif.: Sage.

Mises, Ludwig von. 1920. "Economic Calculation in the Socialist Commonwealth." In Hayek 1935a.

Polanyi, Karl. 1944. *The Great Transformation*. New York: Rinehart.

Ryan, Alan. 2013. "The Planners and the Planned." *Critical Review* 25(3–4): 445–60.

Sahlins, Marshall. 1974 [2004]. *Stone Age Economics*. London: Routledge.

Schumpeter, Joseph A. 1950. *Capitalism, Socialism, and Democracy*, 3rd ed. New York: Harper and Row.

Somin, Ilya. 2013. *Democracy and Political Ignorance*. Stanford: Stanford University Press.

Strong, Michael. 2013. "Some Implications of Hayek's Cognitive Theory." *Critical Review* 25(3–4): 461–72.

Taylor, Fred M. 1929 [1964]. "The Guidance of Production in a Socialist State." In Lippincott 1964.

Vaughn, Karen I. 2013. "Hayek, Equilibrium, and the Role of Institutions in Economic Order." *Critical Review* 25(3–4): 473–96.

Weber, Max. 1904 [1949]. "'Objectivity' in Social Science and Social Policy." In idem, *The Methodology of the Social Sciences*, ed. Edward A. Shils and Henry A. Finch. New York: Free Press.

Peter J. Boettke and Kyle W. O'Donnell

THE FAILED APPROPRIATION OF F. A. HAYEK BY FORMALIST ECONOMICS

ABSTRACT: *Hayek argued that the central question of economics is the coordination problem: How does the spontaneous interaction of many purposeful individuals, each having dispersed bits of subjective knowledge, generate an order in which the actors' subjective data are coordinated in a way that enables them to dovetail their plans and activities successfully? In attempting to solve this problem, Hayek outlined an approach to economic theorizing that takes seriously the limited, subjective nature of human knowledge. Despite purporting to have appropriated Hayek's thought by acknowledging the information-transmitting role of prices, mainstream economists have missed Hayek's point. The predominant tool of formal economics—equilibrium analysis—begins by assuming the data held by actors to have been pre-reconciled, and so evades the problem to be solved. Even the more advanced tools for modeling knowledge in economic analysis, such as the economics of information, assume away either the subjectivism of knowledge and expectations (rendering the coordination of beliefs and plans a trivial matter) or the frictions and "imperfections" of reality (rendering the coordination problem indeterminate).*

Friedrich Hayek is undoubtedly one of the most important economists of the twentieth century. He was often at the center of the century's most significant debates about economic ideas.[1] As a positive scientific economist, perhaps the principal contribution for which Hayek is most widely known is his claim—especially as presented in his 1945 article, "The Use of Knowledge in Society"—that the central economic problem of society concerns the use of dispersed knowledge under various institutional arrangements. During the second half of the twentieth century, mainstream economists would cite Hayek 1945 as an important influence on their work, especially in the economics of information. However, among economists and other scholars who have studied Hayek's work seriously, there is a persistent impression that Hayek is cited but not read, or at least not understood, by many of the mainstream economists who so often claim to have grappled with his ideas. We share this impression and will thus examine the failure of mainstream economics to appropriate Hayek's work on economics and knowledge into its formalist technical apparatus (despite repeated claims to the contrary).

A fundamental puzzle with which Hayek recurrently grapples is the *coordination problem*—the problem of how "the spontaneous interaction of a number of people, each possessing only bits of knowledge, brings about a state of affairs . . . which could be brought about by deliberate direction only by somebody who possessed the combined knowledge of all those individuals" (Hayek 1937, 50–51). The roots of this theme can be seen in Hayek's arguments in the socialist-calculation debate during the 1930s (Caldwell 1988 and 1997; Boettke 1997), in the course of which mainstream economists offered formal proofs to show that central planning could supplant the decentralized operation of market prices.[2] Not only "The Use of Knowledge in Society" but "Economics and Knowledge," published in 1937, stated Hayek's insights into the epistemic problems of economic analysis, which he derived partly from the socialist-calculation debate. Although Hayek's thought continued to evolve over the course of his sprawling intellectual career, these two essays serve as useful foils for examining why Hayek's economic thought resisted formalization so strongly, and why his work has thus far evaded successful appropriation by mainstream economics.

The economics of information, or "information economics," is the most prominent example of how formal theorists have attempted to translate Hayek's ideas into a form that could be easily digested and incorporated by mainstream economics. In this effort Hayek 1945 was seen in the 1960s and '70s as the most concise statement of his understanding of the role of knowledge in the economy. Information economists distilled Hayek 1945 into the argument that information is initially dispersed as incomplete bits across the various members of society; that the central economic problem facing society was how to design institutions or mechanisms for the optimal aggregation, communication, and use of that dispersed information; and that the price system in a free-market economy is an efficient, low-cost mechanism for achieving the optimal solution to that problem (Hurwicz 1969; Grossman and Stiglitz 1976; Myerson 2009). From here, information economists sought to examine the "Hayek hypothesis" in a more rigorous fashion than Hayek had done by constructing models that attempted to formalize the essential aspects of Hayek's argument. Just as had happened during the 1930s, information economists produced numerous articles alleging to refute "Hayek's hypothesis" of the informational efficiency of the price system, and later challenged nearly all claims of the superior welfare properties of free markets over economies with varying degrees of government intervention and planning (Stiglitz 2000 and 2002).

Setting aside these normative considerations, we argue that there are reasons to doubt these formal theorists adequately grasped the central ideas of Hayek's economics, let alone refuted his specific analytical and empirical claims. That there would arise errors in "translating" verbal arguments into formal theory is perhaps inevitable, yet there are aspects of Hayek that *cannot* be adequately formalized, nor is it clear that there would be any benefit from doing so even if it were possible. Hayek thought deeply about the methodological and epistemological foundations of economic theory, especially formal equilibrium-based theory. In highlighting several specific methodological and epistemological problems in the technical apparatus of formalist economics, Hayek foresaw many of the challenges that formal economic theory—especially information economics, game theory, and equilibrium-based analysis more generally—would only begin to grapple with decades later (see Samuelson 2004; Foss 2000; Vaughn 1999). Mainstream economists are inclined to treat Hayek as *just* an informal theorist (see Caldwell 1997; Stiglitz 2000, 1444, 1446; Myerson 2009), such that any failure to formalize his insights stems from their being too "fuzzy" (Caldwell 1997, 1857–58, 1877) to be formalized. But Hayek's position was that formal theory was fundamentally incapable of capturing the heart of the economic process due to the technical limitations inherent in formalism itself. The value of Hayek's informal theorizing is that it captures the dynamism of the market process—explaining, for example, why choice, variety, innovation, and reputation matter for economic development and welfare—and ultimately brings meaning and intelligibility to social phenomena that formalism cannot match or replicate.

The Coordination Problem as a Knowledge Problem

Before we can demonstrate that mainstream economics has failed to appropriate Hayek's insights accurately, we must articulate precisely what those ideas were.[3] In this section, therefore, we outline the core aspects of Hayek's economics, particularly his ideas regarding knowledge and economics, discussing, first, his conception of the central question of economics; next, the methodological, epistemological, and analytical issues that economists must confront in order to improve scientific understanding; and, finally, the propositions and hypotheses that Hayek suggested as solutions to these problems. We intend primarily to construct a concise statement of Hayek's ideas about economics and knowledge—i.e., a "Hayekian framework"—that encapsulates his central insights and enables us to examine why such a framework has evaded the formalism of mainstream economics.

In "Economics and Knowledge," Hayek (1937) articulated a number of ideas that would become major themes in his economic thought and in his broader social theory.[4] First he discussed the limits of formal economic analysis in understanding real-world phenomena, criticizing formal equilibrium analysis, in particular, for distracting economists from the really fundamental problems of economics. At the core of Hayek's critique of formalism was the claim that economic analysis has empirical relevance and conveys understanding about the real world only insofar as it contains explicit assumptions or propositions about how knowledge is acquired, communicated, and used by individual actors.

Next, Hayek set about examining the concept of *equilibrium* and reframing it in terms of the subjective knowledge or "data" held by individual actors, the plans they make and the actions they take based upon this data, and the objective facts that are external to the individual. Hayek emphasized that all claims about equilibria necessarily entail a claim about the knowledge of economic actors: namely, that they have correct foresight or expectations about the objective facts relevant to their situation.[5] For Hayek (1937, 44–45), then, equilibrium refers to the mutual compatibility of plans between individuals and their external circumstances through time, such that the subjective data held in individuals' minds corresponds with that of others and with external, objective facts. In other words, "equilibrium" in a Hayekian sense can be thought of as intertemporal plan coordination, where people can successfully achieve their ends by dovetailing their plans and actions with others and with objective reality (see Vaughn 1999).

Although Hayek was often critical of the equilibrium construct, he nevertheless considered the apparent *tendency towards equilibrium* of the market process as the foundation for, and most important problem of, economic theorizing—where the proposition that such a tendency exists basically means "that, under certain conditions, the knowledge and intentions of the different members of society are supposed to come more and more into agreement," or "that the expectations of the people and particularly of the entrepreneurs will become more and more correct" (1937, 44–45, 51). Hayek maintains that it is "only by this assertion that such a tendency exists that economics ceases to be an exercise in pure logic and becomes an empirical science" (ibid., 44). This point is highly significant in understanding Hayek's argument that the "really central problem of economics as a social science" is the coordination problem that arises from the division of knowledge (Hayek 1937, 50). Keep in mind that the question is, according to Hayek, "how the spontaneous interaction of a number of people, each possessing only bits of knowledge, brings about a state of affairs . . . which could be brought about by deliberate direction only by somebody who possessed the combined knowledge of all those individuals" (ibid., 50–51). As he would later write, "it is a problem of the utilization of knowledge which is not given to anyone in its totality" (Hayek 1945, 78). As such, the coordination problem entails the empirical proposition that there indeed exists a tendency towards equilibrium or coordination within the market economy, which, as we have seen, suggests that the knowledge of market actors tends over time to become more "correct" (Hayek 1937, 44–45, 51). The analytical challenge then becomes examining and articulating "(a) the *conditions* under which this tendency is supposed to exist and (b) the nature of the *process* by which individual knowledge is changed" (ibid., 45, emph. original).

The assumption that such a tendency towards coordination exists might seem dubious at first glance. It is important to recognize, however, that in its most generalized form, this proposition essentially states that *social order* exists. The domain of social science, then, is the shared social reality that emerges from the coordination of the subjective data held in individual minds, the structure and order of which any social science attempts to understand, although it can never be fully grasped by any individual mind (Hayek 1952b, chs. 3–4).

Social science is concerned with the study of social phenomena—culture, language, markets, politics, etc.—but if these "objects" are to be understood, it necessarily implies the coordination of minds. In other words, in a world where a tendency towards coordination, broadly understood, did not exist in any sense—such that we were purely atomistic creatures whose goals, plans, and actions were unintelligible to one another—then *social* phenomena would be inconceivable, and thus, there could be no social science.[6] Further, given the fact that we are fallible beings with limited knowledge and reasoning capacities, there would be little of interest for social science to explain if error and disorder were the predominant characteristics of society: error and disorder are precisely what we would expect, and thus would be uninteresting. As Hayek (1937, 34) put it, "before we can explain why people commit mistakes, we must first explain why they should ever be right."[7] Thus, it is in light of the limits of the human mind that the existence of complex social order can evoke the sense of wonder that drives many social-scientific endeavors.

Formal equilibrium analysis, however, does not directly address the problem of "how the 'data' of the different individuals on which they base their plans are adjusted to the objective facts of their environment (which includes the actions of the other people)" (Hayek 1946, 93). Rather, it "starts from the assumption that people's *knowledge* corresponds with the objective *facts* of the situation, [and] systematically leaves out what is our main task to explain" (Hayek 1945, 91). Hayek traced the source of this confusion, in part, to the uncritical application of formal economic theory, especially the "Pure Logic of Choice"—which was constructed a priori to describe the plans and actions of an isolated individual—to the analysis of the interdependent plans and actions of many people (Hayek 1937, 38–39). Insofar as the Pure Logic of Choice takes the subjective knowledge of an isolated individual as its relevant "data," it follows tautologically that the individual's actions and plans are necessarily in equilibrium with each other. However, in moving from the atomistic equilibrium of an isolated mind to societal equilibria of multiple minds, the meaning of equilibrium, and the nature of the "data" to which it refers, are fundamentally transformed. The data that are assumed as given to the individuals in formal equilibrium analysis correspond directly to the objective facts, leading to equilibrium by definition (ibid., 36–39). But even more fundamentally, Hayek argued, neither the Pure Logic of Choice nor formal equilibrium analysis alone can illuminate the causal relationship between people's subjective knowledge and their experience of the external, objective facts (ibid., 44–48). This means that pure economic theory, especially equilibrium analysis, is incapable of shedding light on the *process* by which people's subjective knowledge is sufficiently adjusted so as to bring about intertemporal plan coordination. In order to do that, Hayek argued in 1937, it is necessary to introduce into economic analysis additional propositions, or subsidiary hypotheses, about knowledge—such as what kind of knowledge is relevant, how it is acquired and communicated, and how much of it people must possess if equilibrium is to be attained.

In "Economics and Knowledge," Hayek (1937, 51) expressed very clearly his dissatisfaction with how it had "become customary among economists to stress only the need of knowledge of prices"—which is notable in light of later formalist treatments of Hayek that attributed to him this very practice. In contrast, Hayek argued that "price expectations and even the knowledge of current prices are only a very small section of the problem of knowledge as I see it. The wider aspect of the problem of knowledge with which I am concerned is the knowledge of the basic fact of how the different commodities can be obtained and used, and under what conditions they are actually obtained and used" (ibid.). In other words, for there to arise a tendency towards equilibrium (or coordination), people must possess some additional knowledge about the underlying "things" being exchanged, in order for the prices of those things to reflect accurately the alternative uses to which they might be put. Yet as Hayek famously argued in "The Use of Knowledge in Society," the knowledge that is relevant to the solution to the economic problem is never *given* to a single mind, but is widely dispersed throughout society as bits of incomplete, subjective knowledge localized to particular times and places. In light of these epistemological conditions, further questions must be answered: How much knowledge must individuals each possess such that equilibrium (coordination), or a tendency towards it, is possible? And what is the role of institutions in the solution to the coordination problem (ibid., 50–55)?

Thus, "Economics and Knowledge" plays a pivotal role in setting the stage for an alternative "Hayekian" framework for economic analysis. First, Hayek reframed the central question of economics as the coordination problem and thus the knowledge problem. Next, he demonstrated that the standard tool of pure economic theory—formal equilibrium analysis—is inadequate for addressing this problem. Finally, he outlined specific analytical and substantive elements of the problem that economic analysis would have to address (and suggested a few ideas for how to proceed to analyze the problem). "The Use of Knowledge in Society" (1945) elaborates on these themes, proposing solutions and hypotheses in response to the questions posed in "Economics and Knowledge"—which he continued to explore in later work, including "The Meaning of Competition" (1946) and "Competition as a Discovery Procedure" (1968). However, in contrast to "Economics and Know-ledge," which largely focused on methodological and epistemological issues of positive economics, "The Use of Knowledge in Society" also returned to the debate over the feasibility (and desirability) of central economic planning. Here, in response to the theoretical and empirical problems he had discussed in 1937, Hayek began to construct a solution emphasizing the operation of social and economic processes within a particular institutional framework.

Most notably, Hayek (1945, 78, 86) argued that the price system acts as a "mechanism for communicating information" about the relative scarcities of resources, and is crucial in a world of dispersed, imperfect knowledge for solving the "problem of how to secure the best use of resources known to any of the members of society, for ends whose relative importance only these individuals know." Within the institu-tional context of a market economy, individuals are free to pursue their desired ends in accordance with their own subjective, tacit knowledge, while the price system extends to them information about the relative scarcities of resources so they may dovetail their plans and actions with those of others (ibid., 79, 84–86). The most important characteristic of the price system, Hayek argued, "is the economy of knowledge with which it operates, or how little the individual participants need to know in order to be able to take the right action" (ibid., 86). That is, prices enable individuals to act as if they possessed more knowledge than a single mind could grasp without the use of the price system. In this sense, prices serve as "knowledge surrogates" (Thomsen 1992, 41, 43–45).

To briefly illustrate, imagine a market for resource Y, which has various possible uses a, b, . . . , z known to several persons A, B, . . . , Z. Hayek suggests that in order for the price of Y to fully reflect the values of these alternative uses, it is sufficient that A knows of a and b, B knows b and c, and so on, where each actor knows only a fraction of the possible uses of Y, as long as, together, their knowledge overlaps in a way that connects all of these separately known facts (Hayek 1937, 53–54). In this example, the price system guides people to conduct themselves as if they had direct access to society's total knowledge. Thus, actor B may not know of use m directly, but since the price of Y reflects m, B plans and acts as if she knew m.

As we have seen, Hayek argued that knowledge of prices alone is not sufficient for market participants to spontaneously coordinate their plans. They must also have some knowledge of the objective facts about the "things" being priced—facts such as the uses of, or substitutes for, these things. The need for knowledge of the facts about things other than their relative scarcities (which are reflected in prices) necessitates an additional mechanism for acquiring and communicating knowledge. Yet Hayek did not base his arguments about knowledge and coordination in the market process upon an explicit "psychological" or cognitive theory of individual learning.[8] Rather, he offered what was essentially an institutional theory of social learning in which individuals are "forced" to adjust their subjective knowledge, expectations, and plans through their interactions with one another and with experiences of common facts (Hayek 1937, 44, 50–54; Hayek 1968, 189).

While the absence of an explicit theory of individual learning is arguably a weakness in Hayek's approach, it may also be one of the major virtues of his economic theorizing. By treating the mind as something of a "black box," Hayek constructed a framework for economic analysis that could accommodate a variety of assumptions and propositions about knowledge, learning, and belief formation, while not being arbitrarily constrained by the internal limits of any particular formal model. Hayek was not trying to justify the heroic assumptions about knowledge that are foundational to mainstream economics, but, quite the opposite, to develop the structure of a social theory that takes seriously the limits of the human mind. Hence, Hayek often seemed content to sketch the basic outline of actors' cognition, without delving into the details.

The Hayekian framework does not require that actors' subjective perceptions necessarily converge upon the objective truth in order to explain the emergence of a tendency towards coordination in markets. Arguably, if one recognizes strict limits to knowledge and cognition, one has already rendered it unlikely that any individual mind could perceive and grasp "truth" in social order (Hayek 1967, 22–42, 82–95). To what, then, could Hayek turn as a solution to the coordination problem?

Competition and the Evolution of Knowledge

Hayek's answer was market competition, which he saw as a mechanism or procedure for discovering such facts as which goods and services consumers demand, which production technologies are the least expensive, and the price at which supply might meet demand—facts that the theory of competitive equilibrium assumes are data (Hayek 1946, 95–96; Hayek 1968).

Market competition embodies many crucial elements of the epistemic process that Hayek argued is a necessary condition for a solution to the problem of coordination in light of radical ignorance. In particular, competition helps to adjust the subjective knowledge of individuals to objective facts. "Competition is essentially a process of the formation of opinion: by spreading information, it creates that unity and coherence of the economic system which we presuppose when we think of it as one market. . . It is thus a process which involves a continuous change in the data and whose significance must therefore be completely missed by any theory which treats these data as constant" (Hayek 1946, 106). In this way, market competition plays a crucial role in Hayek's economic thought as a coordination mechanism that reconciles people's different goals and knowledge, allowing the fullest practicable utilization of the dispersed knowledge in society—and thus guiding individuals to dovetail their plans and actions with those of others, to adjust them when they are incompatible with others, and to discover and correct errors in the market order.

That people may discover facts of which they were previously unaware implies the existence of sheer (or "radical") ignorance or, as Keynes and Knight had put it, "uncertainty." Radical ignorance is a significant element of Hayek's economic thought and marks an important departure from mainstream economics. Competition, he wrote, is principally valuable as a "procedure for the discovery of such facts as, without resort to it, would not be known to anyone, or at least would not be utilized" (Hayek 1968, 179). Thus, the "solution of the economic problem of society is in this respect always a voyage of exploration into the unknown, an attempt to discover new ways of doing things better than they have been done before" (1948, 101).[9] Competition alleviates the problem of radical ignorance—to the extent that such a difficult problem can be dealt with—by testing various entrepreneurs' answers to the question of what consumers want and how most efficiently to sell it to them. Both sides of this equation, though, are equally significant. Not only knowledge of how best to meet demand, but knowledge of what consumers might want, is needed if there are to be coordinative tendencies. Competition provides both types of knowledge. Thus, the Hayekian theory of the market order does not require people to agree upon their particular purposes or ends, but merely to observe the abstract rules of conduct that make market exchanges possible (Hayek 1976, 107–32).

What the Hayekian framework ultimately attempts to offer, then, is a theory in which social-economic order emerges from exchange processes operating between individuals who are fundamentally incapable of ever coming to complete agreement. It would be difficult to overstate the significance of this effort, since it suggests that social order emerges directly from the differences in knowledge, perspectives, and interpretations of individuals, *not in spite of them.*

In light of the analytical need for an impersonal mechanism to adjudicate, adjust, and reconcile people's partial and conflicting knowledge, expectations, and plans, we can better understand Hayek's perspective on market competition as an evolutionary process. First, Hayek argued, the data relevant to economic order change over time, impelling people to adapt to always-temporary conditions (Hayek 1968, 179–81). Given the impenetrable shroud of time and ignorance, trial-and-error experimentation through the competitive market process is among the only established methods for assessing the value to society of alternative courses of action (Hayek 1948, 100–1). The effectiveness of this trial-and-error method is analogous to the theory of biological evolution by natural selection, where economic actors are guided by profit-loss signals and "survival" is determined through market selection. Entrepreneurs who satisfy consumers' demands at the lowest cost and highest quality earn positive profits, which signal socially desirable actions that allocate resources to their highest-valued uses. Entrepreneurs who do not do so, on the other hand, suffer monetary losses and are eventually eliminated via market selection (Alchian 1950). "Competition produces in this way a kind of impersonal compulsion which makes it necessary for numerous individuals to adjust their way of life in a manner that no deliberate instructions or commands could bring about" (Hayek 1968, 189). Competition serves as a critical mechanism for adjudicating between the subjective knowledge held by different persons in society and adjusting actors' subjective data to the objective facts of the situation.

Second, as with evolution, which achieves no *telos*, Hayek did not claim that the market process or the price system were optimal or perfect in any sense, let alone the idealized optimality of formal welfare economics. The market process may never reach a point on the surface of the Pareto frontier, and may never even reach equilibrium (Hayek 1968, 185–86) (competitive processes merely produce a tendency toward equilibrium). Likewise, the price system is unlikely to be perfect in the informational or allocative sense characteristic of a blackboard "social planner solution" derived from a set of simultaneous equations. Hayek argued that such standards are largely irrelevant to any problems of real-world economic phenomena, since they cannot be achieved in the real world by any known means. Rather, real-world competition and market processes should be evaluated only relative to the outcome (or patterned order) that would realistically emerge without free competition (Hayek 1948, 100–106). However, Hayek concluded that the unhampered market economy,[10] compared to its relevant alternatives, is the institutional framework most likely to ever approach such ideals (Hayek 1968, 184–85).

Mechanism Design: The Formalization of "Communication"

Although Hayek had largely turned away from the practice of economic theory by midcentury, his ideas about knowledge and information in economic analysis had a foundational role in the development of both the economics of information and mechanism-design theory. That Hayek was cited but not read, or at least not understood, will become clear if we examine how the leading economists in these areas interpreted Hayek's view of the relationship between prices and knowledge, which are undoubtedly the ideas for which Hayek is most widely cited.

Tjalling Koopmans was a pioneer in the economics of mechanism design, building much of the mathematical foundations for the formal analysis of economic organizations. Koopmans (1977) states that this research agenda was partly inspired by the consensus conclusion that the socialist-calculation debate of the 1920s and 30s showed that the allocation of resources would be efficient under both hypothetical perfect competition and hypothetical central planning. Unfortunately, the debate had stagnated, according to Koopmans, due to the informal nature of the theoretical arguments, which prevented the participants from reaching definite conclusions or postulating rigorous solutions to the problems at hand. Hence, Koopmans constructed a "*pre*-institutional theory of the allocation of resources"—in which an optimal resource allocation is derived from a set of given environmental and informational constraints, independent of any institutional arrangements—to serve as a formal mathematical framework for the design, analysis, and evaluation of alternative economic mechanisms (Koopmans 1951 and 1977, 264–5).

In addition, Koopmans offered one of the first mathematical models purporting to formalize, at least partially, the proposition that the price system communicates information to actors, allowing efficient informational decentralization under certain conditions. However, he largely focused on describing the equilibrium conditions of such an informationally decentralized system, leaving the formal modeling of market processes to others (Koopmans and Beckmann 1957, 60).[11]

Thomas Marschak (1959 and 1969) and Leonid Hurwicz (1969 and 1973) followed Koopmans's work on the theory of mechanism design by examining individual decision making under different organizational structures, or more precisely, the problem of deriving optimal decision rules such that the decentralized actions of individuals will tend to maximize the objective function of the organization.[12] They both recognized that one of the central problems of economic analysis is explaining how information is communicated and acquired. Marschak attempted to tackle the issue, raised by Koopmans, of the need to analyze the mechanisms operating within dynamic adjustment processes in response to changing circumstances. His solution was a formal model of such an informational process (Marschak 1959 and 1969). Within this "process" framework, an economy is comprised of multiple "agents," each of whom has his own vector of states containing bits of information that change at each step as agents "observe" new signals, update their own information, and send new signals according to a defined function (Marschak 1969, 525–26).

Hurwicz (1969 and 1973) continued to refine the theory of mechanism design, in terms of formal rigor, by means of several technical innovations. Perhaps most important, Hurwicz developed a more rigorous, formal definition of informational decentralization—explicitly citing Hayek's influence on his thinking—which would serve as both constraint and benchmark for the formal analysis of alternative mechanisms and allocation processes.

In order to qualify as informationally decentralized, as per Hurwicz's definition, the proposed process or mechanism must "restrict communication to commodity-dimensional messages and also postulate that the only information available to any economic unit concerning the other units is derived from such communication; i.e., except for what can be inferred from such communication, every unit is assumed to be in total ignorance of other units' technologies, preferences, and resource holdings" (Hurwicz 1969, 516). In addition to this stringent formal definition of informational decentralization, Hurwicz proposed other conditions for evaluating the efficiency of a mechanism, the most important, for our purposes, being that a process is *non-wasteful*: Scarce resources must not be misallocated to a less than optimal use, in light of perfect complete information of the environment and an optimal pre-institutional resource allocation (Hurwicz 1973, 18).

Hajime Oniki (1974) would follow these economists by constructing a theoretical framework for organizational analysis that is notable for synthesizing many of the central concepts and ideas of mechanism design theory that Koopmans, Marschak, and Hurwicz had earlier developed. The major problem that Oniki (1974) examined was how to formally analyze and measure the cost of communication in centralized and decentralized economic organizations as part of a broader theoretical framework that might eventually handle more extensive comparative analyses of economic systems.[13] Towards this end, Oniki adopted the approach to modeling communication processes developed by Marschak and Hurwicz; the formal conditions, restrictions, and definitions of information and equilibrium proposed by Hurwicz; and the idea of dispersed information from Hayek (Oniki 1974, 529–34). Thus, we can see this framework as a concise presentation of the major Hayek-influenced themes that the early theory of mechanism design agglomerated and attempted to formalize.

The Economics of Information and the Omniscience Assumption

At the same time that these economists were constructing a relatively new technical apparatus for the theory of mechanism design, another group of economists steadily developed the economics of information using fairly standard tools of price theory. In "The Economics of Information," George Stigler (1961) developed a formal economic theory of optimizing "information search" in markets under conditions of ignorance or uncertainty. This was seen as an important step towards reconciling the Chicago school's equilibrium-always assumption with the economic realities of a world of constant change and uncertainty. Stigler argued that, in a world of uncertainty and ignorance, information is a valuable resource for which rational actors will actively search—or expend resources to collect—so as to reduce their level of ignorance, continuing until their marginal benefit from reduced ignorance equals marginal cost of further search. However, Stigler argued, since there are costs to reducing ignorance—namely, the cost of search—the optimal level of ignorance is greater than zero, and the forces of market competition tend to bring about that level of ignorance.

Stigler, along with numerous other economists, demonstrated that many imperfections and market failures could be re-evaluated as efficient in light of positive information costs, and also provided other insights, including an economic explanation for the social benefits of advertising, reputations, brand names, and various "middlemen" like department stores (Hirshleifer 1973). Thus, Stigler (1961) had a pioneering role in moving from what Jack Hirshleifer (1973, 31–32) described as the *passive* economics of uncertainty, where actors merely react to incoming signals by adjusting their decisions, to the *active* economics of information, in which individuals act purposively to collect, disseminate, and produce information.[14]

Hirshleifer was another pioneer of the active economics of information, whose analysis often emphasized the dynamic, entrepreneurial nature of the market process (Hirshleifer 1971; also see Hirshleifer 1973). In order to formalize their models and theories, however, it was necessary for information economists to adopt mathematically tractable definitions of a number of important concepts (including information, uncertainty, and ignorance). Information, therefore, was treated as something of an objective resource or commodity that can be exchanged and produced and that, in some sense, exists independently of the minds in which it is held. There were even efforts to quantify information in terms of "bits" by applying communications theory (Thomsen 1992, 22–23; Hirshleifer 1973, 33; Oniki 1974). But the economics of information ejected subjectivism from its analysis on an even more fundamental level in assuming that the value or relevance of a particular bit of information can be automatically and unambiguously recognized by an economic agent without the need for interpretation or entrepreneurial "alertness" (Kirzner 1973; Hirshleifer 1973, 32–33; also Lavoie 1985, 52–65).[15] That is, agents were assumed to know *ex ante* the existence, relevance, and value of as-yet-unlearned information; only in this way could they accurately trade the benefit of "acquiring" it against the cost of doing so. All information, then, was treated as a known known whose only unknown aspect was its content, even though this content must determine the value of learning it, at least in part (Evans and Friedman 2011). The economics of information therefore presupposed, in a sense, agents' omniscience. Had it been otherwise, economists of information could not have attributed to agents an accurate calculus of the benefits of learning, and search behavior could not have been forecast except in the empty sense of predicting that agents will try to learn whatever they think it is valuable to learn.

Uncertainty, likewise, was systematically treated in a way that minimized the intractable "genuine" uncertainty associated with Keynes and Knight, in which probability distributions are incalculable for a certain class of phenomena. Genuine uncertainty plays an important role in Hayek's thought because it captures agents' orientation toward an unknown future. But to increase the ease of mathematical modeling, uncertainty was reconceived as a form of probability where actors can simply assign "subjective" probability distributions to every possible state of the world (Hirshleifer and Riley 1979, 1378).

This interpretation of uncertainty had profound implications for another concept of central importance in Hayek's economic thought: ignorance. The only kind of ignorance that exists in the world described by the economics of information is rational ignorance, as exemplified in the decision of an agent not to learn something because she somehow knows that it would not be worthwhile (Boettke 1997, 28). Again, this approach implies "that to make such decisions correctly—as must be the case in equilibrium—agents must know beforehand, among other things, what they are ignorant of and the costs and benefits of the knowledge they could acquire; that is, *they must know what it is they do not know*" (Thomsen 1992, 23; also see Kirzner 1997). In other words, and as we discuss in more detail below, there is no room for *radical* ignorance, or unawareness, within formal economic theory, since there are logical obstacles inherent to formally modeling a situation in which an actor *does not know she does not know* something (Samuelson 2004; Evans and Friedman 2011).

By the 1970s and 1980s, a "new information economics" emerged from the work of yet another group of economists—prominently including Joseph Stiglitz, Sanford Grossman, and George Akerlof—which absorbed and extended several of the core features of both the economics of information and mechanism-design theory. Like their predecessors, the new information economists examined the effects of different informational and incentive constraints on a variety of economic and organizational problems, while many also strove to develop a more general, yet mathematically rigorous, framework for comparative economic analysis based upon formal equilibrium theorizing (see Stiglitz 2000, 1455–56; Stiglitz 1985; also see Myerson 2009). Perhaps unsurprisingly, Hayek was given special attention within the new information economics, particularly in the work of Grossman (1976) and Stiglitz (Grossman and Stiglitz 1976 and 1980), whose interpretation and later formalization of Hayek may have been one of the most important influences on how mainstream economics understands Hayek.

In the Grossman-Stiglitz framework, Hayek 1945 is interpreted as arguing that economically relevant information is initially dispersed across society as incomplete bits privately held by individual agents; that the primary function of the price system is to communicate to agents the information necessary to achieve an efficient allocation of resources; that the competitive mechanism aggregates all private market information into an equilibrium price vector, which summarizes and conveys all such information to every agent in the market; that the equilibrium price is the only bit of information that agents need to know in order to reach the market equilibrium satisfying the standard theorems of welfare economics; and thus that the equilibrium price is a *sufficient statistic* for efficient market outcomes in an informationally decentralized system (Grossman 1976; Grossman and Stiglitz 1976 and 1980). It was this interpretation that Grossman and Stiglitz set out to translate into a formal equilibrium model, which would allow them to analyze rigorously Hayek's informal arguments.

In the formal model (Grossman 1976; Grossman and Stiglitz 1976 and 1980), an economy consists of multiple agents who buy and sell two commodities: one standard good and one risky good with an uncertain value. Each agent, however, is given a bit of private information about the value of the risky good. In making bids and offers for the good, their private information is aggregated by the price, such that in equilibrium all private information is revealed. If information is costless, all relevant information is aggregated by the market price in equilibrium, and the agents reach an efficient outcome through decentralized actions. But if information is costly, agents must choose between observing the market price at zero cost, from which they might then infer market information; or expending resources searching for market information, which will then be instantaneously reflected in the price.

The problem, as Grossman and Stiglitz emphasize, is that the market can never reach equilibrium in a world of costly information where the price system perfectly summarizes private information: At the equilibrium price, there is no incentive to collect additional information and all agents rely on price as a sufficient statistic, but then the price does not reflect all available information and so the market is not in equilibrium. Only when the price system is an imperfect mechanism for aggregating information—i.e., when the price system is noisy—is it possible for there to be an imperfect information equilibrium. Therefore, Grossman and Stiglitz conclude, the notion that the price system is an efficient mechanism for communicating dispersed, private information is false. In turn, it is questionable if the competitive market system is informationally decentralized and economically efficient and even whether it outperforms central planning (Grossman 1976; Grossman and Stiglitz 1976 and 1980).

Following in the footsteps of Grossman and Stiglitz, economists began to develop a highly formalized approach to comparative economic systems analysis. This approach combined information economics with the formal modeling techniques of mechanism design (Myerson 2009; Sah and Stiglitz 1985). This new approach to comparative economics emphasized the operation of alternative economic mechanisms under varying informational constraints, with room to consider the strategic behavior of agents in circumstances of imperfect (asymmetric) information. In line with this approach, Sah and Stiglitz (1985 and 1986) analyze how the "architecture" of the economic system affects how information is communicated and acquired, how decisions are made, and the "aggregate" results of these individual choices in different organizational structures. Sappington and Stiglitz (1987) apply these tools to privatization, examining the costs and benefits of private versus public production of goods in situations with potential principal/agent problems, and suggest a privatization welfare theorem. Myerson (2009) even returns to the socialist-calculation debate, among several other problems of institutional analysis, analyzing several key issues with the formal tools of information economics and mechanism design.[16] However, despite the renewed emphasis on both incentive and information problems in comparative economics, including the socialist-calculation debate, there seems to be little inherent difference between these two problems; indeed, imperfect information can essentially be reduced to an incentives problem (see Myerson 2009), which was exactly the approach that Stigler had originally taken to "the economics of information."

As a result of the efforts described above, mainstream economists constructed a formal, mathematical apparatus that attempted to grapple with Hayek's ideas about knowledge in economics (or rather, their interpretations of these ideas) in a rigorous manner. There are several notable features of the "mainstream Hayekian" perspective that emerged.[17] First, knowledge was treated as identical to objective, albeit decentralized and/or imperfect, information or "data" (Boettke 2002). This objective information is self-interpreting in a strong sense, requiring little or no creativity, insight, or perspicuity if an economic actor is to know its significance. Furthermore, the formal apparatus assumes that the underlying data are the same under all institutional arrangements and that agents have perfect information of their own parameters (production functions, endowments, preferences). The agents behave like automatons, following explicit formal rules that define how they learn, acquire, and communicate information, operating in an essentially mechanical fashion with no role for subjective interpretation. Where agents' own incentives and information matter, they are assumed to behave according to given utility functions and information constraints in a similarly mechanistic manner (Koopmans 1951; Marschak 1969, 525–26; Hurwicz 1969, 514–15; Hurwicz 1973, 16–17; Oniki 1974). This approach is basically able to reduce all problems arising from imperfect, costly, and/ or asymmetric information to a few basic categories, such as adverse-selection and moral-hazard problems. Finally, one of the principal achievements of this formal theory is the argument that even small deviations from perfect information or from the conditions of the fundamental welfare theorems can dramatically undermine market efficiency (Greenwald and Stiglitz 1986; Myerson 2009; Stiglitz 2000 and 2002).

Why the Mainstream Appropriated the "Hayek" It Did

Why did mainstream economics interpret and appropriate the particular version of "F. A. Hayek" that it did—which, as is by now obvious, strays rather significantly from Hayek's actual thought?

The first, and perhaps simplest, reason was a tendency among economists to read *and reconstruct* Hayek's ideas in light of more recent developments in technical economic theory. The formal-mainstream literature abounds with cases where Hayek is explicitly linked to an idea or claim, while the cited work by Hayek does not mention that idea and may directly contradict it. As just one example, Hayek is frequently treated as (a) focusing solely (or at least primarily) on knowledge regarding prices, or price expectations, and (b) arguing that such knowledge is a sufficient condition for attaining market equilibrium. This understanding of Hayek is showcased in the papers by Grossman and Stiglitz (1976 and 1980) that try to formalize Hayek's claims about the informational efficiency of the price system. For instance, after quoting Hayek (1945) on the "economy of knowledge with which [the price system] operates," Grossman (1976, 585) immediately follows with this statement:

> In an economy with complete markets, the price system does act in such a way that individuals, observing only prices, and acting in self interest, generate allocations which are efficient. However, such economies need not be stable because prices are revealing so much information that incentives for the collection of information are removed. . . . It is not enough for traders to observe only prices.

Thus, Grossman implies that Hayek argued that knowledge of prices is the only knowledge necessary for the operation of the market economy. But as we have shown, Hayek was explicit that economically relevant knowledge includes not only knowledge of prices but much more, such as knowledge of alternative uses or substitutes for a commodity and knowledge particular to a time and place (Hayek 1937, 51; Hayek 1945). Further, Hayek sees the price system as a necessary but insufficient condition for promoting (a tendency toward) coordination, or rather, that it is only a portion of the fuller explanation that must include interfirm competition.[18]

A second explanation is that mainstream economics has tended to treat natural-language theorizing simply as an informal, intuitive input into formal theory. But such intuitive theorizing is not necessarily a step towards formalization, nor should it be. Formalism is incapable of capturing some concepts, such as ignorance, with the same level of nuance and detail as informal theorizing. Among other ideas that do not lend themselves to formalization are the significance of change, innovation, and creativity for the vitality of the market order, which Hayek perceptively explored in "The Meaning of Competition" (1946) and "Competition as a Discovery Procedure" (1968), among other writings. We are not saying that Hayek was only, or even primarily, an informal, "intuitionist" economist. However, we believe that mainstream economists have tended to treat Hayek as such, and that this is an important source of their failure to grasp Hayek's ideas (see Caldwell 1997, 1857–58, 1886).

Rather than being unaware of or uninterested in the technical apparatus of formal economic theory, Hayek was deeply concerned with the methodological and epistemological foundations of economics, especially formal equilibrium analysis. This interest is apparent even in his work from the 1930s, when he was still seen as an important professional economist (see Caldwell 1988). It is true that Hayek was less interested in formalizing his theory through mathematical models than with identifying the epistemological limits of technical economic theory as a means of understanding empirical reality. To this end, we believe that Hayek was prescient in his methodological and epistemological critiques, foreseeing a number of critical problems that formal theorists would only begin to grapple with decades after his arguments and that, ironically, are an important underlying cause of the mainstream's failure to appropriate Hayek accurately. Thus, the problem is not that Hayek's informal theory proved too "fuzzy" to be translated to formal theory, but that formal theory was (is?) fundamentally incapable of capturing Hayek's economics due to the inherent technical limitations of formalism itself, which Hayek presciently described.

One of the major problems that Hayek highlighted in his critique of formal economic theory was that its preoccupation with equilibrium analysis had resulted in diminished attention given to the causal processes that underlie economic order, and especially those that solve the coordination problem (Hayek 1937; Hayek 1945, 91). Since then, several prominent neoclassical economists have admitted that significant gaps and problems in the standard theory remain to be resolved, including how the theory deals with dynamic processes and change (e.g., Arrow 1974 and Stiglitz 2002). For example, Stiglitz (2002, 486–87) admits that he has "become convinced that the dynamics of change may not be well described by equilibrium models that have long been at the center of economic analysis. . . . Dynamics may be better described by evolutionary processes and models, than by equilibrium processes."[19]

Hayek's more critical challenge to equilibrium analysis, which remains unresolved by mainstream formalism, is the need for a solution to the coordination problem that accounts in particular for the division of knowledge and labor in society (Hayek 1937, 50–51). As Hayek explained, equilibrium is a coherent concept, and capable of having meaningful content, only insofar as it is defined in terms of the subjective knowledge of individual actors. A fundamental theoretical problem for economics is to explain the mechanisms and processes whereby the subjective knowledge of each is reconciled with that of others and with the objective facts of the world, such that actors are able to successfully dovetail their plans and actions with each other and with other (non-human) aspects of reality. Earlier we described the Hayekian approach to the problem, including the role of prices as knowledge surrogates and the evolutionary mechanisms of the competitive market process. Equilibrium analysis is incapable of explaining how coordination is achieved, or of shedding light upon the necessary conditions and processes for there to arise a tendency towards equilibrium, since it begins with the assumption that the problem has already been solved through the pre-reconciliation of knowledge.

It might be argued that while epistemic assumptions (such as perfect information or rational expectations) that guarantee smoothly operating, "frictionless" markets are instrumentally valuable for the purposes of constructing determinate, tractable models, they can be dropped or modified as needed. However, as economists adopted formal models built upon these epistemic assumptions (explicitly or implicitly) as a central tool for the analysis of informational problems, they began to discover hidden issues deeper than mere mathematical intractability.[20] In their efforts to rigorously explain the mechanisms driving economic outcomes, economists discarded the myriad "imperfections" of reality in order to construct clean, precise models of those operating forces. What they had not realized is the significance, indeed, the necessity, of those imperfections for the existence and operation of real-world market processes (Richardson 1959). It is not simply that formalist economic theory is "unrealistic" because it abstracts away from the frictions and imperfections that appear obvious to casual observers. Rather, by assuming away these imperfections, formalist economics actually renders itself incapable of explaining various phenomena of primary interest to economists: Institutions such as money, contracts, the firm, and even the price system lose their significance and meaning in a mechanistic world of complete information and rational expectations, free from genuine uncertainty and sheer ignorance (Hayek 1937, 55; Malmgren 1961; Radner 1968; Hirshleifer and Riley 1979, 1411–14; Boettke 1997). Such assumptions may even lead to serious logical defects in the theory of competitive equilibrium, where market-clearing behavior can become an almost paradoxical notion.[21] The problem is deeper than simply constructing "dynamic" models of market-clearing behavior, since the underlying challenge is to explain the necessary conditions and processes whereby people with different subjective knowledge are able to spontaneously coordinate their plans and actions with one another.

New Iterations of Omniscience

As the economics of information and the new economics of information prompted ever-greater interest among economists in an originally Hayekian (epistemological) enterprise, the flawed assumptions of the initial models, going back through Stiglitz to Stigler, continued to exert their effect. Thus, the most important new approach to modeling knowledge in economic analysis is arguably the state-space-and-partition model of knowledge, which encapsulates features of rational choice, probability, and decision theory in a general mathematical framework (Samuelson 2004). Although the state-space model has proven highly adaptable to the needs and goals of economics, it contains serious defects inherent to its formal modeling apparatus that cannot be readily eliminated and that diminish the ability of economists to explore epistemic questions.

The standard state-space model begins by defining a set W that contains all possible states of the world w, where every variable is fully specified at each state w of W. Agents are assumed to know W, that is, they know what all the possible states of the world are. This set W is then subdivided into *partitions* containing several possible states of the world, which are assumed to be fixed structural features in the knowledge-belief function of each agent. Agents may be uncertain, then, about what is the true state of the world at any given time, and instead only know which partition contains the true state.

Thus, as in the original economics of information, the economic agent processes information, and knows how to locate the truth, in an automatic and mechanistic manner. The agent learns about the world through information received by direct observation or as an indirect implication of other events or actions—not, for example, by interpreting a conjunction of directly observed and indirectly mediated events and theories through a subjective lens. From these basic elements, the model can be extended and adapted in various respects.

Several axioms that outline what the standard state-space conception can and cannot model have radical implications for its treatment of knowledge. The *axiom of omniscience* states that agents know the set of all possible worlds, and that they know the implications of everything they know. The *axiom of knowledge* states that agents can only know true things, that is, they cannot hold false beliefs. The *axiom of transparency* states that agents know that they know everything they know. The *axiom of wisdom* states that even if agents do not know something, they know that they do not know it (Samuelson 2004, 372–73). Thus, although the state-space model was partly intended to bring nuance and clarity to economics of knowledge and information, it shares with the orthodox formalist theories an inability to deal with Knightian uncertainty and sheer ignorance. A critical feature of Hayekian economic thought, for example, is the existence of radical ignorance, where an agent is ignorant of her own ignorance: A person is radically ignorant of X if she does not know X and does not know she does not know it.[22] The standard state-space model of knowledge cannot capture sheer ignorance, since agents necessarily know the extent of their own ignorance (Samuelson 2004, 398–400). In fact, the state-space model eliminates unawareness by construction (Dekel, Lipman, and Rustichini 1998), and thus the possibility of surprise, as Samuelson (2004, 398) explains:

> The arrival of new information may allow [an agent] to know things are true that she did not previously know, but she must have been aware of the possibility of this new knowledge. Isaac Newton thus may not have

known whether Einstein's theory of relativity usefully describes our world, but in the standard model Newton must have known the theory, and known that he did not know whether it describes our world.

Thus, the state-space-and-partition model fits squarely within the *small-worlds* approach to formal models of probability and knowledge, in contrast to a *large-worlds* view. Small-world models account for every possible contingency and state of the world, and are extended until all uncertainty is eliminated from the model, such that literally every possible state is fully specified and accounted for within agents' probability beliefs (Samuelson 2004, 375). In the small-worlds view, the notion of *discovery* is incomprehensible, since there is nothing left to discover in a fully specified world.

Further, like much of the work in mainstream economics that deals with these issues, the state-space model blurs the distinction between subjective knowledge and objective information. Agents form beliefs and expectations based upon given information, are confident in what they know since they can only know what is true, and can estimate a probability distribution over everything they do not know, which they are confident fully reflects all available information. Learning is a mechanical process in which agents observe bits of information and automatically draw the correct inferences, grasping all the possible implications of their data. In a strong sense, then, we can assign all of an agent's knowledge about the world into one of two categories: For every proposition X about the world, the agent either (1) knows if X is true or false with complete certainty and accuracy, or (2) does not know X, but knows she does not know X and can make a reasonable estimate of the likelihood that X is true.

These difficulties are exacerbated by other assumptions and methodological conventions in modeling knowledge in economic analysis, including the economics of information. Perhaps the most important is the Harsanyi doctrine, which prescribes that economists "should work with models in which agents have common prior beliefs. . . . In this view, two agents whose information and experiences are identical *in every conceivable respect* should have identical beliefs. Any differences in beliefs can then be traced to the effects of differing information or experiences acting on these initial identical beliefs, and any such possibilities should appear explicitly in the model" (Samuelson 2004, 377). In other words, the Harsanyi doctrine states that models should begin with agents who have identical prior probability estimates and beliefs, and who "learn" exactly alike.

Proponents of the Harsanyi doctrine argue that it eliminates explanations of behavior based on differences in beliefs, which they consider lacking in explanatory value—analogous to economists' view of "preference-based" explanations of behavior (Samuelson 2004, 377–78). Although this justification might seem reasonable at first glance, from a Hayekian perspective the Harsanyi doctrine neglects the fundamental problem to be explained, for the question is not why two agents with initially common priors and identical partitions hold different beliefs following different experiences, but how two agents with different priors, knowledge, and beliefs ever actually coordinate their plans and actions with one another in order to successfully achieve their ends.

The state-space-and-partition model of knowledge was developed, in part, as a means of adding rigor to how knowledge is conceptualized, discussed, and analyzed in economics. Despite adding layers of formal rigor and advanced modeling techniques to the economic analysis of information and knowledge, however the state-space models have still not overcome several of the key challenges that Hayek first raised in his 1937 article. The conventional approaches to equilibrium analysis began by assuming that the data given to the actors were "perfect" or pre-reconciled to agree, thereby assuming away the coordination problem. Yet the state-space models begin from what is fundamentally the same flawed premise, namely, that the dispersed bits of subjective knowledge have already been coordinated, such that the actors know or can predict how others will act and can thus successfully dovetail their actions. Thus, a tendency towards coordination and social order is a fully predetermined "outcome" of these formalized models of knowledge and learning, a function of the model's assumptions.[23] Thus, the state-space-and-partition model of knowledge, for all of its technical rigor, suffers from nearly all of the same issues inherent to the older, less "sophisticated" approaches to the formal modeling of knowledge and information in economic analysis. It cannot accommodate radical ignorance and genuine uncertainty—and thus unawareness, discovery, and surprise—within its formal toolset, in addition to ejecting subjectivism and error from its analysis of knowledge.

Any theory that precludes subjectivism, unawareness, error, and discovery must necessarily lose its grasp on the reality of a world of ignorant, fallible agents. By assumption, agents in state-space models know only things that are true, they know the extent of their own knowledge and thus ignorance, and there is no room for two agents who share common prior beliefs to have different knowledge or interpretations of the facts. In fact, in the state-space model, it is *impossible* for two agents with common priors to disagree, or simply to agree to disagree (Aumann 1976; Samuelson 2004, 376).[24] Moreover, the state-space model, combined with the Harsanyi doctrine, cannot comprehend some of the most fundamental aspects of real-world economies, including the competitive market process and the function and operation of the price system, since agents are assumed to be able to coordinate their knowledge and learn the true state of the world with relative ease. Competition and prices are unnecessary at best, because there are no unknowns to discover, and at worst competition is pure waste, since there is no need for a mechanism to adjust knowledge and reconcile plans: The truth can be found and knowledge coordinated directly by the agents.

In the Hayekian framework, by contrast, the tendency towards coordination of the subjective knowledge of actors, which enables them to dovetail their plans and actions with each other and the objective facts of their environment, is not an input to analysis, as with rational-expectations models or the Harsanyi doctrine; nor is it a truism, as with the orthodox neoclassical equilibrium models; it is instead only a *potential* output of a social process. It is important to emphasize, therefore, that the "definite statements about how knowledge is acquired and communicated" (Hayek 1937, 33) that Hayek proposed are not simply assumptions about how hypothetical rational agents would perform mental calculations, form expectations, or update their beliefs. In fact, Hayek seems to have been largely uninterested in examining, theoretically or empirically, such "psychological" elements in economics (e.g., Hayek 1948, 55). Rather, the learning processes that are most significant to understanding the coordination problem, in the Hayekian framework, are social and institutional by nature, not atomistic or psychological. It is almost irrelevant to the Hayekian theory whether or not individuals are modeled as perfect Bayesians or employ heuristics and intuitive rules of thumb when making decisions.[25] What matters is the institutional context within which individuals form expectations, make plans, and act to achieve their goals (Hayek 1946, 95). Thus, the Hayekian framework is less concerned with how individuals learn than with understanding learning in terms of the social processes engendered by adaptive, purposive actors. In some sense, the question is about how social processes "learn" from the dispersed bits of subjective knowledge held by numerous individuals in society.

To be sure, learning can only take place inside an individual's mind, and "social learning" is merely a metaphor meant to convey a sense of how interaction and exchange by purposive actors can generate dynamic social processes that can appear to an observer as orderly, adaptive, and perhaps even super-intelligent. Therefore, we should be clear that the market process—like all complex social processes—is in its formation purposeless, or nonteleological, and that it cannot be said to "adapt" since it has no goals, values, or mind of its own (Buchanan and Vanberg 1991). The orderliness and adaptiveness of the market process is always a result of the actions of individuals, but does not require participants to grasp the full implications of their actions for the overall market order, nor must their subjective knowledge be perfectly adapted or attuned to the changes, adaptations, and evolution of the market order. The competitive market process therefore embodies greater knowledge than any single mind could possess, though not in an intelligible form, because its institutional structure enables individuals to utilize their own subjective knowledge in pursuing their goals, guides them to arrange their goals and actions to dovetail with others as if they had the knowledge necessary to deliberately coordinate with them, and contains endogenous mechanisms that encourage the discovery and spontaneous correction of economic errors and mal-coordinated plans.

Putting the Pieces Together

That Hayek's insights into the epistemic-institutional nature of the market process were neither grasped or adopted by mainstream economists is well illustrated by the contrasting implications that he and they draw from their ostensibly similar concerns with the economics of imperfect knowledge and information.

According to the Fundamental Theorems of Welfare Economics, the "ideal" picture of the market economy is one where society is on the Pareto frontier, defined by a situation where all resources are allocated to their most highly valued uses, such that the marginal rates of substitution are equalized across all the alternative ends to which resources might be put. In this view, the first-best market economy, which is theoretically indistinguishable from an idealized market-socialist society, achieves an equilibrium allocation of resources that is technically and economically efficient, where no resources are wasted. For mainstream economics, markets fail when they do not satisfy the assumptions and conditions that formal theory finds necessary for the existence and stability of competitive equilibrium—e.g., when there are information asymmetries and incomplete futures markets (Stiglitz 2000 and 2002).

Of course, market economies are never "perfect" in any of the senses described above. One might therefore say that real-world markets always fail relative to the idealized blackboard models of competitive equilibrium. But instead of using the perfectly competitive model as the benchmark for evaluating the real-world economic performance of market competition, Hayek (1946, 100) argues for comparative institutional analysis that recognizes the constraints imposed by reality:

> The basis of comparison, on the grounds of which the achievement of competition ought to be judged, cannot be a situation which is different from the objective facts and which cannot be brought about by any known means. It ought to be the situation as it would exist if competition were prevented from operating. Not the approach to an unachievable and meaningless ideal but the improvement upon the conditions that would exist without competition should be the test.

Furthermore, Hayek (1946 and 1968) held that the competitive market process is most important in precisely those situations where empirical conditions stray farthest from the idealizations of general-equilibrium theory. Hence, in "The Meaning of Competition," he (1946, 103–4) argues that

> competition is the more important the more complex or "imperfect" are the objective conditions in which it has to operate. Indeed, far from competition being beneficial only when it is "perfect," I am inclined to argue that the need for competition is nowhere greater than in fields in which the nature of the commodities or services makes it impossible that it ever should create a perfect market in the theoretical sense.

In a world of imperfect knowledge, it is not possible to have entrepreneurial success and economic progress without error and failure. However, this is not simply due to principal-agent problems or incentive-compatibility issues arising from the costs of monitoring agent behavior, enforcing contracts, or collecting information, as is assumed in formalist economic theory.

For example, Sah and Stiglitz (1985 and 1986) model alternative organizational structures—ranging from decentralized to centrally planned organizations—and analyze their performance at evaluating and selecting from potential projects, which are either "good" or "bad," finding that the decentralized "market" organizations accept more "good" projects than do central planners but also fail to reject more "bad" projects as well. In a Hayekian framework, instead of a given pool of potential projects with objectively defined good or bad payoffs, entrepreneurs interpret the meaning of current prices—and anything else that they think is relevant—as producing hypotheses or conjectures about the appropriate future prices of new goods and services, new production methods, and so on, and they act on the basis of these hypotheses in a manner that they believe will yield positive profits. Entrepreneurs experiment with these hypotheses in the market; one interpretation of market "competition," then, is "the deployment by competing capitalist enterprises of various fallible hunches, heuristics, theories . . . that address how, in a specific context, a company can make profits and avoid losses" (Friedman and Kraus 2011, 133).[26]

Given the fallibility and ignorance not only of entrepreneurs but of economists observing them, only *ex post* evaluation of their hypotheses is possible. Even then, however, the "bad" projects are not simply a regrettable but necessary cost of doing business, so to speak. Even where a project or investment is a proven failure and suffers losses, it does not automatically follow that this *individual* entrepreneurial failure represents genuine social waste or deadweight loss. Entrepreneurial failure is necessary, even though it leads to individual losses and lower total wealth in society, because it *reveals* where entrepreneurship is most needed to reallocate resources and adjust plans. In this spirit, Ludwig Lachmann (1978, 18) writes:

> The ability to turn failure into success and to benefit from the discomfiture of others is the crucial test of true entrepreneurship. A progressive economy is not an economy in which no capital is ever lost, but an economy which can afford to lose capital because the productive opportunities revealed by the loss are vigorously exploited.

From a Hayekian perspective, then, the competitive market process may be socially beneficial —even where rivalrous behaviors lead to things that neoclassical economists have often viewed in a critical light, such as duplication of effort or advertising—because it is only through the competitive process that entrepreneurs, consumers, and producers can discover what is most welfare-enhancing for society. Indeed, we have not examined the central-planning alternative because the Hayekian framework makes clear that the facts that may be discovered by competition do not exist apart from a procedure for their discovery and the institutional structure necessary for the operation of that procedure (Hayek 1946, 95–101; Hayek 1968, 179–84).

Finally, in "Economics and Knowledge," Hayek argued that deductive economic theory, or the Pure Logic of Choice, must be combined with empirical propositions about knowledge and learning in order to yield meaningful insights into the real world. For Hayekian economics, institutional analysis partly serves this empirical function. But Hayek (1937, 1945, 1946, 1948, and 1968) often noted that the preoccupation with formal equilibrium theory had led to the neglect of institutions in economic analysis. In an equilibrium state, where actors' knowledge and expectations are aligned, many institutions—such as money, contract enforcement, courts, firms, and even the price system—are made redundant by assumption and otherwise relegated to much more limited roles than our everyday experience of economic reality would ever suggest (Hayek 1937, 55; Richardson 1959; Malmgren 1961; Radner 1968; Hirshleifer and Riley 1979, 1411–14; Boettke 1997). But in situations of dispersed knowledge, imperfect foresight, and radical ignorance—i.e. anything that remotely resembles reality—such institutions are essential to the solution of the coordination problem.

NOTES

1. See White 2012 for an engrossing history of the central economic debates of the twentieth century, which highlights the significant influence that Hayek has had throughout the years.
2. The socialist-calculation debate of the 1920s and 1930s pitted economists critical of central economic planning (Ludwig von Mises, Lionel Robbins, and Hayek) and its proponents (Oskar Lange, Abba Lerner, and others). The debate was touched off by Mises's "Economic Calculation in the Socialist Commonwealth" (1920), which argued that rational economic calculation—required for advanced material production—is impossible without money prices for capital goods, which would be lacking in a socialist commonwealth with collective ownership over the means of production. The socialist economists responded with a theory of market socialism where capital-goods prices would be derived from consumer-goods markets. Hayek's critique of the market-socialist solutions can be found in Hayek 1948, 77–91 and 119–208. See White 2012, 32–67 for an

historical overview of the debate. Boettke 1998 explores in detail the theory of economic calculation and the Austrian critique of central planning.

3. As there are already a number of apt intellectual histories of the development of Hayek's economic thought, including of the "epistemic turn" in his work, we will not be directly concerned with this side of scholarship. Caldwell 1988 examines the history of the intellectual "transformation" of Hayek from technical economist to wide-ranging social theorist concerned with political theory, law, and sociology among other subjects, with "Economics and Knowledge" playing a pivotal role. Boettke, Schaeffer, and Snow 2010 treats the epistemic turn in Hayek's thought from the perspective of his involvement with the socialist calculation debate. Boettke 2002 discusses the epistemic turn within Austrian economics, and identifies this emphasis on the epistemic-cognitive aspect of the market process as the defining characteristic of the modern Austrian school.

4. In addition to the sources mentioned in note 3, Boettke 1990 and Vaughn 1999 also cover this aspect of Hayek's intellectual evolution.

5. Here, and throughout the paper, we use "subjective data" and "subjective knowledge" interchangeably to refer to the "facts" in an individual's mind—e.g. ideas, beliefs, and expectations about the world—as well as their preferences, values, and goals. We use "objective facts" and "objective data" to refer to facts about the world that are external to the individual's mind, and which are, in principle, knowable—e.g., facts about resource availability, the plans and actions of other people, and even "scientific" facts.

6. This is not to say that either societal coordination or the tendency towards it are perfect, ideal, efficient, or optimal in any sense. This also includes their manifestation within the market process; that is, the assumption that there exists a tendency towards coordination in the market economy does not entail any assumptions of the efficiency or welfare properties of such self-ordering forces.

7. Boettke, Caceres, and Martin 2013 pursue this line of thought further in their critique of certain aspects of behavioral economics, particularly what they see as a tendency among behavioral economists to overemphasize the fallibility of real human actors, with the implication being that such "imperfections" stifle the operation of the market process, without also examining how coordination and cooperation nevertheless arise from the efforts of these imperfect actors.

8. At least not in his major works in economics, which are widely cited by formal theorists. However, Hayek was deeply interested in theory of mind from the very beginning of his intellectual career, as evidenced by *The Sensory Order* (1952a), which was largely written decades before being published. Hayek continued to grapple with these ideas later in his career; cf. Hayek 1967, 43–65 and Hayek 1978, 35–49.

9. This passage is perhaps among the clearest where Hayek more or less explicitly discusses the role of creativity, innovation, and invention in the market process, although he arguably never fully developed how such ideas fit within his overarching economic thought.

10. Although by no means a dogmatic proponent of laissez faire, Hayek did support a general presumption in favor of free markets over government intervention, with a high burden of proof for any exceptions.

11. As Koopmans and Beckmann (1957, 60) state, in a passage referencing Hayek 1945:

An important characteristic of the market mechanism just described is the way in which its information requirements are distributed. Each plant owner needs to know only the rents on locations, and the profitabilities of his own plant in each location. The latter information . . . is likely to be more accessible to him than to anyone else. The location rents may thus be looked upon as a condensation of the information present in the entire [market opportunity set] to that smaller number of data that are sufficient, in combination with his own [individual opportunity set], to enable each plant owner to hold his place in an optimal assignment. We meet here with the informational decentralization made possible by a price system, which has been stressed by many economists as one of the main merits of resource allocation through competitive markets.

12. In fact, Marschak (1959, 400) argued that designing incentive-compatible rules was the central problem of the socialist-calculation debate, and that the Mises-Hayek criticism of market socialism was that the central planning board could not properly incentivize the managers of the firms to act as would be required to achieve the efficient economic outcome.

13. Oniki (1974, 540) conceded that a "general approach to the problem of comparing alternative systems would consider the tradeoff between informational costs and allocation errors," while his theory only focused on the former issue. Nevertheless, Oniki's (1974) framework is still valuable for our purposes since it touches directly upon the problems of information and economics that Hayek had discussed.

14. Hirshleifer's notion of a passive economics of uncertainty, in contrast to an active economics of information, casts an interesting light on the following statements by Hurwicz (1973) and Marschak (1969):

It is the function of a resource allocation mechanism to guide the economic agents . . . in decisions that determine the flow of resources. Simplifying to the utmost, we may imagine each agent having in front of him a console with one or more dials to set; the selection of dial settings by all agents determines uniquely the flow of goods and services (trade vector) between every pair of agents and also each agent's production (input-output vector), his "trade with nature." (Hurwicz 1973, 16)

Given his states at the start of a step and the signals received during the step, each agent sends signals to other agents at the end of the step and also modifies his states. Thus each agent's behavior is completely defined by two functions: one function is from received signals and current states to the new states; the other is from received signals and current states to the new outgoing signals. (Marschak 1969, 525)

15. On this point, it is notable that Israel Kirzner (1973, 66) specifically refers to Stigler 1961 as a "treatment of the *non*entrepreneurial aspects of knowledge in the market."

16. The socialist-calculation debate was interpreted to have been fundamentally a comparative analysis of central planning versus a decentralized market economy in terms of allocative efficiency, the incentive compatibility between the central planners and managers, and information costs (i.e., the costs of collecting, aggregating, and utilizing decentralized bits of information). Unfortunately,

however, the debate was "informal" and therefore incapable of offering rigorous conclusions or insights (Hurwicz 1969, 514–15; Marschak 1959, 399–401; Myerson 2009, 60–62; Oniki 1974, 529–34, 540–41; Stiglitz 2000, 1446, 1448).

17. To be sure, there is no single mainstream interpretation of Hayek, and differences in perspectives remain. The following, therefore, are not intended to represent *all* mainstream views of Hayek, but instead to reflect some of the more prominent features that are commonly shared in these views.

18. As Thomsen (1992, 50) explains, Hayek's "point then is not that it is enough (sufficient) for an individual to know prices, in addition to his preferences, resources, and technologies, to act correctly—the target of Grossman and Stiglitz's criticism. Instead, it is that prices *reduce the amount* of detail that he needs to know to do so." Further, the "effectiveness of prices in this role will depend crucially on the existence of a rivalrous competitive process."

19. Arrow (1974, 4) identifies similar issues with neoclassical theory, namely, that it lacks an adequate model of dynamic adjustment processes and disequilibrium changes. Still, he argues that neoclassical (and Keynesian) economic theory is valuable on instrumentalist grounds, especially as a tool of prediction and control. Similarly, in other writings Stiglitz (2000, 1456) appears to remain staunchly committed to equilibrium analysis, even for the purposes of critically examining general-equilibrium theory, arguing that "only with the construction of equilibrium models can one fully confront the inadequacies of the Arrow-Debreu model and its core theorems on existence, optimality, and decentralization" (Stiglitz 2000, 1456).

20. Stiglitz (2000, 1470–71) makes a similar point, although he arrives at this conclusion by a somewhat different path than the one we are pursuing.

21. Consider one of the logical dilemmas posed by the common-knowledge assumption. If a large number of producers simultaneously notice a profit opportunity, where this opportunity is both common knowledge and costly to pursue, then it is unclear to the individual producer whether it will be profitable to pursue that opportunity without additional knowledge about the plans of their competitors, and thus none will actually pursue it: A "profit opportunity which is known by and available to everybody is available to nobody in particular" (Richardson 1959, 233–34).

22. Also see Evans and Friedman 2011 on radical ignorance and economic theory.

23. On "fully predetermined models," see Frydman and Goldberg 2007, 8–13, 26–66.

24. In light of the persistent defects of the formal models of knowledge, such as their lack of allowance for subjective differences of opinion, one might even follow Ludwig Lachmann (1978, 15) in arguing that such formal exercises are in fact irrelevant for a much broader range of problems beyond just those of direct concern to the Hayekian framework: "A method of dynamic analysis which fails to allow for variable expectations due to subjective interpretation seems bound to degenerate into a series of economically irrelevant mathematical exercises."

25. Cf. Tarko 2013 on the emergence of common knowledge under different formal models of knowledge and learning.

26. That market competition involves the testing of competing hypotheses is maintained in Friedman 2006, 475–76; Evans and Friedman 2011, 90–91; and Friedman and Kraus 2011, ch. 4. Friedman and his coauthors, however, do not necessarily credit entrepreneurs either with the ability to formulate the actual hypotheses being tested explicitly; or with the ability to learn from their mistakes

or successes. Instead, following Alchian 1950, they portray mistakes as being punished through a blind process of revenue loss, such that the system may "work" despite the lack of any discovery, or communication, of sound information over time.

REFERENCES

Alchian, Armen A. 1950. "Uncertainty, Evolution, and Economic Theory." *Journal of Political Economy* 58(3): 211–221.

Arrow, Kenneth J. 1974. "Limited Knowledge and Economic Analysis." *American Economic Review* 64(1): 1–10.

Aumann, Robert J. 1976. "Agreeing to Disagree." *Annals of Statistics* 4(6): 1236–39.

Boettke, Peter J. 1990. "The Theory of Spontaneous Order and Cultural Evolution in the Social Theory of F. A. Hayek." *Cultural Dynamics* 3(1): 61–83.

Boettke, Peter J. 1997. "Where Did Economics Go Wrong? Modern Economics as a Flight from Reality." *Critical Review* 11(1): 11–64.

Boettke, Peter J. 1998. "Economic Calculation: The Austrian Contribution to Political Economy." *Advances in Austrian Economics* 5: 131–58.

Boettke, Peter J. 2002. "Information and Knowledge: Austrian Economics in Search of its Uniqueness." *Review of Austrian Economics* 15(4): 263–274.

Boettke, Peter J., W. Zachary Caceres, and Adam G. Martin. 2013. "Error is Obvious, Coordination is the Puzzle." In *Hayek and Behavioral Economics*, ed. Roger Frantz and Robert Leeson. London: Palgrave Macmillan.

Boettke, Peter J., Emily C. Schaeffer, and Nicholas A. Snow. 2010. "The Context of Context: The Evolution of Hayek's Epistemic Turn in Economics and Politics." *Advances in Austrian Economics* 14: 69–86.

Buchanan, James M., and Viktor J. Vanberg. 1991. "The Market as a Creative Process." *Economics and Philosophy* 7(2): 167–86.

Caldwell, Bruce J. 1988. "Hayek's Transformation." *History of Political Economy* 20(4): 513–41.

Caldwell, Bruce J. 1997. "Hayek and Socialism." *Journal of Economic Literature* 35(4): 1856–90.

Dekel, Eddie, Barton L. Lipman, and Aldo Rustichini. 1998. "Standard State-Space Models Preclude Unawareness." *Econometrica* 66(1): 159–73.

Evans, Anthony J., and Jeffrey Friedman. 2011. "'Search vs. Browse': A Theory of Error Grounded in Radical (Not Rational) Ignorance." *Critical Review* 23(1–2): 73–104.

Foss, Nicolai. 2000. "Austrian Economics and Game Theory: A Stocktaking and an Evaluation." *Review of Austrian Economics* 13(1): 41–58.

Friedman, Jeffrey. 2006. "Taking Ignorance Seriously." *Critical Review* 18(4): 469–532.

Friedman, Jeffrey, and Wladimir Kraus. 2011. *Engineering the Financial Crisis: Systemic Risk and the Failure of Regulation*. Philadelphia: University of Pennsylvania Press.

Frydman, Roman, and Michael D. Goldberg. 2007. *Imperfect Knowledge Economics: Exchange Rates and Risk*. Princeton: Princeton University Press.

Greenwald, Bruce C., and Joseph E. Stiglitz. 1986. "Externalities in Economies with Imperfect Information and Incomplete Markets." *Quarterly Journal of Economics* 101(2): 229–64.

Grossman, Sanford J. 1976. "On the Efficiency of Competitive Stock Markets Where Traders Have Diverse Information." *Journal of Finance* 31(2): 573–85.

Grossman, Sanford J., and Joseph E. Stiglitz. 1976. "Information and Competitive Price Systems." *American Economic Review* 66(2): 246–53.

Grossman, Sanford J., and Joseph E. Stiglitz. 1980. "On the Impossibility of Informationally Efficient Markets." *American Economic Review* 70(3): 393–408.

Hayek, F. A. 1937. "Economics and Knowledge." In Hayek 1948.

Hayek, F. A. 1945. "The Use of Knowledge in Society." In Hayek 1948.

Hayek, F. A. 1946. "The Meaning of Competition." In Hayek 1948.

Hayek, F. A. 1948. *Individualism and Economic Order*. Chicago: University of Chicago Press.

Hayek, F. A. 1952a. *The Sensory Order: An Inquiry into the Foundations of Theoretical Psychology*. Chicago: University of Chicago Press.

Hayek, F. A. 1952b [1979]. *The Counter-Revolution of Science: Studies in the Abuse of Reason*, 2nd ed. Indianapolis: Liberty Press.

Hayek, F. A. 1967. *Studies in Philosophy, Politics, and Economics*. Chicago: University of Chicago Press.

Hayek, F. A. 1968. "Competition as a Discovery Procedure." In Hayek 1978.

Hayek, F. A. 1976. *The Mirage of Social Justice*. Vol. 2 of *Law, Legislation and Liberty*. Chicago: University of Chicago Press.

Hayek, F. A. 1978. *New Studies in Philosophy, Politics, Economics, and the History of Ideas*. Chicago: University of Chicago Press.

Hirshleifer, Jack. 1971. "The Private and Social Value of Information and the Reward to Inventive Activity." *American Economic Review* 61(4): 561–74.

Hirshleifer, Jack. 1973. "Where Are We in the Theory of Information?" *American Economic Review* 63(2): 31–39.

Hirshleifer, Jack, and John G. Riley. 1979. "The Analytics of Uncertainty and Information—An Expository Survey." *Journal of Economic Literature* 17(4): 1375–1421.

Hurwicz, Leonid. 1969. "On the Concept and Possibility of Informational Decentralization." *American Economic Review* 59(2): 513–24.

Hurwicz, Leonid. 1973. "The Design of Mechanisms for Resource Allocation." *American Economic Review* 63(2): 1–30.

Kirzner, Israel M. 1973. *Competition and Entrepreneurship*. Chicago: University of Chicago Press.

Kirzner, Israel M. 1997. "Entrepreneurial Discovery and the Competitive Market Process: An Austrian Approach." *Journal of Economic Literature* 35(1): 60–85.

Koopmans, Tjalling C. 1951. "Efficient Allocation of Resources." *Econometrica* 19(4): 455–65.

Koopmans, Tjalling C. 1977. "Concepts of Optimality and their Uses." *American Economic Review* 67(3): 261–74.

Koopmans, Tjalling C., and Martin Beckmann. 1957. "Assignment Problems and the Location of Economic Activities." *Econometrica* 25(1): 53–76.

Lachmann, Ludwig M. 1978. *Capital and Its Structure*. Kansas City, Kans.: Sheed Andrews and McMeel.

Lavoie, Don. 1985. *National Economic Planning: What is Left?* Cambridge, Mass.: Ballinger.

Malmgren, H. B. 1961. "Information, Expectations, and the Theory of the Firm." *Quarterly Journal of Economics* 75(3): 399–421.

Marschak, Thomas. 1959. "Centralization and Decentralization in Economic Organizations." *Econometrica* 27(3): 399–430.

Marschak, Thomas. 1969. "On the Comparison of Centralized and Decentralized Economies." *American Economic Review* 59(2): 525–32.

Mises, Ludwig von. 1920 [1975]. "Economic Calculation in the Socialist Commonwealth." In *Collectivist Economic Planning*, ed. Friedrich A. Hayek. Clifton, N.J.: Augustus M. Kelley.

Myerson, Roger B. 2009. "Fundamental Theory of Institutions: A Lecture in Honor of Leo Hurwicz." *Review of Economic Design* 13(1): 59–75.

Oniki, Hajime. 1974. "The Cost of Communication in Economic Organization." *Quarterly Journal of Economics* 88(4): 529–50.

Radner, Roy. 1968. "Competitive Equilibrium under Uncertainty." *Econometrica* 36 (1): 31–58.

Richardson, G. B. 1959. "Equilibrium, Expectations, and Information." *Economic Journal* 69(274): 223–37.

Sah, Raaj Kumar, and Joseph E. Stiglitz. 1985. "Human Fallibility and Economic Organization." *American Economic Review* 75(2): 292–97.

Sah, Raaj Kumar, and Joseph E. Stiglitz. 1986. "The Architecture of Economic Systems: Hierarchies and Polyarchies." *American Economic Review* 76(4): 716–27.

Samuelson, Larry. 2004. "Modeling Knowledge in Economic Analysis." *Journal of Economic Literature* 42(2): 367–403.

Sappington, David E. M., and Joseph E. Stiglitz. 1987. "Privatization, Information, and Incentives." *Journal of Policy Analysis and Management* 6(4): 567–82.

Stigler, George J. 1961. "The Economics of Information." *Journal of Political Economy* 69(3): 213–25.

Stiglitz, Joseph E. 1985. "Information and Economic Analysis: A Perspective." *Economic Journal* 95: 21–41.

Stiglitz, Joseph E. 2000. "The Contributions of the Economics of Information to Twentieth-Century Economics." *Quarterly Journal of Economics* 115(4): 1441–78.

Stiglitz, Joseph E. 2002. "Information and the Change in the Paradigm in Economics." *American Economic Review* 92(3): 460–501.

Tarko, Vlad. 2013. "Can Probability Theory Deal with Entrepreneurship?" *Review of Austrian Economics* 26(3): 329–45.

Thomsen, Esteban F. 1992. *Prices and Knowledge: A Market Process Perspective*. London: Routledge.

Vaughn, Karen I. 1999. "Hayek's Implicit Economics: Rules and the Problem of Order." *Review of Austrian Economics* 11(1–2): 129–44.

White, Lawrence H. 2012. *The Clash of Economic Ideas*. Cambridge: Cambridge University Press.

Andrew Gamble

HAYEK AND LIBERTY

ABSTRACT: *Hayek's political theory is directed against coercion, which he defines as the intentional control of one person by another. The element of personal intention ensures a clear conceptual distinction between the freedom from coercion— i.e., the "liberty"—that is exercised in the private sphere, and the freedom of choice and opportunity that may be severely constrained by the impersonal, unintentional operation of market forces. Hayek's narrow definitions of coercion and liberty therefore suggest that he was more intent on defending the benefits conferred on us by market forces than on affirming any value intrinsic in freedom—a suggestion confirmed by his lack of interest in species of freedom, such as autonomy, that might conceivably be fostered by state coercion. Hayek's consequentialist defense of liberty, however, was grounded in economic doctrines such as his own view that prices served a vital epistemic function. Given his strictures against the ignorance of modern electorates, Hayek was driven to propose extravagant limits on democracy and to embrace traditionalism; a different Hayekianism might limit inequalities of wealth and encourage the ability to learn from experimentation.*

At first glance Hayek's view of liberty could not be simpler, but it turns out to be considerably more complicated, because he mixes empirical and philosophical claims about liberty and balks at some of the implications of his own theory.

On the surface, Hayek's main theme is the intrinsic importance of economic freedom. In *The Road to Serfdom*, Hayek (1944, 68) declared:

"To be controlled in our economic pursuits means to be always controlled unless we declare our specific purpose. Or since when we declare our specific purpose we shall also have to get it approved, we should really be controlled in everything." "The State," he wrote, "should confine itself to establishing rules applying to general types of situations, and should allow the individuals freedom in everything which depends on the circumstances of time and place, because only the individuals concerned in each instance can fully know these circumstances and adapt their actions to them" (ibid., 56). There are many similar passages in which Hayek identifies economic liberty as the most important aspect of modern liberty, the foundation for all other forms of freedom (ibid., 10, 75).

Hayek was distressed by the turn liberalism had taken in the twentieth century, which led him to seek to rehabilitate the conception of liberty held by those he called the "true liberals" of the nineteenth century (such as Tocqueville, Acton, and Bastiat) and to repudiate the doctrines of the "false liberals" (such as Bentham and the later Mill), which had paved the way for the various forms of collectivism that had dominated the first half of the twentieth century. Hayek's understanding of liberty is closely connected to his understanding of coercion, and of how to minimize it. Liberty (or freedom, which he uses interchangeably with liberty),[1] is contrasted with slavery and is defined as the absence of coercion, whether this comes from other individuals or from the state. Thus, Hayek embraced a negative conception of liberty, which followed the early Mill in emphasizing the importance of all individuals having a sphere in which they can do as they please, free from interference or regulation from outside.

The existence of such a sphere, in which each individual is sovereign and beholden to nobody else, depends on two kinds of protection. It has to be secured against the arbitrary violence of other individuals, and it has to be guarded against the encroachment of the state. The first type of protection requires acceptance of a set of common rules and its enforcement by the state. The state is therefore necessary for the protection of individual liberty, yet at the same time individual liberty has to be protected from the state, which, if not checked, constantly threatens to invade the private sphere of individuals, returning them to a condition of servitude. A paradox of liberty is thus at the heart of the "true" liberal perspective. To enjoy liberty, people must be free from the coercion of others. But that requires entrusting coercive powers to the state, and unless a way can be found to control and limit them, these powers may be used to invade the very sphere of liberty the state has been set up to protect. The emergence of a sphere of individual liberty in the modern era creates a distinctive kind of civilization, but it must always be protected because it is under threat of being eroded or even disappearing altogether.

This threat was, in Hayek's eyes, primarily ideological: He was concerned throughout his career with the threats posed to liberty from the rise of collectivist doctrines and movements. As their influence grew, collectivist ideas came to dominate all major parties, including in many cases liberal parties, and when these parties gained control of the state they increasingly used its coercive powers to shrink the sphere of individual liberty, sometimes deliberately and malevolently, sometimes without being fully aware of what they were doing. Much of Hayek's work is concerned with the threat posed by collectivism and the increasing power of the state, and this makes him appear most of the time as an enemy of the state, constantly counterposing it against the individual and emphasizing the need to protect the individual from the state. Accordingly, Hayek de-emphasized the state's role in protecting individuals from other individuals. But Hayek was by no means unaware of the need for the state. Only if the right kind of state and the right kind of citizens could be created and sustained was there hope for a stable order of liberty.

Hayek's Definition of Coercion

In *The Constitution of Liberty* (1960), Hayek's major restatement of classical-liberal principles, Hayek develops his account of negative liberty through a discussion of the nature of coercion.

He first distinguishes coercion from compulsion. Compulsion exists when an individual is physically compelled by circumstances to behave in a certain way, and therefore has no choice and cannot really be said to be "acting." The circumstances may be natural or they may be the result of human agency. Hayek (1960, 133) uses the example of an individual being physically compelled by another to pull the trigger of a gun. By contrast, coercion exists when an individual is forced by another individual to act in a way that serves the will and purposes of that other individual rather than of the person who is coerced.

This definition of coercion makes intention central. Acts are coercive only if an individual intends to exercise power over others, substituting his or her purposes for theirs. Liberty means being free from such coercion. Therefore, individuals can be free only to a limited extent, since they are unlikely to be able to escape all forms of coercion: the imposition on them of the will of others encountered in families, civil society, and the polity. What may be achievable is for coercion to be limited as much as possible, and liberty maximized as much as possible, by taking account of the fundamental conditions that make liberty possible. This is the constitution of liberty, and it is the elaboration of its principles to which Hayek devoted the second half of his life. As he put it, "the task of a policy of freedom is to minimize coercion or its harmful effects even if it cannot eliminate it completely" (Hayek 1960, 65).

Hayek agrees with those liberals who emphasize that liberty exists when individuals are free from external coercion and able to formulate and carry out their own independent plans of life; he adds that they may then use their local knowledge to decide how to apportion their time between different pursuits and goals. Coercion removes this independence of action, but individuals who are coerced can still choose to act or not to act as the coercer requires. Individuals who are compelled cannot. Coercion in Hayek's account works mainly through threats that change the circumstances facing individuals; as a result, they choose options they would not choose if the circumstances were not being manipulated by the coercer. Their minds have become the tools of the coercer, and they choose the least painful option, but it is crucial to his argument that coercion does not destroy choice even while it may drastically restrict liberty.

Counterintuitively, the result of this argument is that the more effective restraints on individual *choice* represented by compulsion are morally unobjectionable, even while the less effective restraints on individual *liberty* imposed by coercion are to be minimized whenever possible. Since the only circumstances that can be said to reduce liberty are intentional coercive actions, social processes cannot be considered coercive if their effects are not intended by anyone. Crucially for Hayek, this includes market outcomes, such as the distribution of wealth and poverty and the conditions in which individuals have to work. People who suffer from poverty, although severely constrained in their choices and opportunities, are not coerced because their situation is unintended.

Impersonal and unintended social processes—along with natural processes, such as drought or famine—cannot be thought to reduce liberty because no human agent intended them.

Hayek therefore rejects doctrines of positive liberty, which focus on whether individuals have the capacity to fulfil their potential and achieve all they are capable of achieving or might want to achieve. Liberty in this conception takes on substantive forms; to be free is to be able to access particular ways of being and living. But for Hayek all that matters is whether there is a protected private sphere in which individuals can do as they like with a minimum of interference.

Therefore, liberal critics of Hayek often focus on his emphasis on economic liberty to the exclusion of other forms of liberty, such as political liberty and personal autonomy. Hayek did not entirely ignore political liberty, but he attached much less significance to it than to the economic variety. He implied that individuals can enjoy a sphere of personal liberty without having any political liberties at all. Authoritarian governments may in some circumstances invade or threaten the sphere of personal liberty less than democratic governments pursuing a collectivist agenda, and Hayek was in no doubt which kind of government he would prefer in those circumstances.

He was also for the most part uninterested in other forms of freedom that have been so important in defining modern thought, such as the inner freedom arising from overcoming inhibitions and the freedom to become the author of one's own life, an autonomous person with a will to power. Raymond Plant (2010, 64–83), for example, has pointed out that if coercion as defined by Hayek is undesirable, it must be because it is desirable to be able to act autonomously, on the basis of one's own values and thoughts. Yet many of the actions that take place in the private sphere can be criticized as being anything but autonomous. Hayek, however, was suspicious of those currents of thought, which he associated with Rousseau and John Stuart Mill, which emphasized the development of the self, self-fulfilment, and autonomy. Hayek thought such ideas lead inexorably to an extension of egalitarianism and to the demand that individuals be provided with the resources necessary to realize their potential. Such arguments encouraged the steady enlargement of the state in order to provide a level playing field and equal opportunity for all citizens. For Hayek, all such plans for realizing starting-gate equality, however well intentioned, risked subordinating the sphere of personal liberty to the power of the collective as embodied in the state.

Liberty and the Rule of Law

Libertarian critics of Hayek, on the other hand, have complained that despite his clear intention, he fails to protect that sphere from the state. This is because while Hayek's definition of what constitutes a coercive act is narrow by design, its incorporation into his definition of "law" is too vague to limit the actions of state officials very effectively.

Coercion between individuals can be reduced to a minimum, Hayek thinks, under the rule of law: a set of general rules that are the same for everybody and are applied impartially, establishing equal liberty. The best way to protect the liberty of each individual from its violation by others is to ensure that all relations between individuals are governed by general rules, which, because they are impersonal, cannot involve intention, and therefore cannot be coercive.

Hayek's conception of the rule of law is Kantian and very similar to that of Rawls.[2] It is crucial that this conception constrains public officials to enact and enforce only general rules; this will keep them from infringing on the sphere of personal liberty. It is when public officials make arbitrary and discretionary interventions, treating the private sphere of individuals as a matter for public administration, that the state ceases to be a protector of liberty and becomes instead a threat to it. Yet general rules can drastically limit the scope of the individual's sphere of liberty. Any state, no matter how intrusive, might follow Hayek's conception of the rule of law by not naming particular individuals or groups as the targets of its coercion. As long as nobody is singled out for coercion, nobody's liberty can be said to be reduced. Such a state could indefinitely expand its capacities and its budget and limit everyone's freedom of action—or the freedom of action of those who engage in certain generally described actions—in the pursuit of collectively agreed purposes. Indeed, Hayek appears to be content with a wide range of public programs and regulations so long as they conform to the undemanding requirements of the rule of law. His social minimum is quite flexible, to be determined pragmatically, which is why some libertarians see no difference between his position and that of Rawls.

Part of the problem, for libertarians, is Hayek's reluctance to define coercion as physical compulsion. While he acknowledged that force and violence are often the means by which individuals are coerced, he insisted that true coercion has to involve intention and choice on the part of both the coercer and the coerced. This account may actually widen the scope of individual actions that count as coercive and therefore might call for government intervention against them. Although Hayek resisted this conclusion,[3] we have seen that he lacks clear criteria for opposing any general laws as infringements of liberty, since in his terms they are not coercive as long as there is no intent to harm or coerce particular individuals.

The Consequentialist Hayek and the Knowledge Problem

Instead of broadening his definitions of coercion and thus of liberty, however, Hayek (in effect) answers the question of why we should resist socialism, and perhaps less-comprehensive forms of collectivism, on the consequentialist grounds that a society that protects private property is more prosperous, peaceful, and innovative than one that does not. This aspect of Hayek's thought renders moot the idea of liberty as intrinsically valuable, and therefore as warranting close attention to its definition. Yet there can be little doubt that, beginning with Hayek's engagement in the "socialist-calculation debate" of the 1930s, it was a defense of market freedom that was Hayek's main goal (Friedman 1997).

This can be seen in Hayek's broader account of the development of civilization. For him, the growth of civilization is the story of how human beings gradually learned, through trial and error, to discipline and control their natural instincts and make possible the Great Society—a society of strangers based on impersonal exchange and abstract rules.

The emergence of market exchange as a spontaneous order required the elaboration of rules that protected individuals from the arbitrary violence of others and safeguarded a sphere of personal "liberty," or freedom from coercion. In addition, however, it provided a way of coordinating the activities of individuals with widely varying conceptions of the good. They could cooperate with one another without agreeing with one another. Indeed, they learned to trust the satisfaction of their wants to individuals they did not know and would never meet.

In comparison to the story of the growth of a market society, Hayek writes relatively little about the inherent value of liberty for the individual, which he treats as an accepted part of the liberal tradition. He focuses instead on what he thinks has been increasingly neglected:

the extraordinary capacity of a market society to provide for the needs of an ever-growing population at ever-higher levels of satisfaction and quality. This is possible only so long as human societies preserve the basic conditions of liberty. Human societies may always slip back into serfdom or slavery, substituting a planned order for a spontaneous order, *taxis* for *cosmos*. If this is allowed to happen, it would imperil the liberal civilization that alone permits the present level of world population to exist.

This aspect of Hayek's view of liberty is closely related to his account of the nature of knowledge. For Hayek, the division of knowledge in society is even more fundamental than the division of labor.

Human knowledge is necessarily fragmented, limited, dispersed, and decentralized. This characteristic of the human condition makes two basic forms of coordination possible: the personal coordination practiced by hunter-gatherers in tight intimate groups, and the coordination made possible by impersonal exchange in markets, with their long and increasingly complex chains of production and consumption. Personal liberty is not essential for the first type of coordination, but it is absolutely vital to the second type. It is the means by which individuals' knowledge of the particular environment in which they operate can be utilized to provide new goods and services. In this way it is the foundation of innovation and growth; and the more individuals are allowed this freedom to use their knowledge in whatever way they see fit, the more extensive and rapid will be the economic progress of the society. This will occur not because of any central planning or rational design but as the unintended consequence of the decisions of millions of individuals exercising their liberty. Personal liberty does not remove ignorance or prevent mistakes and miscalculations, but it sets in motion a continuous process of discovery through competition, thus increasing the chances of steady improvements in satisfying human needs.

The external counterpart of the subjective knowledge of individual market participants is the price system, which reflects the myriad subjective and changing daily valuations of each market participant. Prices fluctuate as these valuations fluctuate. Thus, prices arise from the exercise of individual liberty, which allows voluntary exchanges at given prices to occur. In turn, though, prices bear down on the individual as an objective constraint, a set of realities that any individual is normally powerless to alter. This constraint embodies the needs of others balanced against the means available for fulfilling them—demand intersecting supply.

A freely fluctuating price system thus imposes on each individual the best available knowledge of how to serve the interests of all, such that resources that are intensely needed by many others are rationed by high prices and entrepreneurs are encouraged to find lower-cost means of meeting others' ends. In this part of Hayek's argument, it is hard to escape the conclusion that liberty is but a means to the end of the satisfaction of overall interests, such that if a better means is found, it should override liberty. Moreover, one can see clearly that the constraints imposed by the economic system may be very great—but since they are not intended by anyone, they cannot, for Hayek, be said to violate liberty.

Upholding a Market Society

A society of individual property owners is likely to be robust in its defense of individual liberty and the rules of the market order that guarantee their property. If wealth is spread widely, citizens will acquire an interest in defending these rules. This is a staple argument of economic liberalism, and at first Hayek embraced it with enthusiasm. Every citizen of the Great Society should ideally be a property owner, since that will ensure both that its basic rules are upheld and defended and, therefore, that economic progress will be fastest: the energies of every individual will be devoted to preserving and enlarging their stock of assets.

A society of property owners may be an ideal for Hayek, but it confronts the obvious problem that most members of modern market economies are without property except for their personal possessions and their own labor power. Assets and wealth remain very concentrated, and in some political economies, after a period of convergence between richest and poorest, the gap has begun widening again. Hayek's response to this problem was complex. He was unwilling to support political intervention to achieve a greater convergence in income or a more equal distribution of property, but in the absence of this being brought about spontaneously, the sociological foundations of his market order look fragile.

One escape route was to treat contract as even more fundamental than property, such that the freedom of individuals to contract with one another, even with only their labor power, became for Hayek the most basic form of liberty. To be able to enter into contracts means being able to make choices, to plan your life, and to preserve your independence and security, even if you acquire no property in the process (Hayek 1960, 140–41). A more radical alternative, and more consistent with his fundamental beliefs about the market order, would have been to make universal individual property ownership a precondition of a free society, but that would have implied that private property was a social right that every citizen should possess, and Hayek firmly rejects the idea of positive rights. To concede the existence of such rights would permit interference by the state to enforce them. For Hayek, state intervention always carries the risk that it will undermine liberty more than it will extend it.

The role of the state should therefore be limited to getting out of the way of the spontaneous interactions of individuals and respecting the patterns thus formed. This seems a consistent libertarian position, but Hayek is unwilling to go all the way with it. If he had done so he might have ended up embracing the arguments of Herbert Spencer.

Hayek and Spencer

There are few references to Spencer in Hayek's writings; those that there are mostly refer to the rule of law. Yet Spencer often seems to anticipate many of Hayek's arguments, particularly in the way he characterizes the perils facing free societies from increasing government interference. Where they differ is that Spencer maintains that competition between individuals must be allowed to run its course if modern society is to survive and prosper. Some individuals will fall into destitution and must be allowed to do so without any interference from the state. A healthy market order requires that all should bear the full consequences of the choices they make. Hayek disagreed.

Spencer argues that in a primitive condition of society, where all start with equal advantages, some individuals turn out to be industrious and prudent; they accumulate property. Others are idle and improvident, or in some cases perhaps just unfortunate, and fall into poverty. Can a poor individual fairly demand relief from a rich one? Spencer's answer is No (Spencer 1994, 9). As he trenchantly expressed the point in *The Man Versus the State*: "Is it not manifest that there must exist in our midst an immense amount of misery which is a normal result of misconduct and ought not to be dissociated from it?" (ibid., 81).

Unlike Hayek (1960, 89), who emphasized that market outcomes were brought about by luck and not merit, Spencer attacked the tendency to think of the miseries of the poor as the miseries of the deserving poor. They were better described as the miseries of the undeserving poor, and therefore as only too well deserved. However, like Hayek's view of liberty, Spencer's view of the poor seems to have been driven by a fear of the political consequences of alternative views. The problem with thinking of the miseries of the poor as undeserved, according to Spencer, was that it encouraged socialist solutions to poverty, which would mean abandoning liberty for servitude.

Long before Hayek penned *The Road to Serfdom*, Spencer warned about "the coming slavery." All socialism involves slavery, he declared, because it involves coercion: "That which fundamentally distinguishes the slave is that he labours under coercion to satisfy another's desires" (Spencer 1994, 96). For Spencer, the most dangerous aspect of socialism was that it destroyed individual independence, and therefore threatened the achievements of modern civilization. As he put it: "The welfare of a society and the justice of its arrangements are at bottom dependent on the characters of its members" (ibid., 105), and these would rapidly decline under socialism, causing disastrous consequences.

Although Hayek's outlook and his rhetoric about socialism are in many respects similar to Spencer's, he resisted Spencer's conclusions. He always rejected the kind of minimal state favored by libertarians such as Spencer (and Nozick). Instead he favored a limited state, albeit one whose boundaries cannot be set in advance or by reference to some fixed principle. Despite this indeterminacy, Hayek wanted to confine the sphere of the state as much as would be necessary to make the sphere of personal liberty expand. In practice, however, he sanctioned quite wide-ranging interventions by the state, including the provision of a social minimum—far beyond what Spencer would have thought justified or Nozick would have thought legitimate.

Spencer's early definition of the minimal state is very precise so as to avoid just such creeping socialism:

> What do [we] want a government for? Not to regulate commerce; not to educate the people; not to teach religion; not to administer charity; not to make roads and railways; but simply to defend the natural rights of man—to protect person and property—to prevent the aggressions of the powerful upon the weak—in a word, to administer justice. This is the

natural, the original, office of a government. It was not intended to do less; it ought not to be allowed to do more. (Spencer 1994, 6–7)

Hayek was happy for the state to do much more. This has led some of his critics to wonder whether his position differs from those of social democrats or egalitarian liberals such as Rawls only in degree rather than in principle. Jeremy Shearmur (2006) has questioned whether Hayek ever fully abandoned the mild socialist beliefs of his youth. Certainly he never adopted the harsh logic that Spencer applied to welfare and the treatment of the poor and the disadvantaged.

A non-biographical explanation for Hayek's deviations from "laissez faire" is the consequentialist character of his thought. His main concern is not the liberty of the individual considered as an a priori principle, but the overall framework of rules that makes the order of liberty possible. His concession to the idea of a social minimum to avoid the worst effects of poverty is primarily based on the political judgment that this can help strengthen the legitimacy of the market order. It is a price worth paying, provided it does not expand to become a universal entitlement. Hayek's judgment is that Spencer's alternatives—allowing people to starve if necessary, or depriving them of their liberty in workhouses—have become too difficult to justify in contemporary liberal democracies. Hayek does not dispute the force of Spencer's argument, but he rules it out on grounds of expediency.

The same is true of Hayek's defense of inequality. Hayek believes that inequality is inseparable from the operation of a market system, and that attempts to suppress or limit inequality will have serious unintended consequences. But he also refuses to accept Spencer's assumption that there is any necessary moral basis for inequality, that the rich are deserving of their good fortune and the poor undeserving. On the contrary, Hayek argues that those who make the largest fortunes, such as bankers and sports stars, are sometimes the least morally deserving or morally appealing Hayek 1976, 72. But gross inequalities in reward, provided they have been properly achieved under the rules of the market, should be accepted because these rules are necessary for the health of the market order and will indirectly benefit everybody.

This is a paradox worthy of Mandeville, if not expressed so colorfully. It is a world away from the simple moral equations of Spencer—or Samuel Smiles or Margaret Thatcher. Hayek advises us to swallow our moral principles about fairness, because these derive from our atavistic hunter-gatherer past and are no guide to appropriate behavior in the Great Society. Instead we should fasten our attention on the higher abstract morality represented by the general rules of the market order. It is a higher morality because these rules make possible the liberty of each one of us, but its consequences are hidden from most of us. Knowledge of these consequences comes from economics, which Hayek presents as a powerful form of practical reasoning whose insights are available only to those who have mastered its deductive mode of analysis.

This is a complex case to argue, and it means that Hayek's system gives rise to possibilities that Hayek did not intend and that he personally rejected.

Hayek always refused to describe what he aimed for in the way of social justice, which he regarded as a meaningless phrase. He preferred as little state intervention as possible, but since he was not prepared to formulate this preference as a strict criterion, he does not have a principled objection to state intervention (under the rule of law) beyond the pragmatic one that unwarranted interventions are those more likely to do harm than good. He accepts the need for a state that is more than a minimal state, but he constantly worries that it could become unanchored and slide down a slippery slope to serfdom or slavery. His concerns are the same as many nineteenth-century liberals, but his priority is not to defend liberty as a right to which every individual is entitled, but, like Spencer, to defend the Great Society, which has made extended forms of liberty possible but is so little understood either by its defenders or its detractors. This approach sanctions much greater involvement by the state in securing the conditions for liberty than Hayek foresaw.

Political Ignorance in a Market Society

The point can be put in a different way. To be fully effective, a Hayekian market order has to be more than just a system of voluntary exchange. It has also to be a political order, a republic, which requires the education of its citizens in the necessity and desirability of a market order so they will maintain and cherish it and refrain from actions and policies that might damage or weaken it.

Formal instruction, deliberation, and debate have their parts to play in this education, but for Hayek the best way to achieve it is by ensuring that citizens are exposed to the market, experiencing its ups and downs, making calculations, and taking risks, above all by owning property. These are life-changing experiences that give all who share them an insight into the nature of the market and the abstract rules required to sustain it. Hayek is not so naïve that he thinks market participants will come to appreciate the abstract reasoning of Austrian-school economics, but he does believe that support and understanding for market institutions and therefore for liberty is the product of practical experience. That is one reason that an expanding state can be a threat to liberty.

Hayek is uneasily aware, however, that the way modern societies have developed has tended to limit rather than to expand the opportunities for citizens to gain direct experience of the market, except as consumers. The growth of public-sector employment and bureaucratic private corporations has meant that most individuals, including Hayek himself, have been security-seeking employees, rather than risk-taking market entrepreneurs. As Hayek noted, a nation of employees is likely to be averse to risk and prone to seek safety, valuing security more than enterprise (Hayek 1960, 121–24). Entrepreneurs are also averse to risk if this is allowed, and will seek security in price-fixing and cartels, which is why competition is so essential if a market order is to flourish. But ensuring competition among entrepreneurs is an easier problem than ensuring that all market agents are entrepreneurs.

This issue leads directly to the greatest paradox of Hayek's account of liberty. An order that guarantees the maximum amount of liberty will produce the most wealth and in the long run will be in the interest of all its members. But how is such an order to be sustained politically? The premise of all of Hayek's writings from *The Road to Serfdom* onward is that the order he so values may have *evolved* spontaneously,[4] but cannot be *sustained* spontaneously. It must have a rational political underpinning if it is to be defended and survive.

The traditional liberal answer to this conundrum has been that economic liberty goes hand in hand with political liberty. In acquiring civil and political rights, people are educated about the security and prosperity made possible by a liberal order, and will vote to sustain it by electing those parties that are pledged to do so. Hayek is dissatisfied with this answer, however, which is why some have questioned whether he is really a liberal at all. Political liberty, he thinks, is no guarantee of economic liberty. It often leads to the invasion of economic liberty, because it allows governments to claim they are acting in the interests of the sovereign people when they override the institutional protections of the private sphere of the market and private property. Democracy may in theory be better than authoritarian forms of rule, but in practice it can be worse, because it provides the cloak of popular legitimacy for setting aside limits that, in Hayek's view, are essential if liberty is to be safeguarded.

Hayek traces the origin of this problem to political ignorance. This has several aspects. The first is institutional. Because there is no price mechanism in politics, the political market is quite unlike the economic market. The valuations individuals form about politics are frequently not based on local knowledge that reflects their experience and their circumstances, but rather depends on information they receive through newspapers and other centralized media as well as messages and images communicated by political parties. The political process comes to be dominated by parties and media that compete with one another as cartels rather than as firms subject to the disciplines of the market and the price system, preventing the kind of accountability that is obtained through the market. In a democratic system there is political competition for votes and power, but policies are aggregated into packages and presented as manifestos, so the individual voter can rarely discriminate among specific policies. It is the whole package or nothing (Buchanan and Tullock 1962).

In this way contemporary democracy tends to breed political ignorance, and the political class comes to be only loosely controlled by the public it serves. Political knowledge comes to be monopolized by elites and the people are shut out from decision making, except for the ritual of an election every few years. As Schumpeter (1943) observed, voters then choose between rival teams of leaders who, over time, may increasingly come to resemble one another, however fractious they appear.

The second aspect of political ignorance is ideational. The modern era has spawned a whole set of doctrines that misconceive the nature of liberty and of the Great Society. Even when these doctrines are well meaning, they can have dangerous consequences if they are put into effect.

Hayek singles out in particular all varieties of socialism, which he thinks is a regression to the mindset of hunters and gatherers (Hayek 1983). By insisting on replacing procedural rules with substantive aims, socialism undermines the basis of the modern market order. Hayek is also strongly critical of many conservative, liberal, and nationalist doctrines, which are also guilty of sanctioning interference by government in the market sphere. The most damaging policies are those that interfere with prices, particularly any form of outright price control, because this prevents prices from performing their signalling function for the market economy, depriving people of crucial economic information that they need to make plans and live independently.

Hayek argues that these false doctrines arise because of what he calls "constructivism" or "constructivist rationalism," whose hallmark is a failure to make proper distinctions between the social and natural sciences, treating the social world as though it were a machine which can be commanded and controlled, rather than as a delicate organism, the full workings of which human beings cannot understand (Hayek 1952). This is another of Hayek's grand paradoxes. The greatest achievement of modern civilization is the creation of the Great Society, with its sphere of personal liberty; but this has come about despite, rather than because, human beings have planned or rationally designed it. Accordingly, we do not understand the basis of the Great Society and may inadvertently destroy it despite the best of intentions. Intellectual error, then, is the great enemy of liberty. But in trying to get us to think more carefully about our society, one may in fact focus attention on its flaws and thus encourage its destruction.

As has often been observed, Hayek was not against rationalism, since rational argument was necessary to understand the true nature of the Great Society. But he rejected constructivist rationalism without explaining how he thought his form of rationalism might predominate, which it clearly needed to do for the sake of liberty. Was it to predominate through force of argument and the acknowledgement by its opponents of intellectual error? Or would it be because the practical consequences of the alternative forms of rationalism would come to be rejected whenever they were put into practice?

The third aspect of political ignorance is sociological. As noted earlier, the Great Society has seen an enormous (and spontaneous) growth of large-scale public and private organizations that make most of their members employees and consumers, not owners and entrepreneurs. This means that most members of the Great Society have little or no direct experience of how markets work, and this ignorance makes them prone to support political parties and to entertain beliefs that are inimical to liberty. Hayek speaks enthusiastically in places about the great boon of modern organization, but in others he entertains his own form of atavism, idealizing a simple society of owners who have direct experience of how markets work. This experience allows them to acquire a set of simple virtues that are necessary for the functioning of an anonymous, extended order— prudence, consistency, honesty, trust—and ensures that they vote for parties committed to the market order (Hayek 1979, 164–65).

For a brief period in a few countries after the aristocratic monopoly on political power had been broken, the votes of large and small property owners were in the majority. But it proved impossible to hold the line, and once the vote had been extended beyond property owners, it became much more difficult to ensure a majority of true liberals in support of the principles of a market order. With the achievement of universal suffrage, the mass parties in both new and established democracies have had to find ways to appeal to a much wider spectrum of classes and groups. From a Hayekian perspective, many of these voters are almost necessarily ignorant of why a market order is so valuable, let alone of what must be done to preserve it (Hayek 1978, 65).

Ignorance is less of a problem in the economy because mistakes can be corrected and individuals can learn to change their behavior. But in politics, while voters can learn about how different parties tend to behave in office and the policies associated with them, choice is much more restricted than it is in market exchange; the nature of the choice that is being made is often unclear because of the aggregation of policies into party platforms and the unknown policies yet to be proposed; and the occasions for individual decision are not daily, as in our activities as consumers, but only once every few years. There is also the problem that some choices in politics can mean the end of choice and so become irreversible by democratic means, for example if they lead to a change of regime and the suppression of democracy, as in Germany in 1933. Consumer choices do not have this finality.

The sociological problem of voter ignorance is compounded, for Hayek, by the growth of the welfare state and the increasing number of voters who are dependent on it in some way for their income. In his constitutional proposals in *Law, Legislation and Liberty*, Hayek favored excluding all those in receipt of state benefits, as well as all those employed by the state, from being allowed to vote in elections for members of his governmental assembly, the lower legislative body. This is because such voters have a material interest in seeing an expansion of government spending and taxation to fund higher wages and benefits.

They would, however, be given a vote (on one occasion only—upon reaching the age of 45) for representatives from their age cohort in the higher legislative assembly, which sets the rules of just conduct within which the governmental assembly operates.

In modern democracies the prospects of re-imposing restrictions on the franchise are not high, although the issue of who should be entitled to vote in modern tax states remains a live one, surfacing in British political rhetoric about "strivers" and "shirkers" and American rhetoric about "makers" and "takers." The suggestion during the 2012 U.S. presidential election that the "takers" make up 47 percent of the population indicates the scale of the problem for a Hayekian democracy, but underestimates it. On Hayek's own criteria, the percentage of people who could be trusted to vote responsibly, because they have a direct experience and understanding of the market order, constitutes a small minority of the electorate. He would have had to disenfranchise himself, as a state employee during most of his career.

From Hayekian Conservatism to Social Liberalism

Hayek's fears at times can seem exaggerated. Widespread ignorance about the foundations of the market order has not prevented parties advocating free-market policies from being regularly elected in many established democracies. But his real anxiety is that liberty can easily be lost because the majority in modern democracies is predisposed to favor state intervention, which appears to them the best way to defend their interests and maintain their security. Hayek despairs of democracy as a form of government because the risks of it being turned against liberty are so high, and in his own lifetime there were many examples of this. Accordingly he seeks to shackle democracy as much as possible, to find new institutional means to prevent popular sovereignty from overriding the constitutional barriers against unlimited government.

The fear of popular sovereignty that pervades his writings also explains his willingness to tolerate authoritarian regimes so long as they safeguarded economic liberty and prevented totalitarianism. But authoritarian regimes were not a long-term solution to the problem, because they lacked legitimacy and sooner or later tended to collapse. The only real solution was to reform democracy so as to entrench liberal values in ways that shackled what democratic governments could do. This inspired some of Hayek's most outlandish thinking: the rational re-design of a new political constitution that would have done credit to the utopian socialists (Hayek 1979, 105–127).

Hayek's defense of economic liberty, coupled with his downgrading of the importance of political liberty, turned his thought in an increasingly conservative direction. He launched an impassioned attack on social justice while at the same time defending corporate power (the issue on which Walter Lippmann parted company with him after 1945) (Jackson 2010). Hayek argued that trade unions posed a much more serious threat to liberty than large corporations, because the latter were disciplined by competition (Hayek 1960, 253–84). As he grew older the conservative cast of his opinions grew more pronounced. He still declared himself in favor of progress, but it had to be a progress that was entirely unplanned and came about accidentally, as a byproduct of the decisions taken by millions of individuals in exercising their liberty, devising their life plans, making mistakes, and adjusting to circumstances. He increasingly emphasized the role of tradition, arguing that Mill and most other liberals were wrong to have set it against reason: Traditions were a surer repository of wisdom than independent, free-thinking intellectuals such as himself (Hayek 1988).

In changed circumstances, Hayek might have presented his argument rather differently. If he had not been so shaped intellectually by his long ideological struggle against socialism, he might have given greater weight to other options for preserving economic liberty, such as finding ways to empower all citizens and to create a more cohesive and fair society. Seeking to minimize opportunities for coercion by reducing inequalities of power between individuals is a long-standing liberal aim. The goal is explicitly Hayekian, but he rejected the means, fearing that egalitarianism would be an excuse to extend the role of the state and shrink the sphere of personal liberty.

Also missing in Hayek's discussion of economic liberty is a surprising lack of enthusiasm for using competition to overturn privilege and reduce rent seeking, which are so prevalent in the public and private sectors of modern economies. Although he endorses the classical-liberal arguments for a strong and active state to intervene in the economy to safeguard the market order, ensuring that all members of the Great Society have the means to be independent within it is not the central focus of Hayek's later writings or of his policy prescriptions, which are dominated instead by his polemics against social justice and his fears about democracy. But it is perfectly possible to derive a social-democratic or social-liberal Hayekian program that is true to the basic principles Hayek enunciated.

A Hayekian social democracy would still be focused on individual liberty as its main goal, but would be neutral as to whether markets, hierarchies, networks, or some combination of the three would be the most appropriate form of coordination. Given Hayek's insights about the limits of human knowledge and the uncertainty that surrounds all human institutions, market failures, government failures, and network failures should all be presumed to be endemic in human institutions. No one form of coordination is likely to be always the best or most appropriate. It follows that Hayekians should have the same skepticism towards markets as they do towards hierarchies and networks.

Moreover, the problem of modern liberty, from this (revised) Hayekian perspective, is broader than that of public ignorance. The well-known failings of representative democracy are indeed manifest in the disengagement and political ignorance of citizens, but deeper problems are the lack of space for experimentation, the lack of feedback from public policies, the difficulty of establishing policy based on evidence, the recurrence of policy disasters, and the rigidity of public opinion and of political ideologies.

A Neo-Hayekian Politics

Where the left sees politics as subordinate to those with market power, the right sees politics as subordinate to special interests. From a Hayekian perspective both should be worrisome, but Hayek and many of those most influenced by him have tended to focus largely on the latter rather than the former. If some of the self-imposed limits on Hayekian politics are removed, however, a series of interesting Hayekian questions are opened up.

First, in a society dedicated to maximizing individual liberty, how big should the market and the non-market spheres be? As Hayek noted, the non-market sphere can be very large indeed in a society that promotes liberty. In the development of modern civilization there has been a gradual enlargement of the sphere of the market, but from a Hayekian perspective there is no simple correlation between the size of the market sphere and the extent of individual liberty. Hayek acknowledged that the price mechanism is not suitable for all spheres of society, so which areas should remain protected from market competition in order to promote individual liberty becomes a central issue.

A second question is how the economic surplus is to be distributed. Through much of human history it has been used to entrench privilege, inequality, social division, and hierarchy. One of the aspects of the Great Society that Hayek celebrates is that in many instances there have been notable advances towards equal liberty for all members of the Great Society, not just an exclusive class within it. But such advances in economic liberty were often won through active measures to equalize power, such as challenges to existing property rights, the breakup of great landed estates, the abolition of serfdom, and the emancipation of women. The winning of political liberties has often been vital for the securing and widening of economic liberty.

Hayek was so concerned about the dangers posed by political liberty in modern circumstances that he failed to emphasize the crucial role it has played in making possible the kind of economic liberty he most prizes. It could do so again.

NOTES

1. Jonathan Wolff (1997) makes an important distinction between freedom and liberty. Freedom implies the possibility of particular actions while liberty concerns the permissibility of types of actions. In these terms, Hayek is much more concerned with liberty than he is with freedom.
2. The relationship between Rawls and Hayek has attracted a lot of attention in recent years, and the possibility of combining their theories has given rise to non-academic "Rawlsekians" (Arthur 2008; Lister 2011). Apart from his use of the term "social justice," Hayek indicated that Rawls's approach to establishing procedural rather than substantive rules was similar to his own, although it is unclear whether he made a detailed study of *A Theory of Justice*.
3. Hayek tries to maintain in *The Constitution of Liberty* that examples of genuine coercion in a market order are very few. But the example he uses of genuine coercion—the owner of the oasis who has a monopoly of the water supply—can easily (as his critics have noted) be applied to many other social situations, including relationships at work, that Hayek insists are non-coercive. Even on his own definition, the incidence of coercion appears potentially much wider than he is prepared to admit. In many social situations, as G. A. Cohen (1995) pointed out, freedom for some means unfreedom for others. Hayek's theory indicates the same, but he chooses to ignore this implication of his own analysis because it would justify a level of intervention by the state to correct it than he is prepared on a priori grounds to approve.
4. A very different view is taken by Karl Polanyi (1945).

REFERENCES

Arthur, Don. 2008. "Hayek & Rawls: An Unlikely Fusion." Evatt Foundation. http://evatt.org.au/papers/hayek-rawls.html.

Buchanan, James, and Gordon Tullock. 1962. *The Calculus of Consent: Logical Foundations of Constitutional Democracy.* Ann Arbor: University of Michigan Press.

Cohen, G. A. 1995. *Self-Ownership, Freedom, and Equality.* Cambridge: Cambridge University Press.

Friedman, Jeffrey. 1997. "What's Wrong with Libertarianism?" *Critical Review* 11(3): 407–67.

Hayek, F. A. 1944. *The Road to Serfdom.* London: Routledge & Kegan Paul.

Hayek, F. A. 1960. *The Constitution of Liberty.* London: Routledge & Kegan Paul.

Hayek, F. A. 1978. "The Atavism of Social Justice." In *New Studies in Philosophy, Politics and Economics, and the History of Ideas.* London: Routledge & Kegan Paul.

Hayek, F. A. 1979. "Epilogue: The Three Sources of Human Values." In *The Political Order of a Free People.* Vol. 3 of *Law, Legislation and Liberty.* London: Routledge & Kegan Paul.

Hayek, F. A. 1983. *Knowledge, Evolution, and Society.* London: Adam Smith Institute.

Hayek, F. A. 1988. *The Fatal Conceit: Errors of Socialism.* London: Routledge.

Jackson, Ben. 2010. "At the Origins of Neo-Liberalism: The Free Economy and the Strong State, 1930–1947." *Historical Journal* 53(1): 129–51.

Lister, Andrew. 2007. "The 'Mirage of Social Justice': Hayek Against (and For) Rawls." *CSSJ Working Papers Series, SJ017.* Oxford: Centre for the Study of Social Justice.

Plant, Raymond. 2010. *The Neo-Liberal State.* Oxford: Oxford University Press.

Polanyi, Karl. 1945. *Origins of Our Time: The Great Transformation.* London: Gollancz.

Schumpeter, Joseph. 1943. *Capitalism, Socialism and Democracy.* London: Allen & Unwin.

Shearmur, Jeremy. 2006. "Hayek's Politics." In *The Cambridge Companion to Hayek,* ed. Edward Feser. Cambridge: Cambridge University Press.

Spencer, Herbert. 1994. *Political Writings,* ed. John Offer. Cambridge: Cambridge University Press.

Wolff, Jonathan. 1997. "Freedom, Liberty, and Property." *Critical Review* 11(3): 345–58.

François Godard

THE ROAD TO SERFDOM'S
ECONOMISTIC WORLDVIEW

ABSTRACT: *At the end of World War II, F. A. Hayek denounced the then-popular idea of central planning by arguing that, if pursued to its logical conclusion, it would entail totalitarianism. But there were at least two problems. First, judging by his example of Nazi Germany, state control over the economy appears to be a consequence, not a cause, of the monopolization of political power. Second, he conflated socialism and mere interference in the market with central planning. Therefore, history did not so much falsify Hayek's prediction as bypass it: Once the vogue for central planning faded in the West, Hayek's book became irrelevant—except, ironically, in Germany. There, it was read as a manifesto for "good planning" through the rule of law. Alongside other "neoliberal" writers, Hayek had a profound (if little acknowledged) influence on the shape of the emerging Federal Republic and, through it, on the whole European institutional framework.*

F. A. Hayek (1944, 37) wrote *The Road to Serfdom* (hereafter *The Road*) as a "political book" and it was received as such. Published in 1944 in Britain and in America, it became a popular phenomenon the following year when condensed versions were issued by *Look* magazine and *The Reader's Digest*. The author met with unexpected public success on a promotional tour of the United States and the book became an object of a polemic during the British general election—a high profile none of Hayek's academic production ever reached. *The Road* became the lodestar of conservatives on both sides of the Atlantic and made Hayek a totemic figure of the right—so much so as to compromise his academic career as an economist (Caldwell 2007a; Hayek 1994, 99–108).

The book uses a prophetic tone to warn against the threat posed by central planning to Britain's and, by extension, the West's liberal order, making an analogy with the rise of National Socialism in Germany. But the 1945 electoral triumph of the Labour party brought the National Health Service, which Hayek implicitly approved, and none of the central planning that he so feared. This paper aims to understand exactly what Hayek got wrong and why. But I also want to recontextualize *The Road* in German political thought and history.

I will first locate the intellectual genesis of the book in Hayek's analysis of central planning and his research on the background of modern political ideas. I will then examine his insights about the association of central planning with totalitarian politics, examining, as well, the misinterpretation of this argument as positing a slippery slope from any economic intervention or redistribution to totalitarianism—a misunderstanding for which Hayek shares some blame because of his conflation of central planning with market interference and "socialism." Then I will consider why his warnings swiftly became irrelevant in English-speaking countries. Finally I will show that *The Road*, despite being primarily aimed at Britain, was most influential in defeated Germany, where its message became part of the emerging neoliberal current of ideas that significantly influenced the country's renaissance, as well as in the pan-European institutions that Germany so powerfully affected. *The Road* took off in Germany because Hayek's positions were closer to those of the proponents of the German social-market economy than to the American libertarianism with which he came to be associated.

Epistemology and Central Planning

The Road must be set in the context of Hayek's intellectual trajectory if it is properly to be understood.

In 1920, Hayek's senior Viennese colleague, economist Ludwig von Mises, launched what came to be known as the "socialist-calculation debate," arguing that socialism—in the sense of a fully centralized economy—was "impossible" because the planning authority would have no basis for rationally allocating capital in the absence of prices for capital goods set by free exchange among private owners. Therefore, "in a socialist state wherein the pursuit of economic calculation is impossible, there can be—in our sense of the term—no economy whatsoever" (Mises 1920, 105). Although the communist movement, both mass and elite, largely ignored this debate, important socialist *economists* such as Oskar Lange took up Mises's challenge and came up with the idea of a socialist market, where central capital allocation would be made through trial-and-error processes and dummy markets. Other authors argued that calculators (computers had yet to be invented) could be used to figure out prices or values to enable planners' decision making.[1]

Hayek was squarely allied with Mises in defending economic decision making through markets, but he never fully subscribed to the aprioristic "impossibility" argument or the "calculational" aspect of it. Instead, his contribution to the debate was to put individual subjectivity at the center of his rationale for decentralized economic decision making. But the market socialists were generally seen as having won the debate.

A second academic controversy weighed even more heavily on Hayek's trajectory because of its greater effect on his reputation. This was the debate in the 1930s with John Maynard Keynes about the latter's *Treatise on Money* (1930).[2] After the 1936 publication of Keynes's *General Theory*, most economists lined up behind him; Hayek, who had become famous as Keynes's foremost academic opponent, found himself the lonely classical liberal voice in academic Britain, frustrated by Keynes's unwillingness to engage in a public debate (Caldwell 1995, 21–34).

These two setbacks appear to have driven Hayek to move away from technical economics and engage in a broader research project, the result of which, "Economics and Knowledge" (1937), is now widely regarded as having been the tipping point in his shift from economics proper to social philosophy. In this paper he enunciated the idea that the price mechanism was much more than a calculation device; instead, it was a decentralized information system for coordinating subjective and changing individual plans. A centralized decision maker, he argued, could not possibly track the "dispersed knowledge" and evolving preferences of millions of individuals in a modern society with the efficiency of the price system.[3] His economics and, later, his political philosophy thus acquired its unique epistemological strand.

Meanwhile, Hayek was writing about the history of ideas and—in publications over twelve years, later bundled in a book (Hayek 1952)—he argued that socialism is the product of a methodological fallacy: the misapplication of natural-science approaches to social problems. The culprits here were the École Polythechnique[4] and such nineteenth-century figures as Auguste Comte and Henri de Saint-Simon. Hayek saw a second key formative influence on socialism in the radical empiricism of the German Historical school of economics, which he thought justified arbitrary government. These French and German sources both fed the intellectual reaction against the *Rechtsstaat* (or law-governed state) that flourished from the late nineteenth century, a reaction that, Hayek maintained, inspired both the Bolshevik and Nazi revolutions.

Refreshingly for an economist, Hayek believed that ideas rule the world. He wholly subscribed to Keynes's view about the influence of "defunct economists," maintaining that "it is ideas, not vested interests, which are dangerous for good or evil" (Hayek 1960, 445n14, quoting Keynes 1936, 331–32). At some point, talented authors originated new ideas, which progressively gain acceptance across intellectual classes, eventually influencing those who make public policy. Thus, liberalism rose to become the governing doctrine of the late nineteenth century thanks to writers such as Smith and the Mills and battles of ideas, like that leading to the repeal of the British Corn Laws in 1846. Socialism, too, was primarily an intellectual movement whose roots must be sought in the history of ideas.

An Economic Theory of Totalitarianism[5]

The Road to Serfdom fuses Hayek's research projects on the epistemological understanding of the price system and the history of economic and political ideas. It also links Hayek's participation in the socialist-calculation debate to his emerging position as a political theorist, for the book erects central planning as the ultimate scourge against which Hayek is fighting. In *The Counter-Revolution of Science* (1952, 156), he argues that the "popularity of "economic planning" is "directly traceable to the prevalence of scientific ideas" typical of the *polytechniciens*. In *The Road to Serfdom* the intellectual history of planning is more muted, emerging in vague allusions to "the uncritical transfer to the problems of society of habits of thought engendered by the preoccupation with technical problems, the habits of thought of the natural scientist and the engineer" (Hayek 1944, 72–73). But the main historical assumption of *The Counter-Revolution of Science* is present in *The Road*, too: that "socialism" means a commitment to the "'conscious direction of all social forces to deliberately chosen goals" (ibid., 73). If this is the case, then central planning is, for socialists, a tautological requirement of their doctrine. "To nearly all those to whom socialism is not merely a hope but an object of practical politics, the characteristic methods of modern socialism are as essential as the ends themselves" (ibid., 83). These means are "economic planning" (ibid., 84), and "what our planners demand is a central direction of all economic activity according to a single plan, laying down how the resources of society should be 'consciously directed' to serve particular ends in a definite way" (ibid., 85).

However, since the *intention* of socialists is for central planning to be accomplished democratically, and since the particular ends they aim to serve are equality and individual freedom, Hayek sees his task as explaining "to the socialists of all parties"—to whom *The Road* is dedicated— that "the unforeseen but inevitable consequences of socialist planning create a state of affairs in which, if the policy is to be pursued, totalitarian forces will get the upper hand" (Hayek 1944, 50). Totalitarianism is thus the "unforeseen consequenc[e]" of "socialism" as Hayek defines it (ibid., 78). Hayek writes that Max Eastman, "Lenin's old friend ... found himself compelled to admit that 'instead of being better, Stalinism is worse than fascism, more ruthless, barbarous, unjust, immoral, anti-democratic,'" and "that it is 'better described as superfascist'" (ibid., 79). "Democratic socialism," Hayek concludes, "the great utopia of the last few generations, is not only unachievable, but ... to strive for it produces something so utterly different that few of those who now wish it would be prepared to accept the consequences" (ibid., 82).

Why? Perhaps counterintuitively, Hayek argues that central planning is both necessarily despotic (i.e., arbitrary as opposed to rule-bound) and that it is structurally inefficient. The second point was proved, to Hayek's satisfaction, in the socialist-calculation debate, while the first point telegraphs the version of liberalism that Hayek would defend as the alternative to central planning: a government that makes and is bound by general laws, not one that issues commands that are aimed at particular individuals. By contrast, the planned allocation of all social resources would require "that every one of our needs is given its rank in an order of values which must be complete enough to make it possible to decide among all the different courses which the planner has to choose" (Hayek 1944, 101). This, in turn, would require "us to agree on a much larger number of topics than we have been used to" (ibid., 104). Since democratic action would not be possible without such agreement, there will be a conflict between socialists' ends and their attempt to use democratic means. "The inability of democratic assemblies to carry out what seems to be a clear mandate of the people will inevitably cause dissatisfaction with democratic institutions" (ibid.), but in any event "if things are to get done, the responsible authorities must be freed from the fetters of democratic procedure" (ibid., 108).[6] As (part of) an explanation of the politics of pre-Nazi Germany and pre-fascist Italy, and as a penetrating examination of the incompatibility of democracy with central planning, one must admit that Hayek was on solid ground. But despite his devotion to the history of ideas, his equation of socialism with central planning, which is pivotal to the whole argument, was reductionist in the extreme.

While Hayek had been a Fabian in his youth, and while the West experienced a vogue for planning that began in the *fin de siècle* and was strengthened by the two world wars, democratic socialists and communists alike would have been surprised to learn that Comtean social-science doctrines were their governing ideas and that, in consequence, central planning was inseparable from their aspirations for freedom, equality, and democracy. Marx was an anarchist; Rosa Luxemburg made "spontaneism" the root of a proper socialism, and Dewey did want "conscious" control to be exercised by society, but not as part of a central plan. Comte played no discernible role in such figures' ideas; *The Counter-Revolution of Science* barely even touches on Marx, not at all on liberal socialists, and ignores alternative hypotheses about the origins and nature of socialist thought.

The issue here, however, is not so much the one-sidedness of Hayek's intellectual history as the fact that a more nuanced view would show that socialism did not *necessarily* mean central planning—to socialists themselves. Far from being as wedded to central planning as to the ideals central planning was supposed to achieve, the left has always shown itself to be far more interested in ends than means—perhaps irresponsibly so. For this reason, central planning turned out to be a fad that ended shortly after the war (although Hayek, failing to realize this, kept up the fight against central planning for the many decades remaining in his long life).

When Hayek (1944, 83) claims that "the dispute about socialism has become largely a dispute about means and not about ends," one hears the voice not of an intellectual historian but of someone who is too absorbed in the daily newspapers of his time—and the voice of an economist. The socialist economists with whom he had debated in the 1930s *were* in favor of central planning. But most socialist intellectuals would never have heard of the problem of "economic calculation," because the question of means has always been important to the left primarily in the sense of "How do we get from the status quo to an ideal society?"—not in the sense with which the economists of the calculation debate were peculiarly concerned: "Is the ideal society practicable?"

If Hayek's "socialism" is narrowly focused on a particular technology, central planning, it is also a broad category that features all modern forms of collectivism, including Nazism. Here Hayek relies on more than the formal name of Hitler's party, highlighting the leftist roots of the National Socialist pedigree in the work of such authors as Werner Sombart and Johann Plenge (Hayek 1944, 181–92). Then Hayek draws analogies between Nazis and Bolsheviks, arguing that the former carried out a full takeover of the German economy that involved a central-command system largely similar to that of the Soviet Union. He deepens the parallel with perceptive comments on the two régimes' distorted morality, which brought the lowest characters to the top of society and debased the very meaning of truth (ibid., 157–80). And *The Road* repeatedly uses the word *totalitarianism*, an Italian concept of the 1920s that was meant since the late 1930s to reveal the shared essence of fascism, Nazism, and communism.

Hayek's analysis, then, was a double affront to the left. First, while Hayek repeatedly acknowledged that most British and European socialists were sincerely committed to political freedom, he dismissed this commitment by emphasizing its incompatibility with planning— which must have seemed a glaring non sequitur to the proponents of democratic socialism. Less intellectually sound was the frequent objection to Hayek's association of Nazi Germany and Communist Russia. This linkage was an anathema to most educated Western opinion because Hitler had gained power by allying with "bourgeois" parties and thanks to support from business interests; and because the Soviet Union was an ally of the West during the war, helping to cement its reputation as the antithesis of the Third Reich. Today, however, the equivalence of central planning and totalitarianism is unobjectionable, and it is widely accepted that full central control of a society's material resources necessarily implies totalitarianism. Hayek may take some of the credit for driving home the point. The point, however, is accepted as much on the left as elsewhere, as the postwar emancipatory virtue of central planning lost its gloss even prior to the rise in the 1960s of the individualistic New Left.

An Ambiguous Warning

At least as problematic as Hayek's central-plan-obsessed conception of socialism are the lessons that have been drawn from it. If "socialism" entails central planning as its means, and if central planning leads to totalitarianism, then if one broadens the definition of socialism, one may impugn as incipiently totalitarian whatever other means are now included under the socialist rubric. This leads to the two issues that have preoccupied readers of *The Road*, as far as I can tell: whether the redistributive, regulatory state (the "welfare state" for short) shares the same totalitarian tendencies as does central planning; and whether, in consequence, totalitarianism is the inevitable consequence of the welfare state.

The second issue emerged immediately after the publication of *The Road*, which was ubiquitously interpreted as arguing that the welfare state would inevitably bring about totalitarianism (Caldwell 2007a, 29). This reading is inadvertently encouraged by passages in which Hayek (1944, 137) comes close to endorsing a slippery-slope argument, as when he writes that "the close interdependence of all economic phenomena makes it difficult to stop planning just where we wish" and that "once the free working of the market is impeded beyond a certain degree, the planner will be forced to extend his controls until they become all-comprehensive." Hayek never draws a line between "planning," "central planning," and mere government interference (as it is usually called) in the market. A sophisticated version of the "inevitability" reading of *The Road* is found in Paul Samuelson's influential textbook, which interpreted Hayek as arguing that "the logic" of *government intervention in the economy*, if pursued persistently, would inevitably undermine political freedoms (Samuelson and Nordhaus 1985, 778–79).[7]

Hayek, however, explicitly denied the unavoidability of totalitarianism. In the original introduction he states that he is not "arguing that these developments are inevitable" (Hayek 1944, 59), and he reports in the 1976 preface that "it has frequently been alleged that I have contended that any movement in the direction of socialism is bound to lead to totalitarianism. Even though the danger exists, this is not what the book says" (Hayek 1976, 19, 55). Rather, his argument is "a warning." Indeed, Hayek always rejected the idea of unavoidable historical processes, as made clear in his discussion of "historicism" (Hayek 1952, 126–41).

Once this underlying vision is accepted, it is easy to dismiss *The Road* by pointing out that some European social-democratic countries came to combine wider political freedoms with much more widespread interventionism than did the United States. Such cases as the full-fledged Scandinavian welfare states, which nobody could accuse of being totalitarian, could thereby be used to prove that *The Road* had been discredited by history.

However, while *The Road* opposed central planning and its allegedly antecedent ideas, it did not oppose the welfare state, whether because it was supposed to lead to totalitarianism or on any other grounds. One might view Hayek's lists of the types of regulation and redistribution that he favored—lists given in *The Road* (particularly chapter XI) and elsewhere (particularly Hayek 1960)—as attempts to back away from the libertarianism that is implicit in an attack on all government intervention in the economy. But Hayek never launched such an attack, certainly not in *The Road*, so the more charitable reading is that Hayek had nothing to back away from. The slippery-slope argument to which I have alluded is an argument about what happens when the government starts to engage in central planning—not when it provides monetary stability and antitrust protection (Hayek 1944, 72) or the regulation of poisonous substances, working hours, and sanitary arrangements (ibid., 86); not when it builds roads, prevents deforestation, fights pollution (ibid., 87), prevents "fraud and deception (including exploitation of ignorance)," i.e., consumer protection (ibid., 88); not when it deals with "problems created by a modern town" (ibid., 95), issues "building regulations or factory laws" (ibid., 118), "enforces a stringent price control" on "whatever monopoly is really inevitable" (ibid., 207); and, most crucially, not when it supplies "a comprehensive system of social insurance" covering "sickness and accident" (ibid., 148)—all of which Hayek favored. "Let a uniform minimum be secured to everybody by all means," he added (ibid., 215). The only instance of government intervention outside of the market that Hayek mentions and *disapproves of* regards labor regulation preventing free choice of occupation (ibid., 86, 121–22, 128–29, 149–53, 154, 213).

Hayek (1944, 148) has a forcefully articulated theory about *how* the state should intervene, "outside of and supplementary to the market system":[8] through "*formal rules* which do not aim at the wants and needs of particular people" (ibid., 113). This allows him both to assimilate almost any intervention *in the price mechanism* to "planning" while stressing that his liberalism is no plea for "inaction of the state" and that "the term "laissez faire" is a "highly ambiguous and misleading description of the principles on which a liberal policy is based" (ibid., 118). So Hayek was no libertarian. The problem is that *The Road* never provides a practicable demarcation criterion to judge when the market process is inadequate and needs to be supplemented by the state (besides allusions to externalities).

Just as Hayek misunderstood socialism through a narrowly econo-mistic lens, however, he was misunderstood by socialists who lacked this lens and thus were unfamiliar with the economists' debate over central planning during the 1920s and '30s. Without this historical background, a careless reader can conflate "central planning" with "the welfare state"— as Hayek had conflated "central planning" with "socialism." Then counterexamples such as Scandinavia can "disprove" the alleged claim that the welfare state leads to totalitarianism. This misreads Hayek as badly as Hayek misread the left. But this particular misreading was not, of course, confined to the left. Conservatives in Britain and the United States also misinterpreted Hayek as a foe of government activism. In recent years, this misinterpretation of Hayek has experienced a revival— as have sales of *The Road*—thanks to populist libertarians such as television commentator Glenn Beck, who equate all economic inter-vention with socialism and then applaud Hayek for showing that socialism leads to totalitarianism.[9] Even some Hayek scholars have furthered this misunderstanding.[10]

Presumably Beck is as unaware of the socialist-calculation debate as most of Hayek's critics were, and therefore does not grasp that for Hayek, central planning is not a metaphor that can be extended to everything the government does. It means nothing less than the replacement of economic allocation by prices with a plan for the deployment of a society's resources, written by the people's representatives and imposed on everyone by law.

Ignorance of Politics

Hayek's narrative of the rise of National Socialism makes it the culmination of a German inclination towards planning initiated by Bismarck's "deliberate organization of economic activity" in the late nineteenth century (Hayek 1944, 191). Thus conceived, Germany's history becomes an illustration of the postwar risk facing the West, where growing acceptance of socialist ideas could lead to a dictatorial endgame. Here Hayek is on shaky grounds, as noted by the economist A. C. Pigou in his review of *The Road*. Pigou stressed that central planning can be not only a "means" to the ends of equality and freedom, but a means to the end of national power—rather than the cause of it. "When men secure command of a country's government and are determined to direct its resources towards building up national power as the supreme end, as undoubtedly Hitler and Mussolini were, they are bound, of course, to work through the method of central planning" (Pigou 1944, 219). In the 1930s, the German command economy was a product of the Nazi takeover of government, not the reverse. Hitler first seized all political power, rapidly established a tyranny if not yet full totalitarianism, and then proceeded progressively to spread state control over the economy, often in a pragmatic fashion. "By 1936 the regime had gathered sufficient strength to draw each and every economic act under its command" (Stolper, Häuser, and Borchardt 1967, 129). So the drift was not from a progressive government control over the country resources towards the abolition of freedoms, but the other way around. The same objection to Hayek's argument is raised by the example of communist regimes, which first seized all power and radically diminished liberty—then began planning the economy (Lindbeck 1971, 64–65).[11]

Hayek's distorted vision of German history reveals a deeper problem with *The Road*: the reduction of politics to economic policy.[12] This starts in its account of the history of ideas, which is seen through a prism of economics and policy, while religion, aesthetics, and literature are practically ignored, leading Hayek to overlook the specific romantic roots of Nazism. Just as important as the distortions in Hayek's approach to intellectual history, however, are the omissions of other factors.

For Hayek, the political process, the actual workings of democracy, are nearly a sideshow to the *longue durée* story of ideas influencing policy. For him, the typology of its economic policy would be enough to define the final nature of a regime: A society with capitalist markets is conductive to political freedom; totalitarianism must stem from central planning.[13] Socialists and Nazis, according to Hayek (1944, 145), "have no difference between them about the question of its being the will of the state which should assign to each person his proper place in society"—an analysis that leaves him blind to the gap between an egalitarian and a hierarchical society.

At one point Hayek opens the door to a broader questioning of the reasons why liberalism had become unpopular (and collectivist ideas so broadly accepted). He detects a tension between the modern rise of (what he would later call "constructivist") rationalism and the necessary epistemological modesty that one must adopt when participating in the complex modern civilization evolving without a set path. Rationalism produces "a new unwillingness to submit to any rule or necessity the rationale of which man does not understand" (Hayek 1944, 211), starting with resistance to "submission to the impersonal and seemingly irrational forces of the market" (ibid., 212). Had he not been blinded by his narrow focus on the type of "rationalism" that produces a "planning mentality" (Hayek 1952), Hayek might have considered the possibility that totalitarianism was a response to the growing tension between rationalism *tout court* and the *lack* of purposefulness of liberalism in the context of mass democracy. Thus, in his otherwise sympathetic review of *The Road*, Joseph A. Schumpeter (1946, 270) falls back on his aristocratic default position to argue that the book missed the question of the compatibility of liberalism and democracy: "The principles of individual initiative and self-reliance are the principles of a very limited class. They mean nothing to the mass of people who—no matter for what reason— are not up to the standard they imply. It is this majority that the economic achievement and the liberal policy of the capitalist age have invested with dominant power." Taking a socially more neutral stance, one could argue, with Marcel Gauchet, that the liberal failure was the aborted attempt to dissolve the political component of social life into the law and the market, and that in response to the void this produced, a mass democracy of empowered rational individuals called for a collective project—or meaning. This was supplied by totalitarianism in the form of a "secular religion" (Gauchet 2007 and 2010; Godard 2011).

Reducing politics to economics, Hayek overlooked the autonomous dynamics of the political process. This explains his mistake in thinking that "socialists" who called for planning would have tolerated Gosplan-type centralization, and his condescending attitude towards "socialists" who professed attachment to liberal freedoms and pluralism.

I venture that Hayek entertained a naïve conception of politics, one that excluded (or dismissed as irrational) the role of emotions, symbols, interests, and confrontation. Otherwise he would have understood the

National Socialist victory in Germany in terms of the party's popular appeal (be it nationalism, anti-Semitism, fear of communism, economic desperation, or other factors) rather than as the product of the rise of economic planning as an ideology. A more explicit expression of Hayek's understanding of politics is to be found in *The Constitution of Liberty* (1960). There, revealingly, his ideal body politic, although democratic, is strongly hierarchical and paternalistic: "Unless some people know more than the rest and are in a better position to convince the rest, there would be little progress in opinion" (Hayek 1960, 110), a view difficult to reconcile with his analysis of dispersion of knowledge. He also paints the politician as necessarily courting conventional views. "His task in a democracy is to find out what the opinions held by the largest number are" (ibid., 112), which misses altogether the figure of the innovative entrepreneur in politics sketched by Schumpeter.[14]

Misunderstanding and overlooking politics, Hayek could only misread the postwar roadmap.

On the Wrong Side of History

Given what I have said, the question arises of the relevance of *The Road*. Arguably, the book's message was obviated when, in the wake of the war, central planning and planning in general were rapidly sidelined; it would have been consigned to the dustbin of history if not for misreadings that gave it a spurious relevance to the interventionist, democratic governments that arose everywhere after 1945. The idea of economic planning was undoubtedly a common one in the mid-1940s; Hayek's obsession with it was echoed by his most perceptive critics, such as Evan Durbin (1945) and Barbara Wootton (1945), who both strongly supported some form of central planning. The then-widespread narrative was that the Depression and, indirectly, the war had been caused by unbridled capitalism, and even a cursory look at the political debates of the time confirms a consensus around this story. Writing contemporaneously with Hayek, Schumpeter (1942, 143) also perceives an "atmosphere of almost universal hostility" to capitalism. Unlike Hayek, who saw mere "risks" to the liberal order, Schumpeter forecast an ineluctable drift to collectivism as "things and souls are transformed in such a way as to become increasingly amenable to the socialist form of life" (ibid., 162).[15] But matters turned out quite differently.

Within three years of the return to peace, the European policy landscape had thoroughly changed. Governments progressively lifted controls and returned to a market economy. Most spectacularly, Germany in 1948 reformed the currency, freed prices, and opened itself up to international trade. As the "Iron Curtain" fell across Mitteleuropa, communists were excluded from Western governing coalitions and their trade-union affiliates were sometimes violently contained. A new liberal paradigm emerged and was soon to predominate, thanks to the combination of soft pressure to emulate West German economic successes and benign American imperialism. In Britain, the Labour government—elected in 1945 on a pro-planning platform—reluctantly lifted rationing and relaxed regulation in the 1948 "bonfire of controls," and the corporations nationalized after the war were quietly given management autonomy (Cronin 1991). In 1945–46, the United States quickly moved out of the controlled war economy and rolled back some of the most interventionist New Deal policies (French 1997; Higgs 2006). This does not mean there was a return to pre-war liberalism; far from it. Instead of a continued drive toward planning, however, a massive shift took place in the focus of political and policy agendas, which moved away from internal stability and foreign policy to concentrate on citizens' welfare (Gauchet 2010; Godard 2011). The liberal ideal of a referee state gave way to that of what I would call a "purposeful state" (a nomenclature that lacks the polemical associations of "welfare state"). This happened through two distinct developments: macroeconomic activism aimed at prosperity, increasingly measured by the new concept of economic growth; and the spread of public social insurance for health, unemployment, and old age (all of which were policy goals explicitly supported by Hayek). Although the spread of social insurance was a continuous process that can be traced from Bismarck's Germany up to the present-day United States, one can locate in the Western Europe of the 1940s the point after which the social state became an untouchable constituent of the democratic compact.

The abstract citizenship of classical liberalism, where the state was conceived as a guarantor of unimpeded private initiative, was thereby transformed into citizenship as an encompassing experience. In purposeful democracy, the state assumes an active commitment to the flourishing of individual welfare; the social state, despite the widespread belief to the contrary, is not a collectivist project. Arguably, the rationale for the market economy was thus radically transformed. Under liberalism it was justified by individual rights; under the purposeful state it became a consequentialist policy. Thus, government intervention became always *in principle* an option—whenever citizens' welfare seems to be at stake. What Popper (1945, 1) called "piecemeal social engineering" became the norm.

The shift towards the purposeful state also implied profound changes in the institutional workings of liberal democracy, as parliamentarism morphed into a centralized system where the head of the executive branch is directly or indirectly elected to the job by leveraging a mass political party. Arguably, this trend began in the Progressive era in the United States (Tulis 1987) and became manifest under FDR, who set the model followed by postwar European heads of government. The British cabinet appreciably increased its power over the legislature throughout the 1940s and 1950s, and European heads of government increasingly used the mass media to communicate with electors above the heads of legislators. Presidentialization goes alongside the generalization of the mass political-party model on the left and on the right—where it was negligible before 1914 but became ubiquitous after World War II, notably with the Christian Democrats and the Gaullists. The two shifts are closely entangled, as the presidentialization of politics depended on using politicians' personal promises to address socio-economic problems.

Hayek (1956, 44) himself recognizes the shift in the Foreword to the 1956 American paperback edition of *The Road*—"the Welfare State has largely replaced Socialism as the goal of reformers"—and in the preface to the 1976 edition, where he explains that "socialism has come to mean chiefly the extensive redistribution of incomes through taxation and the institution of the welfare state" (Hayek 1976, 54–55). The mystery is why Hayek did not voice his hearty approval of these developments, not only because he supported many measures that were undertaken by the purposive state, but because its rise derailed the planning state and ensured that, for the foreseeable future, private property and freely set prices would remain dominant.

The European Road

If *The Road* was often misconstrued as a blast against the welfare state, it found readers in German-speaking Europe where its message was understood the other way around—as an insightful analysis of recent history and as a plea for a system, liberalism, that had never really been tried in Germany. In English, *The Road* was a conservative manifesto; in German, it turned out to be revolutionary. As a result, *The Road*'s actual influence on German politics may have been more profound and lasting than it has been in the English-speaking world, a fact usually ignored by generally American Hayek scholars.[16]

Der Weg zur Knechtschaft appeared in 1945 in a Swiss edition that rapidly found its way north of the border despite Allied censorship.[17] Many Germans readily concurred with the message that central economic planning drastically diminished individual liberty, which was consistent with their current experience: Even in the immediate postwar occupation, as in the Nazi era, Germany was under a command economy. A 1946 letter from Freiburg University economist Walter Eucken to Hayek stresses that *The Road*'s theoretical analysis was empirically validated, as "we in Germany have experienced how incompatible a planned economy and the rule of law are" (Goldschmidt and Hesse 2012, 17).[18]

It is hard to overstate the influence of Eucken's *Freiburger Schule* of market economics (including his colleague Franz Böhm), on the one hand, and that of a pair of exiled German economists, Wilhem Röpke (in Geneva) and Alexander Rüstow (in Istanbul). They were the intellectual godfathers of what came to be known as "Ordoliberalism"[19] (although they would rather call themselves "neoliberals"),[20] which formed the ideological core of the *Soziale Marktwirtschaft* (social-market economy). This strand of liberalism provided the roadmap for the Federal Republic of Germany, and *The Road* was its herald. In the late 1920s, Röpke had introduced Hayek to the Freiburg economists and specifically to Eucken (Hayek 1992, 188–89). The 1945 German edition of *The Road* was eulogistically prefaced by Röpke (and translated by his wife), while Hayek wrote the introduction to an English translation of a book by Röpke a year later (Röpke 1946). Röpke assisted Hayek in creating the Mont Pélerin Society in 1947, the founding meeting of which Eucken attended. In 1962, after retiring from the University of Chicago, Hayek took over Eucken's Freiburg professorship of economics.

The appeal of planning was as prevalent in Germany as in Britain after the war, in both intellectual and political circles on the left and the right. In February 1947, the Christian Democratic Union (CDU), which was to become the country's main postwar governing party, adopted the corporatist Ahlen Programm, which starts by declaring that "the capitalist economic system has not served the public and social interests of the

German people" and devotes one of its five sections to central planning (Konrad Adenauer Stiftung 1997).

In such a climate, with the German civil society flattened by Nazism, the fact that neoliberals won the battle of ideas owes much to a single man, the economist Ludwig Erhard, whose 1948 economic reforms of the (American and British) Bizone of occupation freed prices and established an independent central bank and a new currency, the Deutschemark, in spite of his reluctant foreign overlords and a largely hostile international opinion. Erhard was close to the neoliberals, and his Advisory Council, which provided guidance for the 1948 reform program, had a strong component of Freiburg economists (Wallich 1955, 121). Röpke and Eucken advised Erhard, who met Hayek at least once (Ebenstein 2001, 242) and was influenced by him specifically on the link between economic and political freedoms (Commun 2008, 499). In 1949 Erhard was appointed minister of economic affairs of the nascent Federal Republic; he served in that capacity until he became chancellor in 1963–66.

The Federal Republic made a number of key policy commitments that can be traced to the neoliberals' writings, including monetary stability, free trade in Europe and the world, interfirm competition,[21] and the rejection of Keynesian-style demand management. These choices were influential in shaping the postwar world, as Germany acted as an ally of the United States when Britain and France were reticent followers as in the trade-liberalization process. The institutional principles governing Germany have profoundly influenced the institutional settings of the European Communities, now the European Union, including the concept of independent administrative agencies, proactive antitrust policies, and the idea of "subsidiarity." The difference between Germany on one side and France and Britain on the other side in the late 1940s is that the former enacted a program of reforms designed to re-launch the market economy, whereas the latter two retreated from socialist plans clumsily (notably because of opposition from public opinion) and eventually fell back on a pro-market orientation largely due to American and German influence.

Good Planning

The philosophical closeness of *The Road* and German postwar neoliberalism is wide and deep. Röpke (2004, 95–115) shared Hayek's mostly undifferentiated vision of National Socialist and communist totalitarianism and his critique of "French" rationalism and "scientism" (Hayek 1952). For the Ordoliberals, the market "order" was not a natural occurrence but the deliberate product of a strong state preventing coalitions of interest groups from undermining competition (Streit and Wohlgemuth 2010). For Hayek, too, a free market economy has to be planned for; he uses the words "good … planning" (Hayek 1944, 85) or "planning in the good sense" (ibid.,149). "There is, in particular, all the difference between deliberately creating a system in which competition will work as beneficially as possible and passively accepting institutions as they are…. The attitude of the liberal towards society is that of the gardener" (ibid., 71). Indeed, *The Road*'s vision of a free society is one that many American "liberals" would go along with, as when he writes of the state as "a utilitarian machinery intended to help individuals in the fullest development of their individual personality" (ibid., 115).

The Road was also congruent with the philosophical basis of West Germany at a deeper level. The economistic vision of politics advanced by Hayek could be said to underpin the Federal Republic, the legitimacy of which resides in its material success: "The economy produces legitimacy for the state that is its guarantor" (Foucault 2004, 84). Defeated and occupied Germany may have been the only large country in the world that provided a tabula rasa where the vision of politics reduced to economics could be implemented. Thus, the Hayekian program of liberal restoration became, in Germany, part of a radical project for a brand-new political order.

Ordoliberals drew on a German provincial and specifically Christian morality (the concept of "order" comes from St. Augustine) that one would struggle to find in writings of the agnostic and cosmopolitan Hayek. The former prized liberalism as a bulwark of Christian civilization, the latter valued it as a framework allowing individual autonomy, thus experimentation, thus "unforeseeable free growth" (Hayek 1944, 97). Hayek's Austrian version of economics also distinguished him from his German colleagues, who were keen to empower antitrust bodies to create conditions for competition of the Marshalian equilibrium type. Nonetheless, the political philosophy expressed in *The Road* was closer to that of German neoliberals than to the American conservatives who enthusiastically welcomed the book in 1945. This may be obscured because *The Road* is often read with the hindsight of the later Hayek's increasing libertarian orientation, as recognized by Hayek (1976, 54) himself in the preface to the 1976 edition where he acknowledges that, in *The Road*, he "had by no means sufficiently freed [himself] from all the prejudices and superstitions dominating general opinion."

I suggest, then, relocating the mid-century Hayek. The received narrative makes him a lonely prophet of the free market who came to be listened to only when the postwar boom unraveled in the 1970s and he earned cult status, if not direct influence, in the Thatcher government. I think this is a far too Anglo-centric story and would like to suggest instead the figure of a European Hayek—one who is much more in tune with the actual ideas found in *The Road*.

NOTES

1. To my knowledge, nobody at the time noticed that a socialist country could simply rely on international prices as a guideline for its internal resource allocation.
2. The debate was about economic slumps, which Keynes attributed to discrepancies between savings and investment and Hayek attributed to monetary interventions distorting investment allocations (the "Austrian" business-cycle theory).
3. Focusing on decentralized individual knowledge, Hayek neglected economic actors' ignorance and the sheer random, trial-and-error dynamics of entrepreneurial capitalism testified by business failure (a point made to me by Jeffrey Friedman).
4. Founded in Paris in 1794 by the revolutionary government, the École has been, to this day, a key institution of the French mandarinate and, arguably, the incubator of a vision of centralized, technocratic government.
5. This section draws heavily on suggestions from Jeffrey Friedman.
6. In Hayek's chain of arguments, the way central planning will undermine actual civil liberties is not unlike the result of free markets in Marxist theory: Because most people lack the resources and the actual capacity to use them, civic freedoms remain purely "formal." Implicitly, thus, Hayek refutes the classical liberal dissociation between negative and positive liberty as formulated by Isaiah Berlin (1969).
7. The treatment of *The Road* in later editions of *Economics* did not change significantly after Hayek wrote to Samuelson in 1980 to complain about the misrepresentation of his arguments (Farrant and McPhail 2008).
8. Hayek overlooks the consequences on private economic activity of government provision of such services for free.
9. *The Road* was propelled to the top of the bestseller lists after Beck dedicated a full program to it, drawing parallels between Barack Obama's and Joseph Stalin's governments. See Schuessler 2010 and "'Glenn Beck': Is U.S. Traveling Down 'Road to Serfdom'?" Foxnews.com, 9 June 2010. http://www.foxnews.com/story/2010/06/09/glenn-beck-is-us-traveling-down-road-to-serfdom/.
10. Bruce Caldwell (2010), editor of Hayek's *Collected Works*, writes that the book is "still relevant in our own time," adducing criticism of the 2009 fiscal stimulus

and the 2010 health-care reform, as well as public dissatisfaction with "the machinations of its government."

11. One could also note that Hayek ignores the subjugation of the totalitarian state to the party (Foucault 2004, 196–97).

12. "*The idea of reductionism is that nothing intrinsically new enters at the higher levels*" of explanation, wrote Karl R. Popper (1982, 167). He stressed "the value of the attempt to reduce," but pointed out "that we nonetheless have no really completely successful reductions, where 'successful' means more than just adding to our insight, to our understanding; where it means that one province of knowledge, such as chemistry, has been shown to be completely derivable from another province of knowledge, such as atomic theory" (ibid., 163). I argue that Hayek, at least implicitly, tries to reduce politics to economics, and fails.

13. Thus the rationale of Hayek's support for Pinochet's Chilean dictatorship in the 1970s and 1980s: It did not centrally plan the economy (Fischer 2009, 327; Farrant, McPhail, and Berger 2012).

14. Although Schumpeter's *Capitalism, Socialism and Democracy* (1942) was published two years earlier than *The Road*, the latter does not quote the former. Hayek, however, refers approvingly to it in *The Constitution of Liberty* (1960, 106).

15. Schumpeter (1942), unlike Hayek, believed that socialism was compatible with democracy, at least in Britain.

16. The learned critical apparatus of the thirteen published volumes of *The Collected Works of F. A. Hayek* includes no substantial discussion of Hayek's reception on the European Continent.

17. "Allies agreed to ban books regarded as hostile by one of them—the USSR in this case" (McInnes 1998, 3).

18. From 1938 "the individual blue- or white-collar worker sank back to the status of state serfdom" (Stolper, Häuser, and Borchardt 1967, 156); the worker could not be sacked, but had to accept any assignment anywhere.

19. From the *Ordo* academic journal launched in 1948 by Eucken and Böhm.

20. Alexander Rüstow created the word "neoliberalism" at the 1938 Colloque Walter Lippmann in Paris (Hartwich 2009).

21. Partly in reaction to earlier government-tolerated, and specifically Nazi-backed, cartels, and under Allied pressure to dismantle them, postwar Germany displayed an antitrust commitment that led Erhard in 1958 to create the Federal Cartel Office. The latter's proactive approach has inspired European antitrust policy to this day.

REFERENCES

Berlin, Isaiah. 1969. "Two Concepts of Liberty." In *Four Essays on Liberty*. London: Oxford University Press.

Caldwell, Bruce. 1995. "Introduction." In *Contra Keynes and Cambridge: Essays, Correspondence*. Vol. 9 of *The Collected Works of F. A. Hayek*. Chicago: University of Chicago Press.

Caldwell, Bruce. 2007a. Introduction to Hayek 1944. In Caldwell 2007b.

Caldwell, Bruce, ed. 2007b. *The Road to Serfdom: Text and Documents—the Definitive Edition*. Vol. 12 of *The Collected Works of F. A. Hayek*. Chicago: University of Chicago Press.

Caldwell, Bruce. 2010. "The Secret Behind the Hot Sales of 'The Road to Serfdom' by Free-Market Economist F. A. Hayek." http://voices.washingtonpost.com/shortstack/2010/02/the_secret_behind_the_hot_sale.html.

Commun, Patricia. 2008. "Zur Einführung: Ludwig Erhard (1897–1977)." In *Grundtexte zur Freiburger Tradition der Ordnungsökonomik*, ed. Nils Goldschmidt and Michael Wohlgemuth. Tübingen: Mohr Siebeck.

Cronin, James E. 1991. *The Politics of State Expansion: War, State, and Society in Twentieth-Century Britain.* London: Routledge.

Durbin, E.F.M. 1945. "Professor Hayek on Economic Planning and Political Liberty." *Economic Journal* 55(220): 357–70.

Ebenstein, Alan O. 2001. *Friedrich Hayek: A Biography.* New York: Palgrave.

Farrant, Andrew, and Edward McPhail. 2008. "Hayek, Samuelson, and the Logic of the Mixed Economy." *Journal of Economic Behavior & Organization* 69: 5–16.

Farrant, Andrew, Edward McPhail, and Sebastian Berger. 2012. "Preventing the 'Abuses' of Democracy: Hayek, the 'Military Usurper' and Transitional Dictatorship in Chile?" *American Journal of Economics and Sociology* 71: 513–38.

Fischer, Karin. 2009. "The Influence of Neoliberals in Chile Before, During, and After Pinochet." In *The Road from Mont Pèlerin: The Making of the Neoliberal Thought Collective*, ed. Philip Mirowski and Dieter Plehwe. Cambridge, Mass.: Harvard University Press.

Foucault, Michel. 2004 [2008]. *The Birth of Biopolitics: Lectures at the Collège de France 1978–1979.* Basingstoke: Palgrave Macmillan.

French, Michael. 1997. *U.S. Economic History since 1945.* Manchester: Manchester University Press.

Gauchet, Marcel. 2007. *La Crise du libéralisme.* Vol. 1 of *L'avènement de la démocratie.* Paris: Gallimard.

Gauchet, Marcel. 2010. *À l'épreuve des totalitarismes, 1914–1974.* Vol. 3. of *L'avènement de la démocratie.* Paris: Gallimard.

Godard, François. 2011. "Enchanting Social Democracy: The Resilience of a Belief System." *Critical Review* 23(4): 475–94.

Goldschmidt, Nils, and Jan-Otmar Hesse. 2012. "Eucken, Hayek, and the Road to Serfdom" Freiburg Discussion Papers on Constitutional Economics 12: 4.

Hartwich, Olivier Marc. 2009. "Neoliberalism: The Genesis of a Political Swear-word." *CIS Occasional Paper* 114.

Hayek, F. A. 1937 [1948]. "Economics and Knowledge." In idem, *Individualism and Economic Order.* Chicago: Chicago University Press.

Hayek, F. A. 1944. *The Road to Serfdom.* In Caldwell 2007b.

Hayek, F. A. 1952 [2010]. *The Counter-Revolution of Science: Studies on the Abuse of Reason.* In *Studies on the Abuse and Decline of Reason: Text and Documents.* Vol. 13 of *The Collected Works of F. A. Hayek*, ed. Bruce Caldwell. Chicago: University of Chicago Press.

Hayek, F. A. 1956. Foreword to Hayek 1944. In Caldwell 2007b.

Hayek, F. A. 1960. *The Constitution of Liberty.* Chicago: University of Chicago Press.

Hayek, F. A. 1976. Preface to Hayek 1944. In Caldwell 2007b.

Hayek, F. A. 1992. *The Fortunes of Liberalism: Essays on Austrian Economics and the Ideal of Freedom.* Chicago: University of Chicago Press.

Hayek, F. A. 1994. *Hayek on Hayek: An Autobiographical Dialogue*. London: Routledge.

Higgs, Robert. 2006. *Depression, War, and Cold War: Studies in Political Economy*. New York: Oxford University Press.

Keynes, John Maynard. 1930. *Treatise on Money*. New York: Harcourt, Brace.

Keynes, John Maynard. 1936 [2008]. *The General Theory of Employment, Interest, and Money*. New York: Classic House Books.

Konrad Adenauer Stiftung. 1997. *Das Ahlener Programm der CDU der britischen Zone vom 3. Februar 1947*. http://www.kas.de/wf/de/33.813/.

Lindbeck, Assar. 1971. *The Political Economy of the New Left: An Outsider's View*. New York: Harper & Row.

McInnes, Neil. 1998. "The Road Not Taken: Hayek's Slippery Slope to Serfdom." *National Interest* 51 (Spring): 56–66.

Mises, Ludwig von. 1920 [1975]. "Economic Calculation in the Socialist Commonwealth." In *Collectivist Economic Planning*, ed. Friedrich A. Hayek. Clifton, N.J.: Augustus M. Kelley.

Pigou, A. C. 1944. "The Road to Serfdom." *Economic Journal* 54(214): 217–19.

Popper, Karl R. 1945 [1957]. *The Spell of Plato*. Vol. 1 of *Open Society and Its Enemies*. London: Routledge & Kegan Paul.

Popper, Karl R. 1982. *The Open Universe: An Argument for Indeterminism*. London: Routledge.

Röpke, Wilhelm. 2004. *Democrazia ed economia: L'umanesimo liberale nella civitas umana*. Bologna: il Mulino.

Röpke, Wilhelm. 1946. *The German Question*. London: George Allen & Unwin.

Samuelson, Paul A., and William D. Nordhouse. 1985. *Economics*, 12th ed. New York: McGraw-Hill.

Schuessler, Jennifer. 2010. "Hayek: The Back Story." *The New York Times*, July 9.

Schumpeter, Joseph A. 1942 [1976]. *Capitalism, Socialism, and Democracy*. London: Routledge.

Schumpeter, Joseph A. 1946. "The Road to Serfdom." *Journal of Political Economy* 54 (3): 269–70.

Stolper, Gustav, Karl Häuser, and Knut Borchardt. 1967. *The German Economy: 1870 to the Present*. New York: Harcourt, Brace.

Streit, Manfred E., and Michael Wohlgemuth. 2010. "The Market Economy and the State: Hayekian and Ordoliberal Conceptions." In *The Theory of Capitalism in the German Economic Tradition: Historism, Ordo-Liberalism, Critical Theory, Solidarism*, ed. Peter Koslowski. Berlin: Springer.

Tulis, Jeffrey K. 1987. *The Rhetorical Presidency*. Princeton: Princeton University Press.

Wallich, Henry C. 1955. *Mainsprings of the German Revival*. New Haven: Yale University Press.

Wootton, Barbara. 1945. *Freedom under Planning*. Chapel Hill: University of North Carolina Press.

Paul Lewis

HAYEK, SOCIAL THEORY, AND THE CONTRASTIVE EXPLANATION OF SOCIO-ECONOMIC ORDER

ABSTRACT: *Hayek's later work on the possibility of socio-economic order in decentralized market economies is an exercise in contrastive causal explanation as conceptualized by realist social theorists and philosophers. This interpretation of Hayek's work lends support to the view that Hayek's post-1960 writings can be thought of as an example of comparative institutional analysis. It also provides a means of reinforcing Hayek's own efforts to establish the scientific credentials of his work.*

The past two decades have seen a number of interpretations of the work of Friedrich A. Hayek informed by critical-realist social theory and philosophy. Tony Lawson (1994), Steve Fleetwood (1995), Allen Oakley (1999), and Jochen Runde (2001) have argued that at various stages in his work Hayek adopted, if only implicitly, something closely approximating a critical-realist ontology. Hayek's later work (post-1960) in particular can be seen through a critical-realist lens, for it uses "contrastive explanation," whereby the contrast between two outcomes suggests that different causal mechanisms are at work.

Subjective Interpretation and the Limits of Equilibrium Analysis

In "Economics and Knowledge," Hayek (1937, 33) examined "the role which assumptions and propositions about the knowledge possessed by the different members of society play in economic analysis." According to Hayek, if economic theory is to be applicable to real-world economic problems, then it must take account of two epistemological issues. First, people's actions are informed not by a direct (theoretically unmediated) knowledge of their objective circumstances, but rather by "subjective data"—their subjective perceptions of those circumstances (Hayek 1937, 36; Hayek 1942–44, 44), which are only indirectly and shakily informed by "objective data." Second, objective data are dispersed among the members of society, such that no one person is acquainted with more than a few of the relevant facts. "The knowledge of the particular circumstances of time and place" (Hayek 1945a, 80) thus imposes a "constitutional limitation" on any one person's knowledge, for it implies that no one can possess any more than a tiny fraction of the total knowledge available in society (Hayek 1945b, 14).

Hayek (1937, 37) then goes on to examine the implications of the existence of subjective, dispersed knowledge for general-equilibrium analysis, arguing that "equilibrium exists in this connection if the actions of all members of the society are all [successful] executions of their respective individual plans." This in turn requires that two conditions be met.

First, people will be able to carry out their plans only if they hold *common* expectations concerning external events. For if people based their plans on conflicting expectations about their external environment, then it would be impossible for *any* set of objective facts to make the execution of all of those plans feasible. This requirement is rendered more exacting because, in a society characterized by an elaborate division of labor, the external events that help determine the outcome of any one individual's actions include not only natural events but also the behavior of other people, so that one person's intended actions become part of the set of objective facts that others must take into account in devising their own plans.

The second requirement for the existence of a general equilibrium is, therefore, that people's plans are compatible in the sense that one individual's proposed actions do not disrupt the plans of others. This in turn demands that people are able to form accurate expectations of one another's actions (Hayek 1937, 37–39, 42).

For Hayek (1937, 51, 55), the fact that decentralized market economies typically *do* generate an orderly allocation of resources, in which people are for the most part able to execute their plans successfully, indicates that in practice people usually *do* manage to form reasonably accurate expectations of external events and of one another's actions. However, Hayek also argued that economic theory has been rather unsuccessful in explaining how such plan coordination is actually brought about. The problem stems from the fact that economists have focused almost exclusively on the analysis of equilibrium states, that is to say, on situations in which people's plans have *already* been coordinated, thereby ignoring the question of how (if at all) people actually acquire the information needed to reconcile their plans (ibid., 50–51). Equilibrium analysis takes it for granted that the same objectively correct data— the same knowledge of people's tastes, of what constitutes an economic good, and of the lowest-cost technologies for producing those goods—is *given* to all people, thereby ignoring the subjectivity and dispersal of knowledge that are the epistemic problems to be solved if plan coordination is to be achieved. Given that "the question why the data in the subjective sense of the term should ever come to correspond to the objective data is one of the main problems we have to answer," Hayek is forced to conclude that pure equilibrium analysis is counter-productive, since it "is not concerned with the way in which this correspondence is brought about" (ibid., 39, 44). An understanding of how that happens would require an (empirical) account of the (disequilibrium) causal processes, or tendencies, through which people acquire the knowledge required to form mutually compatible plans (ibid., 33, 46).

However, as Hayek himself admitted, his attempts to provide such an account had largely been fruitless:

> The . . . trouble is that we are pretty much in the dark about (a) the *conditions* under which this tendency is supposed to exist and (b) the nature of the *process* by which individual knowledge is changed. . . . I am afraid that I am now getting to a stage where it becomes exceedingly difficult to say what exactly are the assumptions on the basis of which we assert that there will be a tendency toward equilibrium and to claim that our analysis

has an application to the real world. I cannot pretend that I have as yet got much further on this point. (Hayek 1937, 45, 48)

Despite these difficulties, in "The Use of Knowledge in Society" (1945a) Hayek made significant headway in his analysis of the causal processes in question. This work sees Hayek highlight the coordinating role of freely adjusting market prices. When people act on the basis of their local knowledge, the effects of their actions on the scarcity of various goods is reflected in a change in price. Prices thus convey to others hints about the (local, at times tacit, and always dispersed) knowledge that informs those actions, thereby enabling people to coordinate their actions with one another successfully.

Suppose, for instance, that some entrepreneurs perceive new and lucrative opportunities for the use of a commodity, such as tin. Anticipating future profits, entrepreneurs purchase more tin, which raises its price. The higher price of tin will inform other people of its increased scarcity, inducing them to economize on their use of the resource. The higher price will also lead other entrepreneurs to seek out new sources of supply and to search more assiduously for tin substitutes. In this way people are induced to adapt to changing circumstances without most of them "knowing anything at all about the original cause of these changes":

> The most significant thing about this system is the economy of knowledge with which it operates, or how little individual participants need to know in order to be able to take the right action. In abbreviated form, by a kind of symbol, only the most essential information is passed on and passed on only to those concerned. It is more than a metaphor to describe the price system as a kind of machine for registering change, or a system of telecommunication which enables individual producers to watch merely the movement of a few pointers . . . in order to adjust their activities to changes of which they may never know more than is reflected in the price movement. (Hayek 1945a, 86–87)

On this view, prices act as "knowledge-surrogates," summarizing in a publicly available form the subjective judgements about the value of resources that individuals make on the basis of their local and often tacit knowledge of their situation, thereby enabling other people to adjust their behavior to (constantly changing) circumstances about which they have little or no direct awareness (ibid., 83–90; Hayek 1968, 181–82, 187).

However, as subsequent generations of subjectivist economists such as Ludwig Lachmann realized, the information provided by price signals is insufficient to enable people to dovetail their plans with one another. This requires coordinating not only people's perceptions of their circumstances but also the expectations they form on the basis of those perceptions (Lachmann 1976; Lachmann 1986, 22–58). But there cannot be a mechanical link between people's circumstances and their expectations, since expectations are based on people's subjective *interpretations* of their circumstances—including what current market prices signify about the conditions that will obtain in the future. The problem, of course, is that different people may interpret the same price in a variety of different ways, yielding a diverse spectrum of (subjective) expectations of the future, which in turn underwrite a host of mutually incompatible plans. In a nutshell, then, according to a radical subjectivist such as Lachmann, invoking the informational role of prices does not by itself explain how market economies generate orderly outcomes, because while market prices do indeed convey information about the relative scarcities of goods and the intentions of other people, they do not do so unambiguously.

Rules and Social Order

Hayek's post-1960 writings contain the basis for a convincing solution to the problem posed by the subjectivity of expectations. In addition to prices, Hayek argues, a network of shared formal and informal social rules—such as the laws of property, tort, and contract, and norms of honesty and promise-keeping—disseminate knowledge.[1]

Developing ideas first aired in *The Sensory Order* (1952), Hayek argued that the human mind is a classificatory system whose operation is governed by a system of rules. Perception, along with all the other activities of our minds and much of human action, is a rule-guided activity (Hayek 1962, 43–46, 49–50). Significantly, according to Hayek, people are usually unable to state explicitly many of the rules that govern their perceptions and thus their actions. Our knowledge of these rules tends to be tacit in the sense that, while we know how act in accordance with the rules, we lack the propositional knowledge required to articulate them discursively (ibid., 43–45, 53). For example, everyday life often relies less on the ability to list particular facts than it does on intuitions, routines, and unarticulated perceptions, such as an entrepreneur's hunch about the sort of product that is likely to attract consumers, a production engineer's knowledge of how to solve various technical problems, or a businessman's capacity to glean information about new sources of finance (Hayek 1960, 25; Hayek 1968, 182).

Hayek argues that it is people's reliance on such shared rules that, in conjunction with the information transmitted by relative prices, facilitates social order in decentralized market economies. It is the fact that different people act in accordance with the same abstract social rules, following the same general guidelines about how to interpret and act in various kinds of situation, that makes it possible for them to form reliable expectations of each other's future conduct. This enables them to foresee with some confidence the outcome of their own actions, facilitating (without, of course, guaranteeing) the formation of mutually compatible plans:

> What reconciles the individuals and knits them into a common and enduring pattern of a society is that . . . they respond in accordance with the same abstract rules. . . . What . . . enables them to live and work together in peace is that in the pursuit of their individual ends the particular monetary impulses which impel their efforts . . . are guided and restrained by the same abstract rules. If emotion or impulse tells them what they want, the conventional rules tell them how they will be able and be allowed to achieve it. The action, or act of will, is always a particular, concrete, and individual event, while the common rules which guide it are social, general, and abstract. (Hayek 1976, 12)

Social rules are abstract in that they provide *general* guidelines about how people should act in various *types* of situation, often merely forbidding particular *kinds* of action. However, while such rules do not dictate that a person must take a specific action or pursue a particular goal, they *do* help to establish boundaries within which people are likely to act. This ensures that the general form, if not the precise details, of people's future conduct is predictable enough to facilitate plan coordination (Hayek 1960, 148–61; Hayek 1976, 123–28). In particular, the fact that people draw on shared traditions, customs, and rules in order to act may fend off the radical unpredictability of subjective interpretation. For when it comes to judging the significance of disequilibrium prices, say, people are able to transcend the confines of their subjective points of view by drawing on shared interpretive frameworks. In fact, such rules "could almost be described as a kind of instrument of production, helping people to predict the behaviour of those with whom they must collaborate" (Hayek 1944, 77).[2]

On this basis, Hayek proposes to conceptualize the outcome generated by people's tendency to follow rules as a socio-economic "order" rather than an equilibrium. An "order" is "a state of affairs in which a multiplicity of elements of various kinds are so related to each other that we may learn from our acquaintance with some spatial or temporal part of the whole to form correct expectations concerning the rest, or at least expectations which have a good chance of proving correct" (Hayek 1976 36). The orderliness of social activity manifests itself in the fact that people can, for the most part, implement plans of action in the confident expectation that the contributions from their fellow men required to bring those plans to fruition will in actual fact be forthcoming.

While the rules, customs, and traditions that provide the context for current economic activity were shaped by earlier generations (Hayek 1979 157), their continued existence depends upon current human agency (Hayek 1942–44, 152; Hayek 1967a, 72–80).[3] Each generation in turn reproduces or transforms the rules, ensuring their future existence (perhaps in a modified form). This transformational conception portrays socio-economic order as a never-ending process whereby people draw on pre-existing social structures (such as the legal system) in order to act and, in doing so, either reproduce or transform those structures (Hayek 1942–44, 145–46; Hayek 1979, 157–61). This conception allows us to "meaningfully speak about an order being approached to various degrees, and that order can be preserved throughout a process of change" (Hayek 1968, 184).[4]

Hayek's Institutional Epistemics

For Hayek, the question of economic order is primarily one of knowledge. Only in his work in psychology and social theory, however, did he answer this question convincingly by proposing that shared rules and traditions enable "constitutionally ignorant" people to anticipate one another's actions accurately enough to form mutually compatible plans (Hayek 1960, 29):

> Though at one time a very pure and narrow economic theorist, I was led from technical economics into all kinds of questions usually regarded as philosophical. When I look back, it seems all to have begun, nearly thirty years ago, with an essay on "Economics and Knowledge" in which I examined what seemed to me some of the central difficulties of pure

economic theory. Its main conclusion was that the task of economic theory was to explain how an overall order of economic activity was achieved which utilized a large amount of knowledge which was not concentrated in any one mind but existed only as the separate knowledge of thousands or millions of different individuals. But it was still a long way from this to an adequate insight into the relations between the abstract rules which the individual follows in his actions, and the abstract overall order which is formed as a result of his responding, within the limits imposed upon him by those abstract rules, to the concrete particular circumstances which he encounters. It was only through a re-examination of the age-old concept of freedom under the law, the basic conception of traditional liberalism, and of the problems of the philosophy of the law which this raises, that I have reached what now seems to me a tolerably clear picture of the nature of the spontaneous order of which liberal economists have so long been talking. (Hayek 1964a, 91–92)[5]

In moving away from the concept of equilibrium towards the notion of socio-economic order, Hayek devised in his later work an interdisciplinary social-theoretic approach to the study of economic issues (Hayek 1973, 4). Rather than explaining the market order solely in terms of the actions and interactions of atomistic economic agents, as neoclassical economics would demand, Hayek placed significant explan-atory weight on the causal influence of the social-structural context in which that interaction occurs (Hayek 1979, 158).[6] In the first place, in highlighting the importance of social rules for the coordination of economic activity, Hayek (1945b, 6) portrayed people as intrinsically social beings "whose whole nature and character is determined by their existence in society." People's very capacity to reason, and therefore their beliefs, goals and conduct, are all profoundly shaped (without being entirely determined) by the inherited traditions, customs, and rules of their society: "We should regard human reason as the product of a civilization which was not deliberately made by man but which had rather grown by a process of evolution" (1964a, 86).[7] "Even man's capacity to think is not a natural endowment of the individual but a cultural heritage." Second, Hayek's explanation of socio-economic order reflected this non-atomistic ontology by downplaying the significance of behavioral postulates about the motives (e.g., selfish or altruistic) of human conduct. Instead, he emphasizes epistemic issues, suggesting that the possibility of plan coordination depends less upon people's intentions than on whether institutional arrangements enable them to make effective use of their local, dispersed knowledge. As Hayek put it as early as 1935:

For many years discussion of socialism . . . turned almost exclusively on ethical and psychological issues . . . whether men in general could be trusted to have the moral and psychological qualities which were dimly seen to be essential if a socialist system was to work. But, although this latter question does raise some of the real difficulties, it does not really touch the heart of the problem . . . [namely] the possibility of rational calculation. (Hayek 1935, 119–20, 143)

He made a similar point in "Competition as a Discovery Procedure" (1968), writing that

the term "incentives" is often used . . . with somewhat misleading connotations, as if the main problem were to induce people to exert themselves sufficiently. However, the chief guidance which prices offer is not so much how to act, but *what to do*. In a continuously changing world even mere maintenance of a given level of wealth requires incessant changes in the direction of efforts of some, which will be brought about only if the remuneration of some activities is increased and that of others decreased. (Hayek 1968, 187)

Hayek (1945b, 8–9) described his preferred approach to the analysis of plan coordination as "antirationalistic" in the sense that it is "a view which in general rates rather low the place which reason plays in human affairs, which contends that man has achieved what he has in spite of the fact that he is only partly guided by reason, and that his individual reason is very limited and imperfect":

One might even say that [the anti-rationalistic approach] is a product of an acute consciousness of the limitations of the individual mind which induces an attitude of humility toward the impersonal and anonymous social processes by which individuals help to create things greater than they know. . . . [It] regards man not as a highly rational and intelligent but as a very irrational and fallible being, whose individual errors are corrected only in the course of a social process, and which aims to make the best of a very imperfect material. . . . The chief concern of [proponents of this approach was] indeed to find a set of institutions by which man could be induced, by his own choice and from the motives which determined his ordinary conduct, to contribute as much as possible to the needs of others; and their discovery was that the system of private property did provide such inducements to a much greater extent than had yet been understood. (Ibid., 8–9, 11–12)

However principled they may be, people will be able to generate an orderly allocation of resources only if the prevailing institutions enable them to be confident enough about one another's future conduct to coordinate their plans. While some institutional arrangements, in particular those comprising a liberal polity, help to ensure that that is indeed the case, others, most notably those found in centrally planned economies, hamper or even preclude it. Irrespective of their morality, people's constitutional ignorance will prevent them from developing plans that dovetail unless they act against a backdrop provided by the institutions of private property, money and money prices, and contract and tort law:

> If there were omniscient men, if we could know not only all that affects the attainment of our present wishes but also our future wants and desires, there would be little case for liberty. And, in turn, liberty of the individual would, of course, make complete foresight impossible. Liberty is essential in order to leave room for the unforeseeable and unpredictable; we want it because we have learned to expect from it the opportunity of realizing many of our aims. It is because every individual knows so little and, in particular, because we rarely know which of us knows best that we trust the independent and competitive efforts of many to induce the emergence of what we shall want when we set it. (Hayek 1960, 29)[8]

Thus, Hayek was developing a comparative-institutional approach to social theory, according to which social systems are assessed not by how they affect people's motivation and probity, but by their epistemic capacity to facilitate or hamper people's effective use of dispersed and tacit knowledge (Gray 1998, 40–41, 134–35; Boettke 1999; Boettke and Leeson 2004; Friedman 2005, 26–58).[9] By investigating the social-structural influences on how people acquire knowledge, Hayek was also investigating the possibility of socio-economic order (Hayek 1979, 158).[10]

Complexity and Contrastive Explanation

We can best see Hayek's writings about these influences as exercises in contrastive causal explanation, which means explaining a phenomenon of interest by providing an account of its causal history.[11] Of course, it may not be possible to provide a complete causal history of something as elaborate as the market economy. As Hayek puts it:

> It is evident that this interplay of the rules of conduct with the actions of other individuals and the external circumstances in producing an overall order may be a highly complex affair. The whole task of social theory

consists in little else but an effort to reconstruct the overall orders which are thus formed, and the reason why that special apparatus of conceptual construction is needed which social theory represents is the complexity of this task. (Hayek 1967a, 71)

More specifically, Hayek suggests that systems such as the market are complex because they exhibit few if any significant regularities. In the language used by realist social theorists, they are "open systems," for in the social sciences, "individual events regularly depend on so many concrete circumstances that we shall never in fact be in a position to ascertain them all. . . . The hope may remain illusory that we can discover by observation regular connections between the individual events" (Hayek 1964b, 34).[12]

Therefore, causal explanations cannot be deduced from stable empirical laws because we cannot be sure that the requisite laws are present: "Our difficulty," Hayek (1955, 10) writes, "is precisely that we are unable to ascertain by observation the presence and specific arrangement of the multiplicity of factors which form the starting point of our deductive reasoning."[13] Realist social theorists argue that in such circumstances, far from continuing with a (most likely fruitless) search for stable event regularities, social scientists should aim to uncover the underlying, unobservable causal mechanisms that generate the flux of observable events. That kind of analysis is necessary partly because the social world is an open, or complex, system that rarely displays sharp, stable event regularities that take the form of "whenever event or state of affairs x, then event or state of affairs y." Even seemingly unassailable empirical relationships estimated by econometricians tend to break down when new observations become available (Lawson 1997, 70–85).[14]

Like Hayek, realist social theorists argue that the observed openness of the social world reflects the fact that social systems are multiply caused and are influenced by a varying mixture of both endogenous and exogenous forces, foremost amongst which is the impact of human agency. That is, the complexity of the social world is partly due to the fact that people have the capacity to choose which course of action to pursue. The choice must be in some way free such that, in any given situation, someone could just as easily choose to take action y or action $\sim y$. Genuine choice is thus one source of the openness of the social world, and also requires that the socio-economic world is an open system (Lawson 1997, 8–11).

But purposeful human conduct is possible only if people have some idea of the likely outcomes of their actions, implying that the social world must possess some stable and enduring features upon which people can base their decisions. Given that event regularities are comparatively rare in the social world, realist social theorists argue that the relevant (relatively stable) objects of knowledge must be non-empirical in nature. One example of this kind of knowledge is knowledge of social structures (Lawson 1997, 30–31, 56–58)—contracts, for example. Contracts give economic actors some confidence about the future consequences of their actions by giving them a degree of control over their future income and expenditure. Contracts do not make the future wholly predictable—and so do not give rise to sharp, stable event regularities—but they narrow the range of outcomes that might flow from a particular course of action (Runde 1993, 388–93; cf. Hayek 1955, 17–19; Hayek 1976, 130). Thus, people's tacit or explicit knowledge of social structures such as the legal system, or of norms of honesty and promise keeping, principally informs their actions (Lawson 1998, 357–62; Lewis and Runde 2007, 176n15).

For realist social theorists, identifying such non-empirical structures is central to the explanatory enterprise in social science. Hayek (1955, 10) appears to advocate a similar approach: "Where we have to deal with a complex situation in which observation discloses only very limited regularities, be it in the 'applied' branches of physics or in biology or in the social sciences, we usually ask to what extent our existing knowledge of the forces at work . . . may account for what we observe."[15] On this view, the objective of social science is

> the reconstruction of a hypothetical kind of process which may never have been observed but which, if it had taken place, would have produced phenomena of the kind we observe. The assumption that such a process has taken place may be tested by seeking for yet unobserved consequences which follow from it, and by asking whether all regular structures of the kind in question which we find can be accounted for by that assumption. (Hayek 1967a, 75)

There may, of course, be many causal mechanisms at work (Hayek 1964b, 37; Hayek 1967a, 74). (Indeed, as we have already noted, it is the operation of a multiplicity of often countervailing causal mechanisms—including creative human agency—that accounts for the absence of sharp, stable event regularities.) However, the methodology of contrastive causal explanation suggests that the task of providing satisfactory causal explanations can be reduced to manageable proportions by focusing on a subset of the relevant causal factors, in particular those whose influence is indicated by the existence of differences or contrasts between the history of the phenomenon under investigation (termed the "focus") and the history of another, similar (but not identical) phenomenon (the "foil"). The result will be an explanation that identifies the causes, not of the focus per se, but rather of the difference or contrast between the focus and the foil.

Hayek appears to adopt a similar approach in his account of socioeconomic order. Rather than attempting to do justice to all the influences that have shaped the history and performance of market economies, Hayek concentrates on those causal factors which (in his view) account for the key differences between the history and performance of market economies (the focus) and that of centrally planned economies (the foil). More specifically, according to Hayek, while the existence (and causal influence) of purposeful human conduct is common to both types of economy, the cause of the superior performance of market economies is a social-structural one, namely the capacity of the institutions of the market economy to facilitate a more effective use of knowledge than is possible under central planning (Hayek 1937, 46–55).

By showing how the institutions of a liberal polity enable people to use their local, often tacit, knowledge, and to form accurate expectations of one another's actions, Hayek provides an explanation of the principle—or, in the language used by realist social theorists, the causal process—that explains the production of social order in decentralized market economies. However, these causal theories can explain and predict the general characteristics only of the *type* of outcome produced, not its detailed properties, because a system like the market is too complex to be grasped by our limited minds. Hence, while social theory can account for some of the key *qualitative* features of the market order—in particular its ability to facilitate the implementation of more individual plans than can be achieved in centrally planned economies—and while it can make general or (as Hayek terms them) *pattern* predictions, such as that the absence of the institutions of a liberal polity is incompatible with social order, it does not yield precise explanations or *quantitative* predictions of the detailed outcomes generated by the market (Hayek 1955, 10–17; Hayek 1964b, 26–36; Hayek 1967a, 71–76).

Hayek's commitment to contrastive or comparative analysis is reflected in the way in which, rather than basing his normative case for the market on the (optimal) properties of perfectly competitive equilibria, he makes a comparative institutional claim, namely that a market economy will yield a greater degree of coordination than any other social system yet envisaged.

While Hayek extols the virtues of the market, he is careful not to claim that the outcomes it produces are efficient in any absolute sense. He does not, for example, claim that the allocation of resources produced by free markets will satisfy the criteria for Pareto optimality. Indeed, Hayek thinks that equilibrium analysis ignores the informational problems that real-world markets have to solve, which implies that the normative criteria to which it gives rise, such as Pareto efficiency, provide an inappropriate benchmark for evaluating the merits of real-world market economies. For instance, commenting on the mutual adjustment of plans produced by the price mechanism, Hayek writes:

> Of course, these adjustments are probably never "perfect" in the sense in which the economist conceives of them in his equilibrium analysis. But I fear that our theoretical habits of approaching the problem with the assumption of more or less perfect knowledge on the part of almost everyone has made us somewhat blind to the true function of the price mechanism and led us to apply rather misleading standards in judging its efficiency. (Hayek 1945a, 87)

The relevant comparison is not between a real-world system of competitive markets and some fictitious state of equilibrium, but rather between the former and other, non-market methods of resource allocation:

> The peculiarity of competition—which it has in common with scientific method—is that its performance cannot be tested in particular instances where it is significant, but is shown only by the fact that the market will prevail in comparison with alternative arrangements. . . . We do injustice to the achievement of the market if we judge it, as it were, from above, by comparing it to with an ideal standard which we have no known way of achieving. . . . We judge it, as we ought to, from below, that is . . . against what we could achieve by any other method—especially against what would be produced if competition were prevented. (Hayek 1968, 180, 185)

Thus, Hayek shifts our attention from the more or less absolute notion of efficiency associated with the concept of a competitive equilibrium towards a more relativistic notion (Rizzo 1990, 24–26). The fact that people must decide how to act in a world that is shaped by other people's oft-changing plans implies that there will inevitably be mistaken expectations and failed plans, so that the allocation of resources yielded by the market will not be optimal in the sense of exhausting all possible gains from trade. The market, however, constitutes the most effective means yet known to man of ensuring that people have the information required to correct erroneous expectations, achieving a greater, although still imperfect, degree of plan coordination than is possible under any other social system (Hayek 1945a, 82–83; Hayek 1976, 124–25).

We can approach this point from a slightly different angle if we recall that social rules, which guide people's actions in a market economy, stipulate only the general *kind* of action that people should take in various types of situation. They do not specify the precise actions that people should take. They do not, for example, stipulate that a certain commodity should be bought and sold at a particular price; thus, they do not guarantee that entrepreneurs' expectations about the prices at which they will be able to sell their products in the future will be confirmed. "The abstract rules of conduct can (and, in order to secure the formation of a spontaneous order, should) thus protect only the expectations of command over particular physical things and services, and not the expectations concerning their market value" (Hayek 1976, 124).[16] In the light of their local knowledge, and guided by their awareness of social rules, entrepreneurs form interpretations—conjectures—about what will constitute a profitable business venture. Then, by attempting to implement their ideas, they test the merits of those conjectures in the marketplace.

However, "the best we can attain is not certainty but the elimination of avoidable uncertainty" (Hayek 1976, 125)—through such means as legally enforceable contracts and norms of honesty and promise-keeping. If the entrepreneur's expectations turn out to be overly optimistic, so that the product sells for less than anticipated, the entrepreneur will suffer losses. However, those losses will be perceived by other entrepreneurs, discouraging them from acting on the basis of the same (false) expectations: "The remunerations which the market determines . . . are incentives which as a rule guide people to success," Hayek (ibid., 116–17) argues, "but will produce a viable order only because they often disappoint the expectations they have caused when relevant circumstances have unexpectedly changed. It is one of the chief tasks of competition to show which plans are false":

> The facts that full utilisation of the limited information which the prices convey is usually rewarded, and that this makes it worthwhile to pay the greatest attention to them, are as important as that in the case of unforeseen changes the expectations are disappointed. The element of luck is as inseparable from the operation of the market as the element of skill. (Ibid., 117)

The point, then, is that by following social rules, participants in the market—players in the "game of catallaxy" (ibid., 115)—increase their chances of a successful outcome, albeit without guaranteeing it. By enabling people to respond to circumstances of which they have no direct knowledge—and by providing feedback, in the form of profits and losses, on their efforts to respond to that information—the market system "supplies to each player information which enables him to provide for needs of which he has no direct knowledge and by the use of means of the existence of which without it he would have no cognizance, thus bringing about the satisfaction of a greater range of needs than would otherwise be possible" (ibid).[17]

Complexity and Social Science

Realist philosophy of science suggests that, viewed at a sufficiently high level of abstraction, the study of the socio-economic world proceeds in the same way as that of the natural world. So far as the natural sciences are concerned, both the role of laboratory experiments and the use of control groups in non-laboratory fieldwork trials can be rendered intelligible only if it is acknowledged that the objective is to uncover the existence of unobservable causal mechanisms, not to discover regularities between observable events (Bhaskar 1975, 33–37; Lawson 1997, 27–30, 202–4).

Event-regularity-based, or (as I will term them) Humean, accounts of science downplay the significance of unobservable causal mechanisms and emphasize instead the significance for scientific explanation of event regularities of the form, "Whenever this event of state of affairs, then that (set or spread of) outcome(s)." Such accounts run into grave difficulties when confronted with two widely accepted observations concerning experimental activity in the natural sciences. First, with the notable exception of astronomy, most of the empirical generalizations or regularities that are held to be significant in the natural sciences occur only within the confines of controlled experiments. Second, notwithstanding the first observation, results obtained via controlled experiments are often generalizable, such that they can be successfully applied outside the confines of experimental setups designed to create sharp, stable empirical regularities. These observations pose serious problems for Humeans. For the fact that most of the event regularities regarded as noteworthy by natural scientists occur only under the restricted conditions of experimental control carries for Humeans the unfortunate implication that the existence of the regularities that (on the Humean account of science) constitute the laws of nature depends on *human* intervention. In addition, if the regularities that are the *sine qua non* of deductivist explanations are largely confined to experimental conditions, then a Humean approach is able to explain neither what governs events outside the experimental environment nor the successful application beyond the laboratory of the results obtained therein.

These two observations can, however, be rendered intelligible once it is acknowledged that the natural world is *structured* in the sense that it contains unobservable causal mechanisms that are ontologically distinct from/irreducible to patterns of observable events; and that the natural world—with one or two notable exceptions, such as the astronomical realm—is an *open* system in which events are influenced by a changing variety of often-countervailing unobservable mechanisms. For example, the behavior of a falling leaf typically does not conform to an empirical regularity simply because the leaf is affected in different and conflicting ways by gravitational, aerodynamic, and thermal forces. Experimental activity, according to this non-Humean, realist perspective, is best thought of as an attempt to intervene in the natural world to insulate the activity of one particular mechanism from the impact of countervailing forces. The ultimate objective of such experiments is to engineer a *closed* system in which there is a one-to-one correspondence between the action of a mechanism and ensuing events, so that the impact of the mechanism can be identified empirically. The results obtained in this way are applicable to non-experimental situations inasmuch as the mechanism under investigation is operative even in non-experimental situations— that is, inasmuch as the mechanisms identified in scientific experiments are stable across different contexts.

This line of reasoning suggests that it becomes possible to make sense of the role of experimentation in the natural sciences only if we replace the Humean view with an acknowledgement that the natural world is composed of non-empirical causal mechanisms. If the search for underlying, unobservable causal mechanisms is integral to explaining socio-economic events of interest, then explanation in the social sciences is analogous to explanation in the natural sciences: identifying the underlying causes of observable phenomena of interest and illuminating the general principles that describe the working of the identified causal mechanisms. If this is true, then Hayek should not be charged, as various critics have done, with being "unscientific" because he does not couch his theories in terms of formal mathematical and econometric models.[18] In fact, Hayek's work is scientific in the sense that, like natural scientists, Hayek is searching for underlying causes—in his case, the causes of socio-economic order (Lawson 2003, 34–35, 295n15; Lewis 2003).

This is in keeping with the later Hayek's own approach to the question of the scientific status of economics. Especially after the Second World War, critics who claimed to be doing "real science" dismissed as unscientific Hayek's emerging view of the market as a rivalrous process of discovery (Boettke 1995, 13). Hayek responded by distinguishing between science and scientism. His opponents, he argued, had succumbed to a "scientistic prejudice," engaging in the "slavish imitation of the method and language," but not the true spirit, of science (Hayek 1942–44, 24). In setting such great store on formal mathematical models of equilibrium (which fail to do justice to the importance of subjective, dispersed knowledge) and on the search for observable regularities using large-scale econometric models (ignoring the complexity of the socio-economic world), Hayek's neoclassical opponents had adopted an approach that was

> decidedly unscientific in the true sense of the word, since it involves a mechanical and uncritical application of habits of thought to fields different from those in which they have been formed. The scientistic as distinguished from the scientific view is not an unprejudiced but a very prejudiced approach which, before it has considered its subject, claims to know what is the most appropriate way of investigating it. (Ibid.)

For Hayek (1955, 3–5, 16, 19–21), as for realist social theorists, a truly scientific approach involves ensuring that the methods used by researchers are tailored to suit the nature of the subject under investigation. However, beginning with his 1955 paper "Degrees of Explanation," Hayek argues that economics is a scientific discipline despite the epistemological limitations imposed on it by its complex subject-matter: most notably the inability to generate anything more than explanations of the principle and pattern predictions. Bruce Caldwell (2004, 232–60, 297–306) has perceptively noted that Hayek's view of science evolved. In "Scientism and the Study of Society" (1942–44), Hayek distinguished between the natural and the social sciences in an anti-naturalist fashion, but by the mid-1950s he had begun instead to differentiate disciplines according to whether their subject-matter was simple (closed) or complex (open). Significantly, according to Hayek, the epistemic limitations to which economics is subject are shared by a number of the natural sciences, such as engineering, cybernetics, and evolutionary biology. Far from indicating that economics is unscientific, then, its reliance on explanations of the principle and pattern predictions is symptomatic of the complexity of its subject-matter, and is paralleled by similar limitations in those natural sciences that study complex phenomena (Hayek 1955, 11–14, 18–20; Hayek 1964b, 31–34).

In his commitment to tailoring the methods used by economists to the nature of their subject-matter, and in acknowledging the limitations imposed upon a discipline's ambitions by the nature of its subject-matter, Hayek shows himself to be a true realist.[19]

NOTES

1. While the significance of social rules for the generation of mutually compatible plans is a theme that rises to prominence in Hayek's work in the 1960s, there are passages in his work indicating that he was aware of the importance of social rules and institutions for the generation of social order as early as the 1930s and 1940s. For instance, in "Economics and Knowledge" he refers to the importance of "institutions, such as the press, whose whole purpose is to communicate knowledge" (Hayek 1937, 55; also see 51). Hayek revisits this theme in "Individualism: True and False," where he discusses the importance for plan coordination of "the traditions and conventions which evolve in a free society and which, without ever being enforceable, establish flexible but normally observed rules that make the behavior of other people predictable in a high degree" (Hayek 1945b, 23; also see 1945a, 88). The fact that Hayek alluded to the significance of social rules and institutions as early as the 1930s and 1940s has led to significant controversy among historians of thought over the

extent to which the approach adopted by Hayek between 1937 and the early 1960s in general, and in his essay on "Scientism and the Study of Society" (1945b) in particular, is identical to the one to which he subscribed from the early 1960s onwards. See, for instance, Böhm 1989, Fleetwood 1995, Lawson 1997, 134–51, Oakley 1999, 60–143, Vaughn 1999, Runde 2001, and Caldwell 2004 (296n8, 423–38).

2. See also Ebeling 1986 and Fleetwood 1995, 125–55.

3. See also Fleetwood 1995, 145–46 and Lange-von Kulessa 1997, 276–82.

4. See also Fleetwood 1995, 135–55.

5. See also Hayek 1960, 3.

6. See also Boettke 1999 and Vaughn 1999. The later Hayek's attempts to develop a distinctly social-theoretic approach to the study of economic issues suggests that there may be affinities between Austrian economics and the new economic sociology. For a sample of recent attempts to develop links between the two approaches, see Lachmann 1990, Boettke and Storr 2002, and Lewis 2008.

7. Also see Hayek 1960 and 1973, 17–19

8. Also see Hayek 1960, 156–57.

9. More precisely, the capacity of the market to ensure the effective use of tacit and dispersed knowledge, and thereby to coordinate people's plans, can be thought of as an emergent property of the set of rules that constitutes the market system (Lewis 2012 and 2013).

10. The fact that, in his later work, Hayek focuses on the social-structural causes of socio-economic order should not be taken to indicate that he denies the causal impact of purposeful human conduct, since intentional human agency is the driving force of socio-economic life. However, purposeful human conduct is possible only because institutions—such as private property, the law and other social rules, a common currency, and market prices—give us some assurance of stability when making plans. For Hayek, social structures and intentional human agency are recursively related: Each is a cause and a consequence of the other. Since Hayek's focus in his later work is on the role of social rules and institutions in facilitating human action, the role of intentional human agency per se fades into the background, but it is not denied or entirely neglected (Fleetwood 1995, 146–47; Runde 2001, 13–15).

11. See, for instance, Lipton 1991 and Lawson 1997, 199–226. For more on the relevant notion of (social-structural) causation, see Lewis 2000 and 2005. For related developments in comparative politics, see Somers 1998 and Hall 2003.

12. See also Hayek 1964b, 40–42.

13. See also Hayek 1955, 3–10, 21 and 1964b, 33–34, 40.

14. See also Caldwell 2004, 374–81.

15. See also Hayek 1964b, 40.

16. See also Hayek 1976, 107–32.

17. See also Hayek 1968, 186 and Hayek 1978, 117.

18. Jànos Kornai (1993, 63), for example, views Hayek and Mises's predictions of the impossibility of socialist planning, not as "scientific propositions," but rather as "brilliant guesses." Hayek's contemporary followers lament similar criticisms (Rizzo 1993, 247–51; Boettke 1997, 17 and 21).

19. In *The Sensory Order* Hayek attempted to show in another way that his version of economics was more scientific than that advocated by his intellectual opponents by providing a neuro-physiological (hence "scientific") foundation for his claim that the knowledge on which people act is subjective and dispersed. In doing so,

Hayek hoped to provide a scientific defense for subjectivism and, in the process, expose the positivist approach of his opponents within economics as unscientific. For more on Hayek's "scientific subjectivism," see Hayek 1952, 179–90; Caldwell 1994 and 2004, 259–60; and Horwitz 2005.

REFERENCES

Bhaskar, Roy. 1975 [1997]. *A Realist Theory of Science*, 2nd ed. New York: Verso.

Boettke, Peter J. 1995. "Hayek's *The Road to Serfdom* Revisited: Government Failure in the Argument against Socialism." *Eastern Economic Journal* 21: 7–26.

Boettke, Peter J. 1997. "Where Did Economics Go Wrong? Modern Economics as a Flight From Reality." *Critical Review* 11(1): 11–64.

Boettke, Peter J. 1999. "Introduction: Which Enlightenment, Whose Liberalism? Hayek's Research Program for Understanding the Liberal Society." In idem, *The Legacy of Friedrich von Hayek*. Vol. 1: *Politics*. Cheltenham: Edward Elgar.

Boettke, Peter J., and Virgil H. Storr. 2002. "Post-Classical Political Economy: Polity, Society and Economy in Weber, Mises and Hayek." *American Journal of Economics and Sociology* 61: 161–91.

Boettke, Peter J., and Peter T. Leeson. 2004. "Liberalism, Socialism and Robust Political Economy." *Journal of Markets and Morality* 7: 99–111.

Böhm, Stephan. 1989. "Hayek on Knowledge, Equilibrium and Prices: Context and Impact." *Wirtschaftspolitische Blätter* 36: 201–13.

Caldwell, Bruce. 1994. "Hayek's Scientific Subjectivism." *Economics and Philosophy* 10: 305–13.

Caldwell, Bruce. 2004. *Hayek's Challenge: An Intellectual Biography of F. A. Hayek*. Chicago: University of Chicago Press.

Ebeling, Richard M. 1986. "Towards a Hermeneutical Economics: Expectations, Prices, and the Role of Interpretation in a Theory of the Market Process." In *Subjectivism, Intelligibility and Economic Understanding: Essays in Honor of Ludwig M. Lachmann on his Eightieth Birthday*, ed. Israel M. Kirzner. New York: New York University Press.

Fleetwood, Steve. 1995. *Hayek's Political Economy: The Socio-Economics of Order*. London and New York: Routledge.

Friedman, Jeffrey. 2005. "Popper, Weber, and Hayek: The Epistemology and Politics of Ignorance." *Critical Review* 17(1–2): 1–58.

Gray, John 1998. *Hayek on Liberty*, 3rd ed. London: Routledge.

Hall, Peter A. 2003. "Aligning Ontology and Methodology in Comparative Politics." In *Comparative Historical Analysis in the Social Sciences*, ed. James Mahoney and Dietrich Rueschemeyer. Cambridge: Cambridge University Press.

Hayek, F. A. 1935. "Socialist Calculation I: The Nature and History of the Problem." In Hayek 1948.

Hayek, F. A. 1937. "Economics and Knowledge." In Hayek 1948.

Hayek, F. A. 1942–44 [1979]. "Scientism and the Study of Society." In *The Counter-Revolution of Science: Studies on the Abuse of Reason*, 2nd ed. Indianapolis: Liberty Fund.

Hayek, F. A. 1944 [2001]. *The Road to Serfdom*. London: Routledge.

Hayek, F. A. 1945a. "The Use of Knowledge in Society." In Hayek 1948.

Hayek, F. A. 1945b. "Individualism: True and False." In Hayek 1948.

Hayek, F. A. 1948. *Individualism and Economic Order*. Chicago: University of Chicago Press.

Hayek, F. A. 1952. *The Sensory Order: An Inquiry into the Foundations of Theoretical Psychology*. London: Routledge & Kegan Paul.

Hayek, F. A. 1955. "Degrees of Explanation." In Hayek 1967b.

Hayek, F. A. 1960. *The Constitution of Liberty*. London: Routledge.

Hayek, F. A. 1962. "Rules, Perception and Intelligibility." In Hayek 1967b.

Hayek, F. A. 1964a. "Kinds of Rationalism." In Hayek 1967b.

Hayek, F. A. 1964b. "The Theory of Complex Phenomena." In Hayek 1967b.

Hayek, F. A. 1967a. "Notes on the Evolution of Systems of Rules of Conduct." In Hayek 1967b.

Hayek, F. A. 1967b. *Studies in Philosophy, Politics, and Economics*. London: Routledge & Kegan Paul.

Hayek, F. A. 1968 [1978]. "Competition as a Discovery Procedure." In idem, *New Studies in Philosophy, Politics, Economics and the History of Ideas*. London: Routledge & Kegan Paul.

Hayek, F. A. 1973. *Law, Legislation and Liberty*. Vol. 1: *Rules and Order*. London: Routledge.

Hayek, F. A. 1976. *Law, Legislation and Liberty*. Vol. 2: *The Mirage of Social Justice*. London: Routledge.

Hayek, F. A. 1982. *Law, Legislation and Liberty*. Vol. 3: *The Political Order of a Free People*. London: Routledge.

Horwitz, Steven. 2005. "Friedrich Hayek: Austrian Economist." *Journal of the History of Economic Thought* 27: 71–85.

Kornai, János. 1993. "Market Socialism Revisited." In *Market Socialism: The Current Debate*, ed. Pranab K. Bhardan and John E. Roemer. Oxford: Oxford University Press.

Lachmann, Ludwig M. 1976 [1994]. "From Mises to Shackle: An Essay on Austrian Economics and the Kaleidic Society." In *Expectations and the Meaning of Institutions: Essays in Economics by Ludwig Lachmann*, ed. Don Lavoie. London: Routledge.

Lachmann, Ludwig M. 1986. *The Market as an Economic Process*. Oxford: Basil Blackwell.

Lachmann, Ludwig M. 1990. "Austrian Economics: A Hermeneutic Approach." In *Economics and Hermeneutics*, ed. Don Lavoie. London: Routledge.

Lange-von Kulessa, Juergen. 1997. "Searching for a Methodological Synthesis: Hayek's Individualism in the Light of Recent Holistic Criticism." *Journal of Economic Methodology* 4: 267–87.

Lawson, Tony. 1994. "Realism and Hayek: A Case of Continuing Transformation." In *Capitalism, Socialism and Knowledge: The Economics of F. A. Hayek*, vol. 2. Ed. M. Colonna, H. Hagemann, and O. Hamouda. Aldershot, U.K.: Edward Elgar.

Lawson, Tony. 1997. *Economics and Reality*. London: Routledge.

Lawson, Tony. 1998. "Clarifying and Developing the Economics and Reality Project: Closed and Open Systems, Deductivism, Prediction, and Teaching." *Review of Social Economy* 56: 356–75.

Lawson, Tony. 2003. *Reorienting Economics*. London: Routledge.

Lewis, Paul A. 2000. "Realism, Causation and the Problem of Social Structure." *Journal for the Theory of Social Behaviour* 30: 249–68.

Lewis, Paul A. 2003. "Naturalism and Economics." In *Critical Realism: The Difference it Makes*, ed. J. Cruickshank. London: Routledge.

Lewis, Paul A. 2005. "Agency, Structure and Causality in Austrian Economics: Tensions and Resolutions." *Review of Political Economy* 17: 291–316.

Lewis, Paul A. 2008. "Uncertainty, Economic Sociology and the Causal Explanation of Socio-Economic Order: A Reconstruction of the Work of Ludwig Lachmann." *American Journal of Economics and Sociology* 67: 827–57

Lewis, Paul A. 2012. "Emergent Properties in the Work of Friedrich Hayek." *Journal of Economic Behavior and Organization* 82: 368–78.

Lewis, Paul A. 2013. "Notions of Order and Process in Hayek: The Significance of Emergence." Unpublished manuscript, Department of Political Economy, King's College London.

Lewis, Paul A., and Jochen H. Runde. 2007. "Subjectivism, Social Structures and the Possibility of Socio-Economic Order." *Journal of Economic Behavior and Organization* 62: 167–86.

Lipton, Peter. 1991. *Inference to the Best Explanation*. London: Routledge.

Oakley, Allen. 1999. *The Revival of Modern Austrian Economics: A Critical Assessment of Its Subjectivist Origins*. Cheltenham: Edward Elgar.

Rizzo, Mario J. 1990. "Hayek's Four Tendencies Toward Equilibrium." *Cultural Dynamics* 3: 12–31.

Rizzo, Mario J. 1993. "Afterword: Austrian Economics for the Twenty-First Century." In *Austrian Economics: Tensions and New Directions*, ed. Bruce J. Caldwell and Stephan Boehm. Dordrecht: Kluwer Academic Publishers.

Runde, Jochen H. 1993. "Paul Davidson and the Austrians: Reply to Davidson." *Critical Review* 7(2–3): 381–97.

Runde, Jochen H. 2001. "Bringing Social Structure Back into Economics: On Critical Realism and Hayek's *Scientism* Essay." *Review of Austrian Economics* 14: 5–24.

Somers, M. R. 1998. "'We're No Angels': Realism, Rational Choice, and Relationality in Social Science." *American Journal of Sociology* 104: 722–84.

Vaughn, Karen I. 1999. "Hayek's Implicit Economics: Rules and the Problem of Order." *Review of Austrian Economics* 11: 128–44.

Andrew Lister

THE "MIRAGE" OF SOCIAL JUSTICE:
HAYEK AGAINST (AND FOR) RAWLS

ABSTRACT: *There is an odd proximity between Hayek, hero of the libertarian right, and Rawls, theorist of social justice, because, at the level of principle, Hayek was in some important respects a Rawlsian. Although Hayek said that the idea of social justice was nonsense, he argued against only a particular principle of social justice, one that Rawls too rejected, namely distribution according to individual merit. Any attempt to make reward and merit coincide, Hayek argued, would undermine the market's price system, leaving us all poorer and less free. Like Rawls, Hayek held that we should assess social institutions from behind a veil of ignorance, and he thought that doing so pushed us toward egalitarianism. Most of the distance between Hayek and Rawls at the level of policy stems from Hayek's optimism about the operation of markets, his equivocation about the meaning of central concepts, and his appeal to under-argued slippery slopes. Hayek wavered, however, between claiming that private property and markets benefit everyone, compared to the feasible alternatives, and the principle that they maximize the opportunities of a randomly selected member of society, i.e., aggregate opportunity. Contemporary Hayekians claim that capitalism raises the position of the worst off in the long run, in future generations, whereas Rawlsians insist that inequalities between social positions should benefit the worst off now.*

Friedrich Hayek (1976) famously called the idea of social justice a "mirage." In case there might be any confusion about his view, he also called it a "will-o'-the-wisp" (ibid, 99);[1] an "empty formula" (Hayek 1979a, 3); "strictly," "necessarily," and "entirely" "empty and meaningless" (Hayek 1976, 68, 69, xi); a phrase that "meant nothing at all" (ibid., xii, 33), that had "no meaning whatsoever" (ibid.) and was thus "vacuous" (ibid., 64, 97); "a quasi-religious belief with no content whatsoever" (ibid., xi-xii), a "primitive . . . anthropomorphism" (ibid., 62, 75) or "atavism" (ibid.); a "superstition" (ibid., 66), like believing in witches or the philosopher's stone (ibid., 75); a "hollow incantation" (ibid., xii), like "open sesame" (ibid., 67); a "humbug" (ibid., 90); not an error but merely "nonsense, like the term 'moral stone'" (ibid., 78).

Hayek thought that the idea of social justice was a particularly *dangerous* superstition—"that incubus which today makes fine sentiments the instruments for the destruction of all values of a free civilization" (Hayek 1976, xii)—leading to "the destruction of the indispensable environment in which the traditional moral values alone can flourish, namely personal freedom" (ibid., 67).[2] The phrase "social justice" had become a source of "sloppy thinking and even intellectual dishonesty" (ibid., 80), a "dishonest insinuation . . . intellectually disreputable, the mark of demagogy and cheap journalism which responsible thinkers ought to be ashamed to use because, once its vacuity is recognized, its use is dishonest" (ibid., 97). Hayek was appalled that "social justice" had spawned the evidently ridiculous idea of "global justice."[3] In his later work on the errors of socialism, Hayek called the word "social" a "weasel word," confusingly used to qualify over 160 nouns, from social accounting to social work. He referred to "social justice" as "much the worst use of 'social,'" one that "wholly destroys" the meaning of the word it qualifies, a "semantic fraud." And he noted with alarm that the term had "already perverted the thinking of a younger generation," citing David Miller's recent Oxford doctoral thesis, entitled "Social Justice" (Hayek 1988, 114–18).

Given all of this, one is naturally surprised to find Hayek (1976, xiii) saying that the differences between himself and John Rawls are "more verbal than substantial" and that they agree on "the essential point": that principles of justice apply to the rules of institutions and social practices, but not to distributions of particular things to particular people (ibid., xiii, 100). After all, Rawls often deployed the term Hayek hated in *A Theory of Justice*,[4] using "social justice" as a qualifier of principles and standards (Rawls 1999, 4, 5, 7, 47, 290); conceptions and theories (ibid., 8, 9, 10, 16, 21, 85, 92, 100, 135, 285); convictions and considered judgments (ibid., 18, 34); purposes and ends (ibid., 179, 188); matters, concerns, and standard cases (ibid., 50, 76, 92); and questions and problems (ibid., 39, 78, 92, 118, 132, 135, 136, 174, 479). Rawls also spoke of "the standpoint of social justice" (ibid., 40, 49, 91) and he said that principles of justice "define the appropriate distribution of the benefits and burdens of social cooperation" (ibid., 4, 6, 8).

The phrase "distributive justice" was also the target of Hayek's ire.[5] He claimed that people had misread Rawls, ignoring his point that if a distribution results from just institutions it is just no matter what it is. Yet for Rawls, justice in institutions was itself defined at least partly in distributive terms. If one thinks of the familiar contrast between classical liberalism and social-justice liberalism,[6] Rawls would seem to be a social-justice liberal. So how could Hayek have claimed to be in agreement with Rawls?[7]

The odd proximity of Hayek and Rawls has been noted in the past. From the left, it has been argued (e.g., Connin 1985) that if Hayek can agree with Rawls, there's something wrong with Rawls. From the right, Ayn Rand referred to Hayek's views as "poison."[8] In the middle, some hold out hope for a "Rawlsekian" synthesis (e.g., Lindsey 2006; Wilkinson 2006 and 2008).[9] The prospects for such a synthesis are quite good because Hayek is in some important ways a Rawlsian—at the level of normative principle, but not at the level of policy recommendations. I will outline four main areas of Rawls-Hayek convergence: the importance of "pure procedural justice," the irrelevance of merit, the use of a veil of ignorance, and the principle that inequalities should benefit everyone.

When one presses for a coherent and morally plausible articulation of Hayek's principles, the results are more egalitarian than one might have expected. Although Hayek does not attribute intrinsic moral value to the equal distribution of economic resources, under many empirical conditions his principles allow for policies that limit inequality and benefit the worst off. Hayek manages to avoid these implications by equivocating about the meaning of central concepts and by making implausible slippery-slope arguments about the lack of politically stable intermediate possibilities between a minimal, nightwatchman state and the totalitarian order that would be necessary to achieve perfect equality. There is thus truth in the claim that Hayek and Rawls disagree about empirical (economic and political) questions, rather than about philosophical principles (Arthur 2008).

However, at the level of principle, Rawls's position is significantly more egalitarian than Hayek's in two respects. First, for Rawls political equality can constrain inequalities that satisfy the difference principle. Second, Rawls's difference principle allows for inequality only if it immediately benefits the worst off, whereas Hayek thinks that current inequality is justified if it helps the worst off in the long run.

The Irrelevance of Hayek's Conceptual Claims

While Hayek placed great importance on his conceptual argument against the idea of social justice,[10] his conceptual claims actually do little to undermine the case for social justice.

Hayek's defense of the claim that "social justice" is meaningless starts from the premise that the concept of justice applies only to how people treat each other, not to states of affairs as such (Hayek 1976, 31). When applied to a state of affairs, the terms "just" and "unjust" have meaning "only in so far as we hold someone responsible for bringing it about or allowing it to come about" (ibid.). But while Hayek never tires of repeating that social justice is meaningless, when he is being careful he says that the term is meaningless *in a market economy* (ibid., 64, 67, 68, 69, 81, 91, 96).[11] In a market economy, the distribution of economic benefits is the product of myriad individual actions, each based on different information, in pursuit of widely differing goals, with the result that no one could have foreseen or intended to bring about the resulting distribution. Thus, Hayek argues, it makes no sense to label as just or unjust the distribution that arises in a market economy.

This conclusion is flawed in two ways. First, even if no one can be held responsible for having brought about a particular distribution of benefits in a market economy, there is still an open question about whether people can be held responsible for allowing this distribution to persist: Even if I didn't cause poverty or inequality, I might have the ability and the duty to do something about them after the fact. If I did have such a duty, this poverty or inequality would be wrong, and perhaps even unjust, despite the fact that I didn't originally bring it about.[12] Libertarians might deny that people can rightly be forced to aid each other or share fairly in the benefits of cooperation, but Hayek does not make that argument. In fact, he implicitly rejects it by accepting the legitimacy of state provision of income support for those who can't support themselves in the market.

Second, even if we don't have individual duties to remedy or correct distributive outcomes, we might have a collective duty to design institutions in accordance with distributive principles. Hayek admits that questions of justice arise regarding the design and reform of the rules under which individuals interact. Different decisions about how to delimit rights of property and of contract will have different implications for the distribution of economic advantage. Such decisions could be categorized as just or unjust if there were any duties of distributive justice.[13] Hayek's premise about the interpersonal nature of claims of justice therefore does not advance his case against social justice very far, at least without further normative premises that he does not provide. The real questions are ethical, not conceptual or linguistic.

The Non Sequitur of "Spontaneous Order"

Hayek's fundamental argument against social justice is that it is impossible within the "spontaneous order" of a "great society" or "open society," i.e., a market society,[14] and that we have decisive reasons for preferring market society to the alternatives. To understand what these reasons are and why they must take precedence over social justice, we need to know what social justice is and how it conflicts with the spontaneous order of a great society.

Hayek's idea of spontaneity refers both to the origin of the rules that give rise to social order and to the character of an order even after the rules have been modified by intentional acts of legislation. Originally, human societies were (in part) the product of evolution rather than of conscious design. We didn't start out as the individually rational consequentialists posited by economic theory, but as herd animals that slowly developed complicated social norms and eventually explicit rules. These rule-governed orders were subject to selection pressures. A rule that disrupted social life or weakened the group in competition with other groups would tend to be weeded out. A rule that promoted social cohesion and strength would tend to be selected. Thus, over the course of millennia, systems of social rules evolved that were far more complicated and based on far more information than any single agent with limited cognitive capacities could ever have designed.[15]

However, the fact that a social order originated in evolution does not prove that social justice is undesirable. It may caution us about revising existing rules and practices since they may contain wisdom that is not immediately apparent to our bounded rationality, but there is no particular reason to think that evolution achieves justice. In fact, success in intergroup competition might be achieved by adopting unpleasant norms. Slavery is historically common.

Hayek is not primarily concerned with the spontaneous origin of rules, however, but with the spontaneous character of the order produced by general rules that allow individuals scope to pursue their own purposes. Individual interactions guided by such rules can lead to an order that is spontaneous in that no agent intended to produce it, even if, via legislative revision, the rules originated in deliberate design rather than spontaneous evolution (Hayek 1973, 46). What is crucial is, first, that the rules be general rules that apply to whole classes of people, not local commands issued to particular individuals identified by name or highly specific designation (ibid., 50). Second, the rules should not aim at any purpose except that of ensuring that people treat each other justly—by which Hayek means that they respect a range of primarily negative rights, such as the right not to be assaulted or killed and the right not to have one's property taken.[16] These rights establish a set of protected individual domains (Hayek 1976, 37–38, 103) and allow people to pursue their own distinctive aims according to the information available to them while allowing others to do likewise—which is one of Hayek's definitions of freedom (Hayek 1973, 55).[17]

When social rules have this abstract character, the specific patterns to which interaction gives rise will depend upon a whole range of facts that the designers of the rules could not possibly have known, facts known only to particular people in particular situations.[18]

The free market is the system of abstract rules at the heart of a Great or Open Society, according to Hayek. Market prices are signals about the relative scarcity of resources in relation to people's preferences, and thus serve to allocate resources efficiently. In addition to aggregating dispersed information, the market discovers facts of which no one was previously aware through a decentralized, trial-and-error exploration of production possibilities. The rewards people obtain in a market economy cannot correspond in any strict way to individual merit, because prices provide indications about how people ought to behave in the future, not rewards for how they have behaved in the past. "The prices which must be paid in a market economy for different kinds of labour and other factors of production if individual efforts are to match, although they will be affected by effort, diligence, skill, need, etc., cannot conform to any one of these magnitudes" (Hayek 1976, 80). If the market is to fulfill its twin functions of discovering and aggregating information, it must reward luck as well as skill and conscientious effort.

The best illustration of this point is Hayek's discussion of the relationship of merit and reward within and between occupations. Within a particular occupation, reward will be closely associated with merit (individual ability and industry), but the relative position of different occupations will tend to reflect circumstances beyond anyone's knowledge or control. Demand for different occupations rises and falls with the development of technology and the evolution of preferences. If prices are to direct people to their most productive efforts, prices *must* reflect this kind of luck. The results of the market will therefore often seem unfair, but such unfairness is an essential part of the way the market generates prosperity. The only way to increase the correlation between merit and reward would be to replace free choice guided by market prices (which express people's diverse personal preferences about what they want to consume and produce) with the commands of an authority aiming to reward what it deems virtuous (Hayek 1975, 82). Any attempt to realize distribution according to merit would violate liberty, Hayek (1960, 93–99) claims, in addition to undermining prosperity.

Thus, Hayek's claim that social justice is incompatible with the spontaneous order of a market society has a very narrow target: the desire to ensure distribution according to the principle of individual merit or desert. Hayek (1976, 68–69) recognizes the force of this principle in everyday moral thinking:

> Are we not all constantly disquieted by watching how unjustly life treats different people and by seeing the deserving suffer and the unworthy prosper? And do we not all have a sense of fitness, and watch it with satisfaction, when we recognize a reward to be appropriate to effort or sacrifice? The first insight which should shake this certainty is that we experience the same feelings also with respect to differences in human fates for which clearly no human agency is responsible and which it would therefore clearly be absurd to call injustice. Yet we do cry out against the injustice when a succession of calamities befalls one family while another steadily prospers, when a meritorious effort is frustrated by some unforeseeable accident, and particularly if of many people whose endeavours seem equally great, some succeed brilliantly while others

utterly fail. . . . It is no different with regard to the general feeling of injustice about the distribution of material goods in a society of free men. . . . Our complaints about the outcome of the market as unjust do not really assert that somebody has been unjust; and there is no answer to the question of who has been unjust. Society has simply become the new deity to which we complain and clamour for redress if it does not fulfil the expectations it has created. There is no individual and no cooperating group of people against which the sufferer would have a just complaint, and there are no conceivable rules of just individual conduct which would at the same time secure a functioning order and prevent such disappointments.[19]

In this and other similar passages, the meaning of "social justice" is "distribution according to individual merit."[20] This principle would run counter to the spontaneous ordering of a market economy.

The problem with Hayek's argument is that distribution according to merit is just one conception of social justice. Consider the principles of fair equality of opportunity and that of raising the lowest social position as much as possible. Since neither of these principles requires distribution according to individual merit, neither falls afoul of Hayek's objection. Hayek (1976, 100) comes close to admitting as much at the end of his critique of social justice, when he briefly addresses Rawls's *Theory of Justice*:

> The recognition that in such combinations as "social," "economic," "distributive" or "retributive" justice the term "justice" is wholly empty should not lead us to throw the baby out with the bath water. . . . There unquestionably . . . exists a genuine problem of justice in connection with the deliberate design of political institutions, the problem to which Professor John Rawls has recently devoted an important book.

Although in this passage Hayek talks of "political" rather than "social" institutions, he has to admit that there are different ways of designing the rules of property and contract and that he has not yet provided a reason for thinking that the distributive effects of such decisions cannot be judged just or unjust. He allows that "there is no reason why in a free society government should not assure to all protection against severe deprivation in the form of an assured minimum income" (Hayek 1976, 87). In fact, such a scheme "may be felt to be a clear moral duty of all to assist . . . those who cannot assist themselves," rather than simply being a prudent form of social insurance (ibid).[21] So long as this minimum income is provided outside the market without any other interference with the price mechanism, Hayek says, there is no threat to freedom or the rule of law. The problems he is concerned with, he says, are those that arise when the levels of remuneration for different services are set by authority rather than by the market (ibid.). Hayek provides no reason, here, for thinking that income support or public support of education is not a requirement of social justice, e.g., equal opportunity. His strictures against schemes designed to achieve social justice apply only to attempts to make the distribution of income correspond to individual merit, which would interfere with the setting of market prices.

In *The Constitution of Liberty*, Hayek did provide arguments against redistribution in general, even where the underlying distributive principle is not merit-based.[22] The first is a clearly unsuccessful argument based on the moral constraints on coercion. The basic postulate of a free society, he states, is "the limitation of all coercion by equal law." Given unequal capacities, however, equal treatment guarantees unequal outcomes; achieving equal outcomes, given unequal capacities, would require unequal treatment. Policies such as progressive taxation for redistribution of wealth therefore amount to "discriminatory coercion or privilege," in violation of the fundamental liberal premise of equality under law (Hayek 1960, 87–88).[23]

This argument depends on a familiar equivocation concerning the notion of equal treatment. Treating people with different abilities the same leads to unequal outcomes, but treating them differently does not necessarily amount to treating them with unequal concern and respect. Any standard of "same treatment" needs to specify who needs to be treated the same and in what dimension.

Taken literally, the idea of treating people in the same way might mean that everyone should pay the same absolute dollar amount in taxes, rather than the same percentage. Isn't it unequal treatment if I am required to pay $100 and you are only required to pay $50? Defenders of flat taxation may want to say that equal treatment requires equal taxation relative to total income, i.e., a fixed proportion of income, not equal absolute tax bills. To make this argument, however, they must invoke some normative principle to give content to the bare idea of equality. One needs a theory of justice to determine which forms of differential treatment count as discrimination.

Moreover, Hayek conceded that if state action were necessary to achieve some legitimate objective, but there were different ways of achieving it, then "those [ways] that incidentally also reduce inequality may well be preferable;" he gives the example of different ways of designing the law of intestate succession (Hayek 1960, 88). This concession seems fatal, since the laws of property and contract are enforced by state coercion, and there are more or less egalitarian ways of designing systems of property rights. For example, is inheritance of wealth to be permitted at all?

One might claim that it is a mistake from Hayek's point of view to talk about designing institutions—an example of what he called the constructivist fallacy. Constructivists wrongly assume that order results from the intention of a designing agent, and they neglect the fact that evolved order can be more complex and better adapted than designed orders (Hayek 1973, 8–35). The crucial word here, however, is *can*. Hayek never claimed that social evolution is always optimal. He admits that it can lead down blind alleys and that grown rules may need to be reformed by legislation (ibid., 88–89). This is one reason he denied being a conservative (Hayek 1960, 397).

The concept of spontaneous order, then, does negligible work in Hayek's political-theory project. There is undoubtedly a moral distinction to be drawn between bad things that people do to each other and bad things that just happen. Because it is the product of myriad individual choices based on diverse information, the distribution the market generates is in some respects more like a natural event than a human action. Yet it is a moral rather than just a conceptual question whether we have a duty to help rectify poverty or inequalities we did not cause, and whether it should count as a duty of justice. Furthermore, our collective choices about the structure of social institutions are actions that can be assessed as just or unjust because of their distributive consequences. An awareness of the spontaneous *origins* of institutions suggests, at best, that we tread lightly in overturning them. And an awareness of the spontaneous *results* of institutions does not preclude any egalitarian project except that of assigning compensation according to non-market judgments of value. Neither income redistribution nor any other general government program is barred by respect for spontaneous order.

Liberty, Coercion, and Social Justice

Hayek's conception of liberty, too, fails to open much distance between his position and that of egalitarian redistributionists.

On the one hand, he objected very strenuously to confusing liberty with power or capacity. A conception of liberty as power, he thought, lends itself to socialist attempts to turn "freedom from want" against individual freedom of choice (Hayek 1960, 12–13, 16–19).[24] Hayek therefore insisted that freedom existed only in relationships between people, much as he insisted that justice was a property of intentional, interpersonal conduct. On the other hand, Hayek defined this relationship, in quasi-republican fashion, as the absence of dependence on the arbitrary will of another (Hayek 1976, 12–13).[25] The idea of non-domination[26] provides a strictly interpersonal conception of liberty, one that classifies Robinson Crusoe as free despite the dearth of effective options. Yet it can easily be harnessed to argue for more equal distributive outcomes, to protect people from being subject to the arbitrary will of others in the marketplace.

This argument is facilitated by Hayek's quasi-republican conception of law. Hayek recognized that the threat of state coercion was necessary to prevent interpersonal coercion, but he insisted that the worst effects of the state's coercion could be reduced if it operated only through known general rules whose effect on particular people could not be foreseen at the time the rules were made. Because liberty means not being subject to or unilaterally dependent on someone else's good will, having a framework of known general rules does not make people subject to the arbitrary will of those who made the rules, but permits them to plan their own lives in view of their own ends (Hayek 1960, 133–48).

However, if resources are privately owned and society makes no provision to ensure access to employment, education, and so on, those without property will tend to be subject to the will of those with property, at least when times are bad. Thus, the only way Hayek avoids legitimizing measures to reduce economic inequality in the interests of non-domination is by optimistically assuming that the level of coercion in a market society would not be high. It is only in very exceptional circumstances that control of a resource or a service allows one person to dominate another, he claims (Hayek 1960, 135). A monopolist of an essential good may be able to coerce people into buying that good, but the individual provider of employment cannot normally exercise true coercion because employees can leave and find work elsewhere. Periods of acute unemployment would be "rare exceptions in a prosperous competitive economy" (ibid., 137). Even the threat of starvation that impels someone to take a distasteful job at a low wage is not coercive, so long as the actions that led to this predicament were not aimed at making the person do particular things or serve someone else's will (ibid.).

Hayek is quite right that under ordinary circumstances, I am not coercing anyone if I open a new factory that displaces workers at the old factory and leaves some with no option but to take an unpleasant job. But the fact remains that people in dire straits are *vulnerable* to being coerced, and will thus often be dependent on the good will of others, contrary to Hayek's initial definition of freedom. It is of course an empirical question how common this situation is under the various possible forms of market economy. But Hayek's appeal to liberty and equality under law provide no general argument against the claim that considerations of distributive justice should matter in the design of the institutions of such an economy. To the contrary, Hayek defines coercion in such a manner that deprivation and inequality threaten to create unfreedom—dependence on the arbitrary good will of another person—while law need not do so. Unless his optimistic claims about the operation of a market economy are correct, he has provided a powerful basis for social policies aimed at providing people with a threshold of resources sufficient to allow them to avoid the risk of domination in private life.

That Hayek's concept of liberty was likely to lead him in a social-democratic direction was clear to his early critic, Ronald Hamowy (1961, 32–35). Hamowy claimed that Hayek defined freedom as absence of coercion, and coercion as the manipulation of someone's environment with a view to benefitting oneself.[27] This definition counts beneficial but self-interested offers as coercive. For example, if I offer to buy you beer and pizza to convince you to help me move, I am manipulating your environment—the options available to you—for my own benefit. But intuitively speaking it is clear that I am not coercing you.

Hayek correctly responded that his definition of coercion deemed only option-reducing manipulations of a person's environment as coercive. Yet this response does not resolve the problems posed by monopolies in essential resources. If I am the owner of a spring in the desert and you are starving of thirst, I might let you drink from my oasis if you agree to work for me for one full year without pay. It seems that I am not coercing you because I am not threatening you with harm. And since you don't have any options, I am not threatening to take them away; I am, in fact, increasing your options with a mutually beneficial but exploitative offer and can thereby get you under my thumb.

Hayek claims that such examples are not typical of a competitive market economy. But let's bracket his optimism. The example of a monopoly of an essential resource suggests that what is crucial is not whether your action worsens or enhances someone's set of options, but the facts of absolute deprivation and relative inequality. If there is enough deprivation and inequality—if one person is poor enough to want to sell himself and the other is rich enough to buy him[28]—then the person on the top end of the relationship can effectively dictate the conduct of the other, treating the other person as a thing, substituting his will for that of the other person because the other person has no choice if he or she wants to survive.

In his response to Hamowy, Hayek (1961, 28–30) dealt with the case of a monopoly of an essential resource by counting failures to fulfill positive duties of aid as harms:

> The instance I discuss in my book is the situation in which somebody has acquired control of the whole water supply of an oasis and used this position to exact unusual performances from those whose life depends on access to that water. Other instances of the same kind would be the only doctor available to perform an urgent life-saving operation and similar cases of rescue in an emergency where special unforeseeable circumstances have placed into a single hand the power of rescue from grave danger. They are all instances where I should wish that those in whose hands the life of another is placed should be under a moral and legal obligation to render the help in their power even if they cannot expect any remuneration—though they should of course be entitled to normal remuneration if it is in the power of the rescued. It is because these services are regarded as rights to be counted upon that a refusal to render them except on unusual terms is justly regarded as a harmful alteration of the environment and therefore as coercion.

According to this position, if I make my performance of my positive duty of aid conditional on exorbitant demands, I will be guilty of coercion. Here Hayek follows Mill.[29] This appeal to positive duty brings the case of the monopoly of an essential resource within the ambit of his definition of coercion, but cannot be squared with Hayek's description of his method in Chapter 9.5 of *The Constitution of Liberty*:

> The existence of . . . an assured free sphere seems to us so much a normal condition of life that we are tempted to define "coercion" by the use of such terms as "the interference with legitimate expectations" or "infringement of rights" or "arbitrary interference." But in defining coercion we

cannot take for granted the arrangements intended to prevent it. The "legitimacy" of one's expectations or the "rights" of the individual are the result of the recognition of such a private sphere. . . . Only in a society that has already attempted to prevent coercion by some demarcation of a protected sphere can a concept like "arbitrary interference" have a definite meaning. (Hayek 1960, 139)

In this passage, Hayek says that we cannot assume any specific set of rights and duties in defining "coercion," but must rather design our rights and duties so as to minimize coercion in an unmoralized sense.[30] Yet if we are designing rights and duties to minimize coercion, we can't use claims about positive duties to define coercion.

Pure Procedural Justice and the Irrelevance of Merit

We have seen that Hayek's critique of social justice is really a critique of distribution according to individual merit, as long as society is a scheme of cooperation governed by general rules that allow broad scope for individual liberty. His sympathy for Rawls is therefore readily intelligible, given Rawls's commitment to pure procedural justice and his denial that desert is a fundamental principle of justice. Rawls, too, argued that principles of justice apply to institutional rules rather than to distributions directly.[31] The basic structure of society is a public system of rules—for example, rules about property and contract. Distributions of goods and income across individuals arise because people make choices in light of the options the rules make available. Under a different set of rules they would choose differently, and a different distribution would result.[32] If the rules are just, the distribution that results from voluntary interaction within the constraints of the rules is just, no matter what it may be.

Distributive justice thus involves an element of pure procedural justice. The rules are not a means to bring about a particular result, as in the case of more or less perfect procedural justice (e.g., splitting a cake by the "you cut, I choose" rule, or the rules of a criminal trial). Distributive justice is more like gambling; if the bet was freely entered into under fair conditions, the result is fair no matter what it is. Thus, one cannot take a stock of goods distributed across particular individuals and judge it to be just or unjust independent of the institutional system from which it resulted by way of choices and agreements made in good faith (Rawls 1999, 76).

It will be objected that although principles of justice apply to institutional rules, not distributions, Rawls defines just institutions partly in terms of distributions; for example, a just institution should provide fair equality of opportunity and should raise the position of the worst off. However, the distributions in question are not distributions across particular individuals, but distributions across social positions. We choose systems of institutional rules based on the distribution of positions they make available. Then individuals interact within the constraints set by the rules, and the resulting distribution across individuals is just by definition.

The rationale for focusing on social positions is that people are born into different starting points in life that make it more or less likely that they will be able to succeed. People are born with different levels of innate talent and, assuming that liberty must permit private childrearing in some form, we will never have full equality of opportunity across social positions. Moreover, even if we did, and even if there were no differences in levels of innate talent, the market would still involve a substantial element of luck. People who are willing to work and play by the rules will suffer unmerited failure; others less meritorious will win success.

> The extent of one's contribution (estimated by one's marginal productivity) depends upon supply and demand. Surely a person's moral worth does not vary according to how many offer similar skills, or happen to want what he can produce. No one supposes that when someone's abilities are less in demand or have deteriorated (as in the case of singers) his moral deservingness undergoes a similar shift. All of this is perfectly obvious and has long been agreed to. (Rawls 1999, 273–74)

Since everyone depends on the cooperation of others, we ought not take advantage of this morally arbitrary luck to claim a greater share of what we produce together—not unless this inequality will make everyone better off. We ought therefore to assess the design of economic institutions from the perspective of someone in the lowest social position. This doesn't mean that we have to maximize the income of the least-responsible individual—say, someone who is unwilling to work or follow the laws. Rather, we should assess economic institutions from the point of view of someone willing to work and follow the laws, but who happens to have been born without a lot of innate talents (at least not talents currently in demand) or born into a family at the bottom end of the distribution of income and wealth.

Rawls's principles thus have a hybrid character in relation to pure procedural justice. Distributions across individuals are just so long as they result from interaction within just institutions, but just institutions are defined in part by their tendency to produce the right distributions across social positions. Appreciating this hybrid character is essential to understanding how Rawls's principles avoid two prominent criticisms. The first is the Nozickean argument that liberty upsets patterns; the second is the Dworkinian claim that the difference principle is not sufficiently sensitive to ambition.[33]

Nozick's argument is well known. Assume a just distribution, whatever one thinks that is, and then let individuals engage in fully informed and voluntary exchange. The resulting distribution will no longer fit the specified pattern. To get back to the right pattern the state will have to coercively extract some of what individuals justly acquired and give it to others, which doesn't seem right (Nozick 1974, 160).

The ambition critique has the same structure. Start with an equal distribution of land between two equally talented gardeners, Ian the industrious and Christine the contemplative.[34] Next, let them make fully informed and voluntary decisions about work, leisure, and consumption. Ian works hard in the garden so that he can afford to buy things, while Christine only works a little, because she takes pleasure in walking in the woods and watching the sun set. After a time, Ian and Christine will have unequal wealth. By the difference principle, this inequality is only permitted if it benefits the least-well-off person—Christine. To ensure that justice is preserved, government may have to take some money away from Ian and give it Christine, which again doesn't seem right.

The mistake in both of these cases is the application of principles of justice to distributions across specific individuals, taking their conduct as fixed, instead of applying the principles to institutional rules, within which individuals then makes choices. If individuals engage in voluntary transactions within the framework of just rules, the resulting distribution is just, *regardless* of the pattern it produces. But just rules are defined partly in terms of ensuring that there is fair equality of opportunity[35] and that the lowest social position is raised. If a progressive income tax is necessary to achieve these goals, then distributions of rights over resources are just to the extent that they are compatible with such taxation. There can be no just distribution of resources that does not allow for institutions necessary to maintain fair equality of opportunity and the difference principle, if these are indeed valid principles of justice. That is to say, there can be no just distribution of absolute property rights.[36]

Now take the example of the two gardeners. If the rules defining property, contract, inheritance, etc., are just, then any distribution between Ian and Christine that results from their decisions is just *no matter what it may be*; this is the idea of pure procedural justice. But these rules will not be just unless they protect people's basic liberties, secure fair equality of opportunity, and permit inequalities only if they raise the lowest social position. If property or other rules do not satisfy these principles, then the distribution that results will not be just, but not because of the extra inequality between individuals that results from the decisions they have made about work and lifestyle. Rather, the problem would lie in the extra inequality between social positions that results from collective decisions about the design of institutions.

The Nozickian and Dworkinian critiques of the difference principle are structurally similar in that they focus on distributions across individuals, taking institutional context for granted. It is therefore not surprising that the position-based pure-procedural-justice response to the Dworkinian objection about ambition has the same structure as the property-rights response to the Nozickean objection about liberty.

Hayek's Principles of Social Justice

One of the standard objections to Hayek's claim that social justice is a mirage is that he himself subscribes to a principle of social justice, namely, the principle of maximizing utility. For example, Hayek (1976, 63) speaks of a market order as "an impersonal process that brings about a greater satisfaction of human desires than any deliberate organization could achieve." Hayek has been accused of contradicting himself at this point. If principles of social justice can't be used to assess the outcomes of the market's spontaneous order, then it should not be possible to assess the market according to the utilitarian standard (Johnston 1997; Lukes 1997).[37]

One response is to claim that Hayek is talking about desirability, not justice (Feser 1997, 596–97; Tebble 2009, 592). This victory for Hayek would be purely verbal. We need to identify our first principles of institutional assessment, even if we refuse to call them principles of justice. Moreover, since these principles guide the decisions we make about the design of social institutions, Hayek has no grounds for refusing them the label "principles of justice." The decisions we make about our social rules are things we do to and with one another, and they give rise to public agencies that do things to people, such as enforcing rules of property and contract. Such decisions are forms of interpersonal conduct, and so can be just or unjust, according to Hayek's account.

A second response is to admit that Hayek accepts some principles of institutional design, but to insist that first amongst these is respecting and protecting human freedom—a principle that will be undermined by any attempt to achieve a particular distribution of rewards. But as before, this response is plausible only in regard to attempts to achieve distribution according to individual merit—as well as attempts to achieve perfect economic equality. Even if liberty comes first, and even if it always conflicts with merit-based distribution, other kinds of distributive considerations might have a secondary role in designing institutions.

It is misleading to describe Hayek as a utilitarian, however.[38] Hayek (1976, 115) speaks of giving people the opportunity to satisfy their *needs*, rather than doing whatever will maximize satisfaction of whatever desires they happen to have. The standard objections to maximizing *utility* therefore do not pose a serious challenge to Hayek.[39]

The objections to designing institutions that will *maximize* the total sum of utility (in the aggregate, without regard to its distribution) are more serious. Yet here again, Hayek is not a consistent utilitarian. Consider, for example, this comment about the absurdity of complaining about distributive injustice in a market economy:

> It has of course to be admitted that the manner in which the benefits and burdens are apportioned by the market mechanism would in many instances have to be regarded as very unjust if it were the result of a deliberate allocation to particular people. But this is not the case. Those shares are the outcome of a process the effect of which on particular people was neither intended nor foreseen by anyone when the institutions first appeared—institutions which were then permitted to continue because it was found that they improve for all or most the prospects of having their needs satisfied. To demand justice from such a process is clearly absurd. (Hayek 1976, 64)

This passage sets out two different arguments against complaining about the injustice of a market-generated distribution. The first is that doing so would treat the unintended, unforeseeable product of the interaction of a great many agents as if it were the consequence of the actions of a single agent. The second is that the market improves the prospects for (most) everyone to satisfy their needs when compared to the previously existing, feudal economic order, and presumably also when compared to a planned economy.

A few pages later, Hayek (1976, 70, emph. added) says that "we consent to retain, and agree to enforce, uniform rules for a procedure which has greatly improved the chances *of all* to have their wants satisfied, but at the price of all individuals and groups incurring the risk of unmerited failure."[40]

"Unmerited failure" is the lack of distribution according to merit, which is what people think of as social justice. Hayek's point is that it is "absurd" to prefer this type of social justice at the expense of everyone being worse off. This is the familiar leveling-down objection to equality: that it is irrational to forbid deviations from distribution according to merit if these deviations can make everyone better off than they would be under a system that ensured a closer fit between merit and reward. This objection implies that we accept the market economy because it increases (most) everyone's opportunity for need-satisfaction as compared to the historical baseline, and as compared to the alternative of a planned economy.

Here Hayek runs into problems. First, is the criterion that everyone—or just most people—be better off? "Most people" will bring Hayek's position closer to utilitarianism, but he needs to say "everyone" to sustain his claim about the absurdity of complaints of social injustice. Second, what is the appropriate baseline of comparison? No one wants to go back to the feudal order, but are there really only two viable alternatives to it—a planned economy and a pure market order? If we must compare three or more options, including some form of social democracy, most comparisons of pairs of options will show improvements for some at the expense of losses for others, with the result that the Pareto criterion will not rank the alternatives. If so, we must decide whether a given alternative is justified because everyone would be better off than if society were *maximally* equal—or whether everyone has to be better off than they would be if society were *more* equal (otherwise we default to the more equal alternative). The latter, more demanding criterion is of course the Rawlsian position.

Hayek avoids confronting these questions by switching to a different sense of "improving people's chances." In the passages above, when Hayek speaks of improving everyone's chances of having their needs satisfied, he means that every person's opportunity for need satisfaction is greater in a market economy than it would be under some alternative, baseline scenario—either the historical status quo or a planned, egalitarian economy. In other passages, however, Hayek (1976, 129) speaks of maximizing the chances of anyone picked out at random: "Since rules of just conduct can affect only the chances of success of the efforts of men, the aim in altering or developing them should be to improve as much as possible the chances of anyone selected at random."[41] In other words, although Hayek initially talks of improving everyone's chances no matter what their social position, as compared to some alternative social order, he switches to the principle of maximizing anyone's chances, prior to having been born into a particular social position.

The latter principle involves maximizing aggregate opportunity for need satisfaction. Maximizing expected opportunity means being willing to accept that some may have very small chances in life in order that others who would have had greater chances anyway can have still greater chances. That would be fine if people voluntarily undertook this gamble before being born. However, if I am born into the lowest social class I will naturally complain that I didn't get a chance to refuse this gamble.

A more plausible view is that to benefit all, inequalities must benefit those who have less, rather than those who have more. The worst off may get more in the unequal distribution of a competitive market economy than they would in an egalitarian centrally directed system (Hayek 1979a, 14), but do they get more in Hayek's ideal society than they would under any feasible liberty-preserving alternative?

Hayek (1976, 131) admits that "it might seem reasonable so to frame laws that they will tend more strongly to improve the opportunities of those whose chances are relatively small." He doesn't deny that this is reasonable at the level of principle, but he does deny that it is feasible: Improving the opportunities of those with less "can rarely be achieved by generic rules" (ibid.). Yet this is exactly what policies such as income support and subsidized education do.

Hayek (1976, 130–31) also had an unfortunate tendency to conflate the maximization of aggregate income with the maximization of opportunity. In his Australian lectures, for example, he said that "the productivity-enhancing function of prices . . . depends on their informing people where they will find their most effective place in the overall pattern of activities—the place in which they are likely to make the greatest contribution *to aggregate output*. If, therefore, we regard that rule of remuneration as just which contributes as much as possible to increasing the chances of any member of the community picked out at random, we ought to regard the remunerations determined by a free market as the just ones" (Hayek 1979a, 9–10).[42] Yet the relationship between income and opportunity is clearly convex. Earning $100,000 as opposed to $50,000 makes a big difference in the extent of one's opportunities, but earning $1,000,000 as opposed to $950,000, not nearly as much. Hayek simply cannot leap from maximizing average opportunity to maximizing average income.

One reason Hayek did not worry about these philosophical nuances may have been that he thought that no matter which of the various plausible distributive principles one prefers, a small-state market society that protects private property is best. After implausibly arguing that there is no way to help the least well off with generic rules, Hayek (1976, 131) goes on to claim that "the fact which . . . has contributed most during the last two hundred years to increase not only the absolute but also the relative position of those in the lowest income groups has been the general growth of wealth which has tended to raise the income of the lowest groups more than the relatively higher ones." Hayek cites an interesting statistic: Someone whose income was in the 50th to the 60th percentile of the American income distribution in 1940, but descended to the 30th–40th percentile group by 1960, still had a higher absolute income in 1960 than in 1940. Thus, during this period, the incomes of lower part of the distribution were growing fast enough so that after twenty or thirty years, people in that part of the distribution were making more than the higher-ups used to make. But it is no longer true that income is growing so fast in the lower deciles of the income distribution that descending in the distribution will generally be consistent with one's income growing.[43]

Hayek's Original Position

The final point of similarity between Rawls and Hayek is that they both employed the device of choice under uncertainty to think about principles of institutional design.

How would you design society if you had to choose where your children would be born? You wouldn't choose an aristocratic society, Hayek argues, despite the attractions of that lifestyle, because your children would likely end up being peasants. Instead you would choose a modern industrial society that "did not offer such delectable plums to a few but offered better prospects to the great majority" (Hayek 1976, 132). This thought experiment does not support Hayek's principle of maximizing aggregate chances over the Rawlsian principle of improving everyone's chances as compared to a baseline of equality.

In the footnote that accompanies this passage, Hayek explains that he himself faced such a choice in deciding which foreign country to place his children in during the early days of the Second World War. Should he send his children to the United States, Argentina, or Sweden? The choice he would have made for himself, knowing his skills and talents, was not necessarily the one he would make for his children, whose talents were yet to develop. Starting out from zero, one would choose America, because their chances there—averaging over all the positions they might occupy—would be greater than in the Old World, with its sharp social distinctions (assuming that they would be placed with a white American family, Hayek says).

However, the choice amongst these alternatives does not distinguish between Hayekian and Rawlsian principles. Was Hayek's decision motivated by the fact that *average chances* were better in America than in Europe, or by the fact that the chances *for those in the lowest position* were better in America than in Europe? Suppose, for example, that Hayek had been choosing between sending his children to Canada or the United States. Suppose that the chances of any child picked at random were greater in America, but that the chances of the least innately talented child would have been greater in Canada.[44] Which country would Hayek have picked?

The main formal difference between Hayek and Rawls on this point is that, like the economist John Harsanyi (1953, 434–45), Hayek allows the agent knowledge of the probabilities of occupying various social positions behind the veil of ignorance, while Rawls does not. Rawls asks what principles of institutional design one would choose, not knowing the precise level of social and technological development, whereas Hayek asks which of a given set of institutional setups one would choose knowing the relevant empirical facts. Thus it would be feasible in Hayek's setup to gamble on a society with greater average chances at the cost of enduring a worse fate if one ended up in the lowest social position—whereas in Rawls's setup, without any reliable way to calculate probabilities of ending up in one position or another, we maximize the level of the lowest position. Yet Hayek's example of placing one's children forces the question of whether one would really gamble on avoiding the lowest position.[45] Would he not have been tempted to give priority to the worst off to ensure that his children would at least be helped, to the maximum feasible extent, if their talents or upbringing did not suit them to the demands of the market in their place and time?

Remaining Differences between Hayek and Rawls

The upshot of this discussion is that Hayek's basic philosophical and normative assumptions do not by themselves dictate his conclusions about law and policy. What generates these conclusions is a set of empirical claims, in particular claims about feasibility.

The most striking example of this occurs in Hayek's rejection of the value of equal opportunity. Hayek (1976, 84–85) accepts formal equality of opportunity, "*la carrière ouverte aux talents*," and he admits that "there is also much to be said in favor of government providing on an equal basis the means for the schooling of minors," although he doesn't say that this is a requirement of social justice. He then goes on to point out that such measures "would still be very far from creating real equality of opportunity," which would require that government "control the whole physical and human environment of all people" (ibid.).[46]

The obvious response is that even if complete equality of opportunity would require a totalitarian state, it is a principle of justice that we attempt to achieve fair equal opportunity *until* it threatens liberty; then we must stop. At this point Hayek has recourse to the slippery slope. The more government succeeds in equalizing opportunities, the stronger the demand to remove remaining handicaps. "This would go on until government literally controlled every circumstance which could affect any person's well-being." Thus "any attempt" to realize equality of opportunity beyond government provision of services that can be justified on other grounds "is apt to produce a nightmare" (Hayek 1976, 84–45).[47] The claim that the political slippery slope presents us with an either/or choice between personal liberty and equality of opportunity is not convincing.[48]

Although the conclusions that Hayek reached about policy were not egalitarian, the fundamental normative principles he accepted do not by themselves block—and in many plausible circumstances support— policies that aim to bring about a more equal distribution of economic resources. His conception of liberty as independence of will, as well as his claim that rule by law makes coercion less coercive, open the possibility for state action that reduces the occurrence of private domination. Once we acknowledge conceptions of distributive justice not based on individual merit and the possibility of institutional orders intermediate between pure socialism and pure capitalism, Hayek's espousal of the principle that inequalities should benefit all opens the door to redistribution—in the name of *social justice*. Or, to be more precise, since the idea of redistribution wrongly suggests a punctual reallocation of resources in violation of established rules, it opens up the possibility of designing social institutions with a view to equalizing distributive outcomes across social positions.

There are two important respects, however, in which Rawls's view is more egalitarian than Hayek's. The first has to do with the importance of equal political liberty. Rawls (1999, 197–98 and 247) was aware of the possibility that inequalities that satisfy the difference principle might be so great as to undermine the fair value of political liberties. He thought that unless we take steps to limit the extent of socio-economic inequality or insulate the political process from it, the more advantaged will come to control the society, despite the formal equality of their votes. Hayek was much less worried about this possibility. His main concern was that the perception of legitimacy attached to democracy would encourage legislatures to venture beyond the proper function of making law, giving rise to a discretionary power of command that would inevitably become the object of political struggle. Instead of limiting itself to enacting general, negative rules of individual conduct, legislatures would become involved in the business of day-to-day government, turning the state into a tool for extracting resources from some in order to buy the votes of others. Hayek's solution was to restrict the scope of state action so that it could not be used in this way, and to reform legislatures so that they could be insulated from interest-group politics (e.g., by electing representatives over the age of 45 to a single 15-year term, after which point they would be guaranteed alternative public employment) (Hayek 1979b, 445–52).

The second remaining difference is more purely normative and concerns the justification of economic inequality. Recent "bleeding-heart libertarians" have claimed that Rawls misunderstood the institutional implications of his difference principle. Jason Brennan (2007, 292–93) argues that a society that uses the state to provide a wide range of public services and to redistribute income so as to satisfy the difference principle—a Rawlsian "property-owning democracy," which Brennan calls "Fairness Land"—will have lower growth rates, as compared to a society that relies more heavily on the market—"Pareto-Superior Land." The result is that the worst off in Fairness Land will eventually be worse off than they would have been had the society opted for the classically liberal institutions of Pareto-Superior Land. The lesson Brennan draws is that societies that directly aim to satisfy the difference principle may be less successful at doing so than societies that subscribe to more traditional liberal ideals.

However, as John Tomasi (2012, 236) points out, if a society adopts or maintains free markets and private property because this setup best satisfies the difference principle, Pareto-Superior land *is* Fairness Land. The real issue is not about intentions but about what counts as satisfying the difference principle. According to Brennan and Tomasi, the difference principle requires "maximizing the material shares of the least well-off over time" (ibid.). This, I take it, is also Hayek's view: Society should maximally benefit the worst off *in the long run*, and a society based on private property, free markets, and limited government will do just that. Assuming that classically liberal institutions generate higher growth rates overall and at the bottom end of the distribution, Brennan and Tomasi take it for granted that a consistent Rawlsian ought to endorse this institutional scheme. With higher shared growth rates, at some point everyone, including the worst off, is better off than they would have been under more interventionist, less market-friendly Rawlsian institutions. "At what point," then, "do the least advantaged (and everyone else) in Fairness Land object that they were given a bad deal?" (Brennan 2007, 294).

This objection will be met with another, more powerful objection on the part of the worst off from earlier generations. Unless the growth rate differential is massive, the worst off who are making the sacrifice at time 1 will not be the same worst off who are made better off at time 2. Maximizing long-run growth out of concern for the worst off over the long run means that the worst off in generation 1 must accept inequality that makes them worse off for the sake of raising the prospects of the worst off in generation 2, who will be better off anyway.

In contrast, the orthodox Rawlsian position is that inequality between positions now should raise (or at least not lower) the lower position compared to what it could otherwise have been, not that inequality now may be justified because it raises the worst off in the long run. Growth *is* required, but as part of the just-savings principle, which has a definite target: the attainment and preservation of just institutions. There is no need to go on maximizing indefinitely, in Rawls's view. Except where economic development is necessary for realizing equal basic liberties, justice doesn't require that the least well off accept more inequality today for the sake of maximizing the level of the lowest position in the long run.[49] The focus of Rawls's principle is how we divide what we produce together today, and what this decision says about the relationship between citizens. In contrast, Hayek is more concerned with maximizing the range of choices people have in the long run—a position that is in some tension with his definition of liberty as independence of will rather than effective range of choice.

*　　　　　*　　　　　*

Despite these differences with Rawls, Hayek is in some important ways a closet liberal egalitarian who reaches inegalitarian policy conclusions only by means of equivocation and imagined slippery slopes. What, then, remains of distinctive value in his writings about social justice?

On the left, markets are sometimes viewed as inherently objectionable because they let people callously use each other for selfish gain; only to the extent that they make everyone better off are markets to be tolerated despite this injustice.[50] One lesson Hayek has to teach us is that markets and private-property rights are important not just because they are efficient at producing wealth, but because they allow people with very different values and purposes to cooperate in beneficial ways, despite their many disagreements about how society ought to allocate its resources. The great discovery of market society is not how selfishness can be made to serve the public interest, according to Hayek, but how people with radically different ends can be led to cooperate, each acting for his or her own purposes, in a way that benefits others (Hayek 1976, 3–4, 109–10).[51]

Second, markets allow us to explore through decentralized trial and error the great many ways of producing the things we want or might discover we want. This process encourages innovation, facilitating unpredictable social and cultural change. Experiments in living also require experiments in producing.

In short, Hayek teaches us that capitalism has virtues other than simply generating wealth. However, what Hayek resists teaching us is that the legal framework of capitalism can be designed to reduce inequality in the name of justice.

NOTES

1. See also Hayek 1973, 142.
2. See also Hayek 1976, 62.
3. "There is apparently no end to the violence that will be done to language to further some ideal and the example of 'social justice' has recently given rise to the expression 'global justice'! Its negation, 'global injustice,' was defined by an ecumenical gathering of American religious leaders as 'characterized by a dimension of sin in the economic, political, social, sexual, and class structures and systems of global society.' It would seem as if the conviction that one is arguing for a good cause produced more sloppy thinking and even intellectual dishonesty than perhaps any other cause" (Hayek 1976, 80).
4. Although I will be citing the revised edition of *The Theory of Justice* (1999), Hayek would have read the original edition (1971). However, the many small differences (and some larger differences) between the two works do not affect any of the points at issue between Hayek and Rawls.
5. Cf. ch. 9 of *The Mirage of Social Justice*, entitled "'Social' or Distributive Justice," as well as 137 and elsewhere. See also Hayek 1979a, 4; Hayek 1988, 118.
6. I take these terms from Gaus 2007, 84.
7. In a later interview, Hayek partially retracted his endorsement of Rawls, alleging that Rawls had changed his position by the time of *Theory*. However, Rawls's position on justice and institutions did not change (see n31 below).

> BUCHANAN: Let me raise another point here. In I believe the preface to the second volume of your *Law, Legislation, and Liberty*, you say—the mirage of social justice—in one sentence you say that you think that you're attempting to do the same thing, essentially, that John Rawls has tried to do in his theory of justice. People have queried me about that statement in your book.

> HAYEK: Well, I perhaps go a little too far in this; I was trying to remind Rawls himself of something he had said in one of his earlier articles [Rawls 1963], which I'm afraid doesn't recur in his book: that the conception of correcting the distribution according to the principle of social justice is unachievable, and that therefore he wanted to confine himself to inventing general rules which had that effect. Now, if he was not prepared to defend social-distributive justice, I thought I could pretend to agree with him; but studying his book further, my feeling is he doesn't really stick to the thing he had announced first, and that there is so much egalitarianism, really, underlying his argument that he is driven to much more intervention than his original conception justifies.

The text of these interviews is found in Hayek 1983. The video is available at http://hayek.ufm.edu/index.php?title = Category:James_Buchanan; the discussion of social justice starts at 21:35.

8. In a letter to Rose Wilder Lane in 1946, Rand wrote: "As an example of our most pernicious enemy, I would name Hayek. That one is real poison" (Long 2005, 312).

9. The most comprehensive statement of a Rawls-Hayek synthesis is the "bleeding-heart libertarianism" (http://bleedingheartlibertarians.com) of John Tomasi, particularly chapter 5 of *Free Market Fairness* (2012). Claude Gamel (2008) also downplays the extent of the gap between Hayek and Rawls.

10. In the Preface to *Mirage*, Hayek explains that the publication of the volume was delayed by the fact that he had struggled with its central chapter. He had been trying to argue that people would never agree about what social justice required, and that any attempt to make remunerations accord with justice "would make the market unworkable." He felt that he was "hitting into a void," however, until he finally realized that "the Emperor had no clothes on," because the phrase "social justice" simply had no meaning (Hayek 1976, xi).

11. See Mack 1983, 571–72 and Lukes 1997, 68. Similarly, in *The Constitution of Liberty* Hayek (1960, 11–22) argues that liberty is primarily a characteristic of a relationship between people, not of an individual's power, capacity, or effective range of choice.

12. "A state of affairs that no one has intended or foreseen may, nevertheless, require action to alleviate suffering or deprivation, and failure to take such action may be justly condemned as unjust" (Lukes 1997, 72). See also Plant 1991, 92–93 and Tebble 2009, 591.

13. This is a point that others have made in response to Hayek. David Miller (1999, 108–9) notes that "it is possible to study the distributive outcomes of a market and to consider how a change in the ground rules might alter these outcomes." Miller offers the example of laws against discrimination by sex or race in the labor market, which do not abolish the market but merely change its ground rules. "Essentially the same process occurs when the respective rights of landlords and tenants are changed, when consumer protection legislation is introduced, when cartels to fix prices are made illegal, and so forth" (ibid.) David Johnston (1997, 610) also discusses the more or less predictable distributive consequences of legislative decisions about how to design and frame the market.

14. Thus, Hayek (1976, 33) says that it is misleading to call states of affairs just or unjust "in the case of a spontaneous order," where "the resulting state was not the intended aim of the individual actions. . . . What is called 'social' or 'distributive' justice is indeed meaningless within a spontaneous order and has meaning only within an organization."

15. Hayek (1973, 72–123) argues that law did not originally mean legislation and that, originally, judges did not interpret legislative acts but articulated, specified, and attempted to render consistent pre-existing social rules that no one ever consciously invented.

16. I say "primarily" because this is how Hayek generally describes them; e.g., Hayek 1976, 37–38 and 103; Hayek 1979b, 130–32. However, he offers no argument that positive duties could never be sufficiently general to count as part of a system of rules that would be characterized by spontaneous order, and elsewhere he does concede the existence of positive duties of aid; see the discussion of Hayek's response to Hamowy below. In "Justice and Individual

Rights," the Appendix to chapter 9 of *Mirage*, Hayek criticized the idea of positive social and economic rights, according to which every citizen or human being is entitled to particular benefits. Because a right to a benefit implies a duty on someone's part to provide it, recognition of such rights would require that the spontaneous order of the market be replaced with "a deliberately directed organization," in which people would no longer be able to use their knowledge for their own purposes, but would have to do as instructed by their rulers (Hayek 1976, 103). There are many ways of ensuring that children have education and health care, however, short of replacing the market with a Soviet-style command economy. Here as elsewhere it seems that Hayek is motivated by fear of the slippery slope.

17. See also Hayek 1979a, 4.

18. "The particular content of the order will depend on the concrete circumstances known only to the individuals who obey the rules and apply them to the facts known only to them. It will be through the knowledge of these individuals both of the rules and of the particular facts that both will determine the resulting order" (Hayek 1973, 46).

19. See also Hayek 1976, 79, 80, 85, 91, and 94. Elizabeth Anderson (2005) also remarks on the narrowness of Hayek's result. What Hayek saw, according to Anderson, was that distributive principles based on assessments of individual merit were incompatible with any social order involving a substantial degree of individual freedom. Given the role of chance in the market, distribution according to merit would require constant state surveillance and interference in order to correct deviations from its standard of merit, leading to "the ultimate busybody state" See also Don Arthur (2008): "For Hayek, 'social justice' meant allocative justice—the demand 'for an assignment of the shares in the material wealth to the different people and groups according to their needs or merits.'"

20. The narrowness of Hayek's critique is also clear in his later attack on the errors of socialism. He remarks that "social justice" has come to mean "distributive justice," but that distributive justice is "irreconcilable with a competitive market order." He recognizes that people might be happier if the "relative economic positions of individuals" were just. "Yet the whole idea behind distributive justice—that each individual ought to receive what he morally deserves—is meaningless in the extended order of human cooperation" (Hayek 1988, 118).

21. "Hayek concedes that people may have obligations to help each other even when those so obliged did not cause the distress to be alleviated—indeed, when this distress is the result of an impersonal, spontaneous order" (Lukes 1997, 73). Don Arthur (2008) notes that unlike Ludwig von Mises, Hayek consistently supported government provision of a minimum income and public subsidy of education, and was for this reason criticized by libertarians such as Ayn Rand. Along with other critics, Tebble (2009) suggests that Hayek's admission that government can provide a minimum income is incompatible with his earlier claim that distributive justice is unfeasible, since a public minimum will lead to there being less inequality than there would otherwise have been. In contrast, I think that Hayek's support for some form of income support outside the market simply shows that he was rejecting only a very specific kind of distributive justice, i.e., the kind that is based on individual merit.

22. In this work, Hayek (1960, 87) distinguished patterns of distribution in general (e.g., more or less equal) from distribution according to individual merit: "Our objection is against all attempts to impress upon society a deliberately chosen

pattern of distribution, whether it be an order of equality or inequality. We shall indeed see that many of those who demand an extension of equality do not really demand equality but a distribution that conforms more closely to human conceptions of individual merit and that their desires are as irreconcilable with freedom as the more strictly egalitarian demands."

23. See also Hayek 1979b, 102–104, and Hayek 1979a, 39. Hayek's argument in *Social Justice, Socialism and Democracy* (1979a) is less about fairness than about a slippery slope towards an expansion of discretionary political power. Any deviation from equal treatment under law, even "discrimination" to help the least fortunate (especially when labelled "social justice"), threatens to "open the floodgates to arbitrariness," by which Hayek means the use of government to extract resources from some in order to buy the votes of others.

24. See also Hayek's disparaging remarks about Roosevelt's Four Freedoms (Hayek 1976, 101–6).

25. But see Gamel 2008, 115. Gamel argues that Hayek has a negative conception of liberty, claiming that if Hayek were true to his conception of liberty as the absence of coercion, he ought not support state provision of a minimum income, and that if he really believed such a policy is legitimate, he would have to endorse a more positive conception of liberty. In contrast, I take Hayek's conceptions of liberty and coercion to be fundamentally republican in character, making his support for state provision of a minimum income consistent.

26. See Pettit 1997, 51–80.

27. What Hayek (1960, 20–21) actually said was that "by 'coercion' we mean such control of the environment or circumstances of a person by another that, in order to avoid greater evil, he is forced not to act according to a coherent plan of his own but to serve the ends of another." He also says that coercion occurs "when one man's actions are made to serve another man's will, not for his own but for the other's purpose" (ibid., 133). Coercion implies that "the alternatives before me have been so manipulated that the conduct the coercer wants me to choose becomes for me the least painful one" (ibid.).

28. Cf. Rousseau 1762, book 2, ch. 11.

29. "There are also many positive acts for the benefit of others, which he may rightfully be compelled to perform; such as, to give evidence in a court of justice; to bear his fair share in the common defence, or in any other joint work necessary to the interest of the society of which he enjoys the protection; and to perform certain acts of individual beneficence, such as saving a fellow-creature's life, or interposing to protect the defenceless against ill-usage, things which whenever it is obviously a man's duty to do, he may rightfully be made responsible to society for not doing. A person may cause evil to others not only by his actions but by his inaction, and in either case he is justly accountable to them for the injury" (Mill 1859, 224–25).

30. A conception of coercion is moralized if it counts as coercive only those threats of harm that violate people's rights, such that laws against murder don't count as coercive because one has a right not to be murdered. A conception of coercion is unmoralized if it counts fully justified threats as coercive nonetheless.

31. Hayek picks out a statement of this point from Rawls's 1963 "Constitutional Liberty and the Concept of Justice" and comments that he cannot find a comparably clear statement of the view in *A Theory of Justice*. In his later interview with Buchanan, Hayek suggests that Rawls's views changed. However, there is no reason to think that this is so. Rawls's 1963 paper said that the

task of identifying a just distribution of things to particular people had to be abandoned as mistaken in principle. In *Theory* the same ideas recur in Rawls's discussion of pure procedural justice: "If it is asked in the abstract whether one distribution of a given stock of things to definite individuals with known desires and preferences is better than another, then there is simply no answer to this question" (Rawls 1999, 76). In both works, however, he insisted that the basic institutional structure of society could be appraised as just or unjust in terms of its consequences for the distribution of benefits and burdens across social positions. In "Constitutional Liberty and the Concept of Justice," we find Rawls arguing that "inequalities as defined by the institutional structure or fostered by it are arbitrary unless it is reasonable to expect that they will work out to everyone's advantage" (Rawls 1963, 75). By "inequalities," he said that he meant "differences in the benefits and burdens attached to [offices or positions] either directly or indirectly, such as prestige, wealth, and liability for taxation and compulsory services." People don't object to the existence of different positions, but to the rewards attached to them. "Thus [people] may complain about the pattern of rewards and honors set up by an institution (e.g., the privileges and salaries of government officials) or they may object to the distribution of power and wealth which results from the various ways in which men avail themselves of the opportunities allowed by it (e.g., the concentration of wealth which may develop in a free-enterprise economy allowing large entrepreneurial and speculative gains)" (ibid.). In "Justice as Fairness" (1958, 47), he had already made clear that justice was the first virtue of social institutions or "practices," and that practices included "markets and systems of property" as well as "trials and parliaments."

32. "What a person does depends upon what rules say he will be entitled to, and what a person is entitled to depends on how he acts. The distribution which results is arrived at by honoring the claims determined by what people undertake to do in light of these legitimate expectations" (Hayek 1976, 74).
33. Philippe Van Parjis (2003, 216) has argued that when understood to apply across social positions, the difference principle is "far more responsibility-friendly (or ambition-sensitive) and hence less egalitarian (in outcome terms) than is generally understood,"
34. See Kymlicka 1990, 72–75.
35. It is also worth pointing out that Rawls (1999, 265, emph. added) defines his equal-opportunity principle in terms of social positions: "Although the internal life and culture of the family influence . . . a child's motivation and his capacity to gain from education, and so in turn his life prospects, these effects are not necessarily inconsistent with fair equality of opportunity. Even in a well-ordered society that satisfies the two principles of justice, the family may be a barrier to equal chances between individuals. For as I have defined it, the second principle only requires equal life prospects in all sectors of society [i.e., across all sectors] for those similarly endowed and motivated. If there are variations among families in the same sector in how they shape the child's aspirations, then while fair equality of opportunity may obtain between sectors, equal chances between individuals will not. This possibility raises the question as to how far the notion of equality of opportunity can be carried; but I defer comment on this until later (§77). I shall only remark here that following the difference principle and the priority rules it suggests reduces the urgency to achieve perfect equality of opportunity." "Perfect" equality of opportunity would require equality of opportunity within

as well as between sectors; fair equality of opportunity requires only equality across sectors, averaging over the idiosyncratic differences between individual families within each social position.

36. This critique of Nozick's argument about liberty and patterns is originally due to Cheyney C. Ryan (1977) and G. A. Cohen (1995). (Cohen's Wilt Chamberlain paper was first published in 1977.) See also Kymlicka 1990, 102–27 and Wolff 1991, 73–118.

37. "Hayek contradicts his claim that impersonal orders should not be judged against standards of justice by using just such a standard—a utilitarian standard—to justify the paradigm case of a spontaneous order, the market" (Lukes 1997, 74). "The claim that the market generates greater aggregate wealth than any alternative economic order constitutes a prediction about a determinate outcome of a spontaneous order. If the market order can be defended by reference to this particular outcome, it is not evident why other particular outcomes, such as the generation of an equal distribution of wealth, could not constitute a valid basis for the defense of alternative social arrangements" (Johnston 1997, 87).

38. John Gray (1982), Steven Lukes (1997, 74), and David Johnston (1997, 613) attribute a utilitarian principle to Hayek, i.e., maximal aggregate preference satisfaction.

39. Among the standard objections to taking utility as the variable to be maximized are that some people may get utility from injustice, that some people may be better at producing utility than others, and that if we believe in individual responsibility it is the opportunity for welfare that we want to maximize, not its actual achievement.

40. See also Hayek 1976, 72.

41. See also ibid., 32.

42. Also: "If it were . . . true that the central direction of the means of production could effect a collective product of at least the same magnitude as that which we now produce, it would indeed be a grave moral problem how this could be done justly. This, however, is not the position in which we find ourselves. For there is no known way, other than by the distribution of products in a competitive market, to inform individuals in what direction their several efforts must aim so as to contribute as much as possible *to the total product*" (Hayek 1988, 7, emph. added).

43. See, for example, the U.S. Census bureau's historical income table for families from 1947 to present, which gives the upper limits in 2007 dollars of the quintiles of the income distribution: http://www.webcitation.org/query?url = http%3A% 2F%2Fwww.census.gov%2Fhhes%2Fwww%2Fincome%2Fhistinc%2Ff01AR.html& date = 2009-04-12.

44. The example is suggested by the case that Thomas Nagel (1979, 123–24) puts forward of a family that has two children, one of whom is disabled, and must choose between moving to a troubled neighborhood in the city, which will bring a small benefit to the disabled child due to access to medical services and special education, or to a pleasant semi-rural suburb, which will bring larger benefits to the other child.

45. I note in passing that the differences between Rawls and Harsanyi can be overstated. Rawls argues for maximin only in the dimension of social primary goods, things like income. Part of the reason for "maximinizing" these goods is that the parties care little for gains in this dimension, beyond some level, but greatly fear falling below this level. They want to protect their so-called moral

powers, which are the ability to form, revise, and pursue a conception of the good (the contents of which they don't know) and the capacity to have and act in accordance with a conception of justice. Having some income and wealth is essential for that; having a lot is not (Rawls 1999, 134–35). In other words, past a certain point, greater amounts of social primary goods make a sharply declining contribution to the parties' fundamental interests as citizens. For a discussion of the relationship between utilitarianism and Rawls's Section 26 argument for maximin, see Mandle Forthcoming.

46. See also Hayek 1960, 92–93.

47. See also Hayek 1976, 137–42 and Hayek 1960, 100.

48. Hayek (1979a, 11) has another, even less-plausible argument against state action in service of fair equality of opportunity, which is that it will reduce the incentive parents face to work hard and make maximally productive decisions so as to be able to pass on wealth to their children. Here, Hayek seems to be saying that we should not sacrifice any bit of aggregate wealth for the sake of fair equality of opportunity.

49. "It is also characteristic of the contract doctrine to define a just society as the aim of the course of accumulation. . . . In this respect, justice as fairness contrasts with utilitarian views (§41). The just savings principle can be regarded as an understanding between generations to carry their fair share of the burden of realizing and preserving a just society. . . . Finally, the last stage at which saving is called for is not one of great abundance. . . . Justice does not require that early generations save so that later ones are simply more wealthy. Saving is demanded as a condition of bringing about the full realization of just institutions and the equal liberties. . . . It is a mistake to believe that a just and good society must wait upon a high material standard of life. What men want is meaningful work in free association with others, these associations regulating their relations to one another within a framework of just basic institutions" (Rawls 1999, 257).

50. The view I have in mind here is G. A. Cohen's, as reflected in his comments about how capitalism "corrupts humanity" in the envoi to his *If You're an Egalitarian, How Come You're So Rich?* After many years of service at a dress-making factory, Cohen's father was abruptly dismissed, simply because maxim-izing shareholder profit required it. Cohen (2000, 181) uses this incident to illustrate the way in which "business turns human producers into commodities."

51. "In the Great Society we all in fact contribute not only to the satisfaction of needs of which we do not know, but sometimes even to the achievement of ends of which we would disapprove if we knew about them. We cannot help this because we do not know for what purposes the goods or services which we supply to others will be used by them. That we assist in the realization of other people's aims without sharing them or even knowing them, and solely in order to achieve our own aims, is the source of strength of the Great Society. So long as collaboration presupposes common purposes, people with different aims are necessarily enemies who may fight each other for the same means; only the introduction of barter made it possible for the different individuals to be of use to one another without agreeing on ultimate ends" (Hayek 1976, 109–10). This insight has been emphasized recently by Gerald F. Gaus (2010, 374–75) in his "jurisdictional" account of property rights.

REFERENCES

Anderson, Elizabeth. 2005. "So You Want to Live in a Free Society (1): What Hayek Saw." *Left2Right* blog, May 27. http://left2right.typepad.com/main/2005/05/so_you_want_to_.html.

Arthur, Don. 2008. "Hayek & Rawls: An Unlikely Fusion." Evatt Foundation. http://evatt.org.au/papers/hayek-rawls.html.

Brennan, Jason. 2007. "Rawls' Paradox." *Constitutional Political Economy* 18: 287–99.

Cohen, G. A. 1995. *Self-Ownership, Freedom, and Equality.* Cambridge: Cambridge University Press.

Cohen, G. A. 2000. *If You're an Egalitarian, How Come You're So Rich?* Cambridge, Mass.: Harvard University Press.

Connin, Lawrence J. 1985. "On Diquattro, 'Rawls and Left Criticism.'" *Political Theory* 13(1): 138–41.

Feser, Edward. 1997. "Hayek on Social Justice: Reply to Lukes and Johnston." *Critical Review* 11(4): 581–606.

Freeman, Samuel, ed. 1999. *John Rawls: Collected Papers.* Cambridge, Mass.: Harvard University Press.

Gamel, Claude. 2008. "Hayek et Rawls sur La Jusice Sociale: Les Différences Sont-Elles Plus Verbales Que Substantielles?" *Cahiers d'economie politique* 54: 85–120.

Gaus, Gerald F. 2007. "On Justifying the Moral Rights of the Moderns: A Case of Old Wine in New Bottles." *Social Philosophy and Policy* 24(1): 84–119.

Gaus, Gerald F. 2010. *The Order of Public Reason: A Theory of Freedom and Morality in a Diverse and Bounded World.* Cambridge: Cambridge University Press.

Gray, John. 1982. "F. A. Hayek and the Rebirth of Classical Liberalism: A Bibliographical Essay." *Literature of Liberty: A Review of Contemporary Liberal Thought* 5(4): 19–101.

Hamowy, Ronald. 1961. "Hayek's Concept of Freedom: A Critique." *New Individualist Review* 1(1): 28–31.

Harsanyi, John C. 1953. "Cardinal Utility in Welfare Economics and in the Theory of Risk-Taking." *Journal of Political Economy* 61(5): 434–35.

Hayek, F. A. 1960. *The Constitution of Liberty.* London: Routledge and Kegan Paul.

Hayek, F. A. 1961. "Freedom and Coercion: Some Comments and Mr. Hamowy's Criticism." *New Individualist Review* 1(2): 28–32.

Hayek, F. A. 1973. *Rules and Order.* Vol. 1 of *Law, Legislation and Liberty.* Chicago: University of Chicago Press.

Hayek, F. A. 1976. *The Mirage of Social Justice.* Vol. 2 of *Law, Legislation and Liberty.* Chicago: University of Chicago Press.

Hayek, F. A. 1979a. *Social Justice, Socialism, and Democracy.* Sydney: The Centre for Independent Studies.

Hayek, F. A. 1979b. *The Political Order of a Free People.* Vol. 3 of *Law, Legislation and Liberty.* Chicago: University of Chicago Press.

Hayek, F. A. 1983. "Nobel Prize-Winning Economist Friedrich A. von Hayek." Interviewed by Earlen Craver, Axel Leijonhufvud, Leo Rosten, Jack High,

James Buchanan, Robert Bork, Thomas Hazlett, Armen A. Alchian, and Robert Chitester. University of California, Los Angeles, Library Center for Oral History Research. http://archive.org/details/nobelprizewinnin00haye.

Hayek, F. A. 1988. *The Fatal Conceit: Errors of Socialism.* London: Routledge.

Johnston, David. 1997. "Is the Idea of Social Justice Meaningful?" *Critical Review* 11 (4): 607–14.

Kymlicka, Will. 1990. *Contemporary Political Philosophy: An Introduction.* Oxford: Clarendon Press.

Lindsey, Brink. 2006. "Liberaltarians." *New Republic,* December 4.

Long, Roderick T. 2005. "Praxeology: Who Needs It." *Journal of Ayn Rand Studies* 6 (2): 299–316.

Lukes, Steven. 1997. "Social Justice: The Hayekian Challenge." *Critical Review* 11(1): 65–80.

Mack, Eric. 1983. "Hayek on Justice and the Market: A Reply to Macleod." *Canadian Journal of Philosophy* 13(4): 569–74.

Mandle, Jon. Forthcoming. "Utility." In *The Rawls Lexicon,* ed. Jon Mandle and David Reidy. Cambridge: Cambridge University Press.

Mill, John Stuart. 1859 [1977]. "On Liberty." In *Essays on Politics and Society.* Vol. 18 of *The Collected Works of John Stuart Mill.* Toronto: University of Toronto Press.

Miller, David. 1976. *Social Justice.* Oxford: Oxford University Press.

Miller, David. 1999. *Principles of Social Justice.* Cambridge, Mass.: Harvard University Press.

Nagel, Thomas. 1979. *Mortal Questions.* New York: Cambridge University Press.

Nozick, Robert. 1974. *Anarchy, State, and Utopia.* New York: Basic Books.

Van Parjis, Philippe. 2003. "Difference Principles." In *The Cambridge Companion to Rawls,* ed. Samuel Freeman. Cambridge: Cambridge University Press.

Pettit, Philip. 1997. *Republicanism: A Theory of Freedom and Government.* Oxford: Oxford University Press.

Plant, Raymond. 1991. *Modern Political Thought.* Oxford: Wiley-Blackwell.

Rawls, John. 1958 [1999]. "Justice as Fairness: Political Not Metaphysical." In Freeman 1999.

Rawls, John. 1963. "Constitutional Liberty and the Concept of Justice." In Freeman 1999.

Rawls, John. 1971. *A Theory of Justice.* Cambridge, Mass.: Harvard University Press.

Rawls, John. 1999. *A Theory of Justice,* rev. ed. Cambridge, Mass.: Harvard University Press.

Rousseau, Jean-Jacques. 1762 [1913]. *The Social Contract & Discourses.* London: J. M. Dent & Sons.

Ryan, Cheyney C. 1977. "Yours, Mine, and Ours: Property Rights and Individual Liberty." *Ethics* 87(2): 126–41.

Tebble, Adam James. 2009. "Hayek and Social Justice: A Critique." *Critical Review of International Social and Political Philosophy* 12(4): 581–604.

Tomasi, John. 2012. *Free Market Fairness.* Princeton: Princeton University Press.

Wilkinson, Will. 2006. "Is Rawlsekianism the Future?" *Cato at Liberty* blog, December 4. http://www.cato-at-liberty.org/is-rawlsekianism-the-future/.

Wilkinson, Will. 2008. "The Rawls in Rawlsekianism." Blog post, April 8. http://willwilkinson.wordpress.com/2008/04/08/the-rawls-in-rawlsekianism/.

Wolff, Jonathan. 1991. *Robert Nozick: Property, Justice, and the Minimal State.* Stanford: Stanford University Press.

Alan Ryan

THE PLANNERS AND THE PLANNED

ABSTRACT: *Much of what makes Hayek so controversial can be found in* The Road to Serfdom, *the theoretical basis of which is provided by* The Counter-Revolution of Science. *The first book, a polemic against the "planning mentality," did not defend complete laissez faire, but argued that planning disrupts the coordination between prices and supply and demand; that effective planning is thus impossible in a modern industrial society; that it is coercive; and, of course, that it leads to totalitarianism. In* The Counter-Revolution of Science, *Hayek argued that the "planning mentality" is the result of the hubristic attempt to reconstruct society along scientific lines. But the likes of Edward Bellamy envisioned a planned but free society, while John Dewey contrasted planning, where people collectively choose their goals, against a planned economy that is coercively imposed. Hayek's welcome strictures against a scientistic society and an overly ambitious social science aside, his binary approach to intellectual history distorted through oversimplification.*

This essay may be thought self-indulgent; if it is, I apologize. Fifty years ago, I read Hayek in the course of getting myself an education in the philosophy of social science and theories of history. I therefore read him alongside Karl Popper and John Stuart Mill—whose letters he had done so much to rescue after they had been scattered in all directions and many of them, together with others of Mill's manuscripts, destroyed by enemy action when the Chancery Lane branch of the National Provincial Bank was bombed in 1941.

I read *The Road to Serfdom* (1944) and was not much moved; it did not seem to me that Clement Attlee had launched Britain on the primrose path to a Stalinist nightmare, nor that the Conservative governments in the 1950s, practicing "Butskellism"—the social and economic policies of (the Labour leader) Hugh Gaitskell and (the Conservative) R.A.B Butler—were any more likely to lead to the gulag and the concentration camp. *The Counter-Revolution of Science* (1952) was another matter; it was evidently all of a piece with Popper's *Poverty of Historicism* (1957) as well as *The Road to Serfdom*, and fascinating. The mixture of philosophical critique, political polemic, and history of ideas was deeply engaging even if not always absolutely persuasive. What follows is not a contribution to Hayek scholarship, but a second look at these two books and the connections between them, with the benefit of hindsight and against the background of a couple of alternative views on planning, democracy, and the *hubris* of social scientists: one from an American socialist whom Hayek does not mention; the other from an American liberal democrat whom Hayek mentions only in passing.

Hayek's career in Vienna, London, Chicago, and Freiburg im Breisgau defies summary. Although in his later years he became an icon of the American libertarian right, he was not a libertarian in the American sense and he disliked the term a good deal. He may perhaps not have been wholly at ease in an American setting at all; he kept his British citizenship, although, like his close friend Popper, he was eventually buried in Vienna. It may be significant that Hayek spent only eleven years at the University of Chicago, as against twenty at the London School of Economics; that in Chicago he was a member of the Committee on Social Thought rather than a member of the economics department; that the last decades of his very long life were largely spent in southern Germany; and that although many of his most enthusiastic followers are to be found in America, he had more impact on British economic and political life than anywhere else.[1]

Part of the reason, paradoxically, is that the British political system is highly centralized, and that once Sir Keith Joseph and the *Institute of Economic Affairs* had persuaded Mrs. Thatcher that Hayek's *Constitution of Liberty* (1960) rather than Harold Macmillan's *The Middle Way* (1938) should be the Conservative Party's bible, she had no difficulty remaking the party in her new image. It helped that Reagan came to power only a few months later than Thatcher, and that he, like she, had advisers and confidants who were admirers of Hayek.

In the face of his appeal to iconic conservative figures such as Mrs. Thatcher, it is somewhat paradoxical that Hayek was insistent that he was not a conservative. Many of his admirers took no notice and insisted that he was: They were self-confessed conservatives, they held the same views as he, *ergo* he was a conservative. His problem was not unprecedented; Herbert Hoover bitterly resented being cast as a conservative, thinking himself an old-fashioned liberal devoted to "rugged individualism." By the end of his life, he admitted that this was probably a lost cause. Hayek refused to accept that it was a lost cause; he saw himself, rightly, as a "classical liberal" or, as he sometimes said, a "Burkean Whig," sharing Burke's belief in the importance of tradition—the inexplicit, and perhaps inexplicable, understandings and attachments that allowed a society to spontaneously develop along productive lines—along with Burke's attachment to the economics of Adam Smith's *Wealth of Nations*. It is impossible to guess what Burke would have made of Darwin and modern evolutionary theory, but it is not hard to see the similarities between Burke's attachment to a loosely evolutionary account of the development of a legal and political system, exemplified by the development of the English common law, and Hayek's preference for British liberalism over its Continental counterpart. Classical liberals were committed to Smith's "simple system of natural liberty" and, allowances duly made for the greater sophistication of subsequent economic theory, that is what Hayek was committed to as well.

Although Hayek was an extremely accomplished economist, this was not the reason for his post-1945 importance. Gunnar Myrdal is said to have resented having to share the Nobel Prize for economics in 1974 with someone he thought of as an ideologue. But Hayek's allies frequently thought less of him as an economist than as a political theorist and a social thinker in a broad sense. Milton Friedman was sometimes very rude about parts of Hayek's economics, but quite sure that *The Road to Serfdom* was one of the great books of the twentieth century. Keynes was both a rival of Hayek in the 1930s and (by most reckonings) the victor in their contest to produce a compelling account of the causes of, and possible cure for, the Great Depression; but he too thought highly of *The Road to Serfdom*. Isaiah Berlin, on the other hand, did not, although he thought well of Hayek's critique of historical inevitability, and thought Hayek more acute than Popper about the differences between history and natural science.

Before embarking on what makes *The Road to Serfdom* and *The Counter-Revolution of Science* interesting today, even if no more completely persuasive than they were when they were written, I should say why it is not surprising that Keynes admired the former work—he died some years before the latter was published as a substantial book, but had doubtless read the first sections when they were published as articles in *Economica* in 1941 and 1942. Keynes was a "new liberal" in the sense in which L. T. Hobhouse and Bertrand Russell were: They believed in a more activist state and thought the state had a role in civilizing its citizens, as well as a role in ensuring their health and sustaining them in unemployment, ill health, or old age. But many new liberals shared two anxieties more or less equal and opposite in nature.

One anxiety—expressed very clearly by Beveridge (1909 and 1942), the begetter of the British welfare state—was that workers who were not impelled by the fear of starvation would simply not work. The question was what to do about them. They could hardly have their benefits withdrawn and be left to die in the gutter. More than thirty years before he published the *Report* that laid the foundations for the post-1945 British welfare state, Beveridge imagined there might be a need to create work camps in the countryside in order to solve the problem. Hayek himself quotes Sir Richard Acland, the founder and leader of the Common-wealth Party, suggesting that the work-shy should be sent to "agreeable" camps in the countryside and put to work.

Comment on the attractiveness of *Arbeit macht frei* in post-1945 Britain is otiose. An interesting question is why impeccably practically minded public administrators and economists might think in such extreme terms. I have only two (rather feeble) suggestions. One is that it was part of the *déformation professionelle* of economists used to thinking of pure cases; if we remove the familiar disincentive to idleness provided by a market system that will not pay those who will not work, we need some other disincentive, and what incentive more obvious than imprisonment? The other anxiety was Hayek's own. It was a slippery-slope argument. If we — collective "we" operating through the medium of the state—took responsibility for some aspects of individual welfare, why not others? If taking responsibility for more and more aspects of individuals' welfare turned out to be complicated, we would need more and more control over their behavior to ensure that they really did live the decent lives we had in mind for them. It is in effect the road to Huxley's *Brave New World*. Isaiah Berlin, knowing the vast distance between Stalin's Russia and anything that his friends in the British Labour Party might put their names to, could easily dismiss Hayek's fears; Keynes, knowing what schemes might be hatched in the imaginations of his friends—Bertrand Russell (who thought that Huxley had stolen the idea of a brave new world from him) and the Webbs (who thought Stalin had created a new civilization) among them—saw the warning as useful and necessary.

The Road to Serfdom

The Road to Serfdom sold very well as a book from the outset, but paper shortages both in Britain and the United States limited the number of copies that could be printed and circulated. When it was reduced to less than a quarter of its length and published in the *Reader's Digest*, it rode on the back of the magazine's circulation of 160,000. The condensation was said by Hayek himself to be astonishingly successful; it is certainly a striking simplification of an argument that was not in the first place very complicated, and which could be reduced to essentials by the omission of the long discussion of the nineteenth- and twentieth-century progenitors and defenders of fascism. It found an enormous American audience, predisposed, as the 1946 midterm elections revealed, to believe that nothing but a return to the world as it was before the New Deal would save America from Bolshevism, at worst, "creeping socialism," at best.

That the book was a huge success in the United States was not because it was particularly directed at the United States. Although Hayek invoked a number of American proponents and critics of planning in his general denunciation of the planning mentality, most of his targets were British (and not infrequently colleagues or former colleagues at the London School of Economics), while the argument that socialism led to fascism by quick and inevitable steps was largely based on evidence from Germany and Italy, and the similarities between Stalinism and Nazism were obviously based on Russian as well as German evidence.

The basic structure of the argument against planning was simple enough, but the hinterland to it was equally interesting though less visible. The hinterland was the old problem of socialist calculation. *If* it was possible to calculate the optimal allocation of the productive resources of a society, central planning ought in principle to be able to ensure that the economy harnessed everyone's skills and energies, as well as the productive capacities of all available raw material and technologies, thus securing without friction a result that the private-property-based free market could only approximate in a roundabout and trial-and-error fashion.

It is plain that some such vision animated Marx and, as we shall see, the late nineteenth century American socialist Edward Bellamy, among many others. Marx could see in capitalism only obstacles to the efficient production of all that we need, and thought that with the abolition of the private ownership of the means of production all that would remain would be relatively simple technical questions whose solutions were rationally unchallengeable. There would be no deep conflicts of interest remaining after the destruction of capitalism and irrational challenges were not be expected either.

Hayek learned his economics from those who had demonstrated that the calculation problem could not be solved. Intuitively, it is obvious enough that Marx's vision is internally incoherent: Only if both our wants and abilities are stable and predictable can the optimization calculation be performed. But it is an axiom of Marx's social vision that we shall become unpredictably more interesting creatures, possessed of greater abilities, developing new wants, and will therefore no doubt imagine both new goods to consume and new ways to produce them. To achieve what Marx wanted we would have to be able to predict the unpredictable.

Hayek's argument presupposed the impossibility of achieving the complete non-coercive control of the economic machine anticipated by Marx. What *The Road to Serfdom* did, and very effectively, was to spell out the disasters to be expected from an attempt to create the utopia envisaged by Marx. Because Hayek belonged to what one might call the "and moreover" school of polemic, it is not easy to recreate the structure of the argument. It is probably more sensible to seize on three or four salient points before turning to the way in which *The Counter-Revolution of Science* provides the underpinnings of *The Road to Serfdom*.

First, Hayek did not defend what he thought of as laissez faire. He was sure—and I think never budged from his view—that governments needed to perform a substantial number of the tasks that any welfare state tries to perform, such as providing unemployment and disability benefits, health care and pensions. But this was not in the interest of promoting equality for its own sake, only in the interest of insuring the unlucky against non-culpable misfortune. Even when attacking the myth of social justice later in life, he seemed concerned to make nothing more than the conceptual point that misfortune that could not be laid at the door of a human agent was *only* misfortune, not injustice, and that alleviating it was humanitarianism, not social justice.

A second point Hayek emphasized in *The Road to Serfdom* was that planning in the sense at issue was incompatible with democracy. This must be true in the terms in which the discussion proceeds. Inasmuch as a global plan is legitimated by its rationality, it is not a matter of what anyone in particular wants; if individuals are free to vote to reject bits of it, the plan collapses. Therefore, even if the plan might be instituted or initially legitimated by referendum or plebiscite, it could not thereafter be subjected to democratic revision.

Third, the incompatibility of plan and popular government is an aspect of the larger problem that trying to institute a global plan must increase the role of coercion in social and economic life. Whereas participants in a market economy cannot coerce anyone else to act in a particular way, work at a particular occupation, pay a particular price for a good, and so generally on, a planned economy rejects the "signaling" function of prices and in effect militarizes the economy. People must work as directed or face physical sanctions; goods must be sold at the price dictated, regardless of resulting gluts or shortages; and anyone who reintroduces flexibility by raising or lowering a mandated price will be arrested as a black marketeer. The thought that there are only two options—coercion or free exchange—is perhaps the leading idea that liberals of Hayek's persuasion extracted from Locke, or more exactly from Locke via Kant. There are innumerable ways in which one might justify the existence of private property, including property in our own persons and labor, but one very powerful route is the argument that it provides the basis for the most minimally coercive and maximally voluntary system of economic coordination.

The fourth point in *The Road to Serfdom* is that what is by now emerging as a thoroughly totalitarian system will encourage the rise of the worst sort of person to positions of power. Not everyone who works to administer a totalitarian system of authority will be as intrinsically evil as a monster such as Heydrich, but the system will reward people in proportion to their ruthlessness. This is not to deny that many people— the Communist Party of the Soviet Union was obviously full of them— will try to keep out of sight, doing enough to placate their bosses without excessively alienating those whom they are meant to be pushing around. They, however, neither want to rise to the top nor have any prospect of doing so. The ambitious, on the other hand, will have to be energetically ruthless, and the more unprincipled and brutal they are, the speedier their ascent. This is not at all like Hannah Arendt's depiction of Eichmann, of course, nor even very like many other writers' depiction of someone like Speer, but it fits a good many of Hitler's and Stalin's associates. One might wonder perhaps whether a keen student of Machiavelli would have offered the more nuanced thought that both lions and foxes are likely to rise to the top of a totalitarian system, but that the man who rises to the very top will be the one who is both lion and fox.

The penultimate point worth picking out is more nearly Orwellian, but it is central to Hayek's hatred of totalitarianism. Hayek was a significant philosopher and historian of ideas who thought that the aspiration for total control is the death of a concern for truth. Against Hayek one might contend that Marx himself was, for the most part, bleakly honest about the prospects of revolution, the competence of his fellow revolutionaries, and much else. Nonetheless, the track record of the Soviet Union justifies Hayek's argument. Essentially, the argument is that once a country is committed to a plan—think of Stalin's Five-Year Plans—those whose authority and prestige hinges on the success of the plan have too much to lose by allowing doubts about its success to be ventilated. Covering up what everyone knows is one part of the story; the other is that little by little the criterion of truth comes to be whatever the party or its leadership dictates. *The Road to Serfdom* was written before Lysenko was allowed to destroy Soviet plant breeding, but he is the poster-child for Hayek's point.

The final point to emphasize is one that takes us back to the beginning. Proponents of a planned society commonly insisted on the extent to which modern industrial societies were in the grip of forces too strong for individuals to control. There is an obvious tension between a belief in historical inevitability and in the necessity of planning, but most enthusiasts for a planned economy, at least most of those whom Hayek went after in *The Road to Serfdom* and *The Counter-Revolution of Science*, were historicists in his and Popper's sense of the term. History had, so to speak, brought us to the point where we had to take conscious control of our productive powers *as a society*. This was not the banality that individuals should use forethought and common sense to plan their individual futures, but the claim that society as a whole should use its collective intelligence to plan its future.

What *The Counter-Revolution of Science* argued, and what *The Road to Serfdom* depended on, was the claim—multiple claims really—that there was no such entity as society as a whole. There were patterns of interaction between individuals, but these had to be understood from the inside as the unintended outcomes of intended actions. There were genuine patterns, otherwise the discipline of economics would have been impossible. But these were not "natural" in the sense in which the patterned interactions of physical and chemical phenomena are natural. Even the latter, Hayek sometimes seemed to suggest, owed a good deal of their "meaning" at least to human conceptualization; but at all events, patterned human interaction *had* to be understood as resting on the intentions and understanding of conscious human agents.

Then the deep paradox struck. The emphasis on impersonal forces and the downplaying of the significance of individuals would lead to a society in which we were at the mercy of individuals—but, as in a feudal society, individuals who were armed with the powers of the legal system and the coercive machinery that backed the law. They would decide whether we were employed or starved, where we lived, where we could travel, and so on down the line. It was no accident that communist societies were riddled with corruption; wherever the powerless are at the mercy of officials, and especially of underpaid officials, bribery in one form and another is to be expected. A society in which we were at the mercy of unintended and undirected misfortunes, such as a lack of demand for the goods and services by which we had hoped to make a living, may be very bad news; nonetheless, the misfortunes are not directed at us, and there is no suggestion that if we contrive to avoid them we shall be pursued and punished. Indeed, if we can find new and legitimate ways of making a living, we shall thrive and prosper. "Serfdom" really was the right term, for Hayek's polemical purposes, since the threat was of a new feudalism.

The Counter-Revolution of Science

The underpinnings of *The Road to Serfdom* were provided by *The Counter-Revolution of Science*. It is not a work to summarize lightly, although the overarching theses are straightforward. One is that the totalitarian state is history's revenge on the *hubris* of Enlightenment enthusiasts for the scientific reconstruction of society; the search for heaven on earth under the aegis of the omnicompetent state infallibly leads to hell on earth. Hayek's long discussion of the ways in which the subjective nature of social interaction defeats the attempt to find laws in the strict sense of natural laws of human behavior is both interesting in its own right and crucial to demolishing the very possibility of the utopian project of the Enlightenment rationalists. It belongs with the anti-utopianism of Berlin's essays on the same subject, written around the same time.

From this distance one might wonder why so many writers took up this theme simultaneously; one would suppose that the war had sufficiently discredited both fascism and communism. The answer, of course, is that it had not. Certainly fascism was thoroughly discredited outside Spain and Portugal; communism was anything but. In both France and Italy, the communist party secured between a fifth and a quarter of the popular vote for almost two decades after the war. Even in countries where communism had never gained much of a foothold, such as Great Britain, communist organizers wielded a disproportionate influence within the trade unions; the name of Bert Ramelson will be familiar to any Briton over the age of 50. The *Daily Worker* sold well, and it took several years before gratitude to the Soviet Union for its part in the destruction of Nazi Germany was wholly replaced by fear of its ambitions in Europe and disgust at its murderous and repressive behaviour at home and throughout the Soviet bloc.

It was therefore of the essence to argue, as Hayek did at length in *The Road to Serfdom*, that fascism was simply the bastard child of socialism. The greater part of *The Counter-Revolution of Science* is almost a prolegomenon to that task since it traces the socialist pedigree to the man who sometimes seems to be, in Hayek's mind, the *fons et origo* of every disaster to befall the twentieth century. This was not Marx but Comte.

Marx emerges as just one of Comte's disastrous offspring—as it turned out, the most influential of those who put the poisonous mixture of German historicism and French positivism into circulation—but not its originator. The role of Comte comes as something of a surprise to the unwary reader, because Hayek spends a great deal of time on Saint-Simon, tracing his impact on his German contemporaries and juniors in immense scholarly detail. Only late in the narrative does Hayek tell us that the works of Saint-Simon that had the greatest impact were those that were (very probably) written by Auguste Comte.

Whatever else we might think, it is exceedingly hard to deny that Comte was a passionate anti-liberal. Many positivists, especially in Britain and America, combined a generally liberal worldview with an attachment to a Comtean ethic of *"vivre pour autrui,"* and perhaps with an ability to overlook Comte's own foibles (such as his wish to see Clothilde de Vaux accepted as the Religion of Humanity's version of the Virgin Mary). But Hayek insists that Comte himself was no milk-and-water anti-liberal; Mill's description of Comte's views as "liberticide" was all too accurate (Mill 1855, 214). No more than Lenin did Comte believe that freedom of thought and speech possessed any value once the "scientific" view of social change had been established.

I want to raise one question about all this, as much from a history-of-ideas perspective as anything else. For Hayek, the crucial dividing line is between individualists and collectivists, historicists and their critics, those who would abolish private property and individual choice in favor of the planned society, whose similarity to an army on the march did not escape Hayek or anyone else. This rides roughshod over another distinction to which it is odd that he did not—here at least—pay more attention. To put it crudely, it is the dividing line between Saint-Simonians and Marxists; the former think in terms of "industrial society" and the latter in terms of "modes of production" built around particular forms of private property. The latter think in terms of exploitation and the extraction of surplus value from the direct producers, the former in terms of rational and irrational forms of management. The latter cannot but think in terms of violent revolution, the former in essentially evolutionary terms.

In the middle of the twentieth century, it was for many commentators an open question whether the Soviet Union and Western industrial societies might not converge on an almost identical pattern of production, with large, bureaucratically managed undertakings driven by a desire for security and predictability, profoundly averse to gales of creative destruction. This was to imagine the non-violent euthanasia of capitalism and communism alike: Communism would abandon the pursuit of worldwide proletarian revolution, make undertakings more responsive to consumers, relax censorship, and permit something closer to genuine democracy, while capitalism would rely on government to smooth the adjustment to new technologies, provide an educated and cooperative workforce, operate a welfare state, and sponsor the scientific research on which a modern industrial economy depended. Cut-throat competition would be a thing of the past, although there would be plenty of scope for the kind of competition illustrated by the choice between a Ford and a Chevy or an Apple or Samsung smartphone.

The notion that what was on offer was one or other variety of an "industrial society" was deeply depressing to Marxists who hankered after old-fashioned class conflict culminating in a genuine socialist revolution. It was no more attractive to people of Hayek's persuasion, who hankered after the return of a more nearly Victorian capitalism. One reason for wondering why Hayek did not explore the differences between the Saint-Simonian and Marxian visions of capitalism and their socialist successor economies is that the Saint-Simonian vision provides the basis for an account of a liberal corporate state in which the usual liberal freedoms are preserved along with representative democracy. The Marxian vision does not. But if some sort of corporate liberalism is possible that does not bring with it the horrors of a totalitarian state of the Soviet or Nazi variety, Hayek's "either/or" loses its persuasive force.

Bellamy's Looking Backward

Hayek spends a great deal of time in *The Road to Serfdom*, and the great majority of *The Counter-Revolution of Science*, drawing up a bill of indictment against French and German intellectuals and radicals of the nineteenth century. However, one writer with whom he does not engage spent a great deal of ingenuity trying to evade the grim predictions of *The Road to Serfdom*.

Edward Bellamy's *Looking Backward*, a utopian novel written in 1887, was hugely successful; it was second only to *Uncle Tom's Cabin* among nineteenth-century best-sellers. Significantly, Bellamy did not call his utopia a "socialist" one, because he thought the word smelled of gasoline—the crucial ingredient of what were later known as Molotov cocktails—and reminded people of marital infidelity and atheism. It was a "nationalist" utopia; it arose as the culmination of the rise of the great trusts, which eventually coalesced into the one national trust that produced and distributed everything everyone needed or wanted.

The title of *Looking Backward* referred to the trope that animated the book: Its hero had fallen asleep in the Boston of 1887, deeply unhappy with a world rife with class conflict, insecurity, wasteful (as he saw it) competition and the prospect of wars over markets and imperial prestige. He had been reawakened in the Boston of the year 2000 to find that the economy was in the hands of the one great trust; that classes no longer existed; and that everyone worked for twenty years at an occupation of their own choosing to which they were suited by talent and training, and then spent their leisure years on whatever avocation they wished.

Dr. Leete, the Bostonian of the year 2000 who explains the workings of utopia to the sleeper, Julian West, is at pains to insist that the ultra-planned society is wholly non-coercive. It is, of course, true that everyone must work at something or other, but everyone receives an identical share of the national output in the form of a pre-figured credit card, containing so many "credits" for use within the next year (money having been abolished). The calculation problem has been solved, though we are never told how, and consumers have complete freedom of choice in how they will allocate their credits. Meanwhile, everyone works for a few years as a common laborer—which is the obvious analogue to national service—and thereafter chooses the occupation that best suits them. Given that incomes do not vary, what does vary is the hours of work expected; a process of *tatonnement* takes place to adjust the numbers coming forward to the amount of work required, and if there are any goods whose production would require workers to work in an entirely unacceptable fashion, they are not produced at all.

The question is not whether Bellamy's utopia could be realized, nor whether it would not be intolerably boring if it were. Dr. Leete is not to the modern taste. The point is rather that on the face of it, devices to avoid all the horrors that Hayek insists must inevitably attend the search for a planned economy can be created and can work. Or to put it more tartly, Bellamy's utopianism begs hardly more questions than does Hayek's dystopianism.

Dewey's Liberalism and a "Planning Society"

Among the ranks of those one might count as "new liberals," Dewey occupies a fairly prominent place. For our purposes, his significance is that he combined a passionate belief in democracy—a term he interpreted in a particularly wide sense—with a belief in making modern industrial society more rational, better organized, and more productive of a good life for all the citizenry.

Dewey would have met with blank disbelief Hayek's insistence that planning and democracy are incompatible. If anything, Dewey would have retorted that democracy and an unplanned economy are incompatible. Dewey, of course, was not an economist, although his brother George was (and was indeed the first president of the American Economics Association). More to the point perhaps, Dewey was notably uninterested in setting out the details of the institutional arrangements he thought should govern a modern democracy and a modern industrial economy. He certainly believed in industrial democracy, and thought that democracy in the workplace was an essential complement to political democracy. As in Bellamy's novel, however, it was never clear quite what mechanisms he thought we needed to employ if it was to be achieved.

Be that as it may, Dewey certainly did not like the idea of a "planned economy," suggesting instead that what was needed was a "planning" economy.

Dewey was animated by the idea that we might collectively work out what sort of life we wished to live together and how we were to do it. Because he opposed the idea of fixed goals of any sort, he was inclined to think that the great value was what he termed "growth." Unlike the growth of plants, which tends towards a species-specific and fixed end, growth in the case of the human species is open-ended. This is not the place to explore the difficulties of Dewey's view, which are obvious enough; Dewey's position was not foolish, but it was elusive. He retained enough of what Hegel summarized in his notorious claim that "the owl of Minerva flies only with the falling of the dusk" to allow himself some room for maneuver; we might not be certain when *in media res* whether we were "growing" or "retrogressing," but we would know it on reflection.

The evolutionary perspective suggests that we could stand back a little from our immediate concerns and ask whether the species *Homo sapiens* is thriving or the reverse, and with hindsight come to a consensus about the answer—though whether an answer is valid for more than short periods and circumscribed geographical areas is another matter. Nor, of course, would any answer be invulnerable to a critic who just disliked the human race for whatever reason, or who was sincerely convinced that some divinely instituted program lay behind the ups and downs of human history to make sense of it all. We can dislike a thriving community of mosquitoes and by the same token think the human race better off never to have existed; and we can see ourselves as playthings of the gods, or, more satisfyingly, as actors in the divine comedy. Pragmatism cannot stop us from doing so, though one may suppose we shall be few in number and easily ignored.

My object, however, is not to provide Dewey with a metaphysics for which he never saw the need. It is only to suggest that Dewey's concept of a "planning" as against a "planned" society is not vulnerable to Hayek's strictures in *The Road to Serfdom*. Indeed, Dewey was, like other writers at *The New Republic* around the time of the First World War, inclined to think that it was unplanned capitalism that was more likely to recreate serfdom. Social mobility and a wide-open economy might have characterized the early days of American capitalism, but by the early years of the twentieth century, the rich were in a fair way to locking up the social, economic, and political systems. The actual operation of the individualist system was at odds with its ideological justification. When Herbert Croly said in *The Promise of American Life* (1909) that he was advocating the pursuit of Jeffersonian goals by Hamiltonian means, he meant that if the promise held up to the world by the American Revolution was to be fulfilled, there needed to be a concerted political effort to achieve it. It could not be left to chance, and it would not be handed to Americans by destiny or fate.

Dewey was more cautious about putting his trust in politicians, but the doctrine is not dissimilar. Dewey was also unwilling to talk about "the State," having a profound skepticism of the Hegelian tendency to elevate its role in history. As the title of *The Public and its Problems* (1927) suggests, his preferred category was "the public," and his view of democracy was that it was a problem-solving device. The problem to be solved was overcoming the disorganized condition of a world in which "rugged" individualism had degenerated into merely "ragged" individualism.

There is much to be said against conceiving of a democratic society as a quasi-scientific community formulating and resolving its "problems." But the one thing that can't be said is that it is a road to serfdom.

NOTE

1. It is perhaps rash to say so; Eastern Europe was at one point full of passionate disciples in a way in which Britain never was. Hayek was influential among Conservative politicians, subscribers to the IEA, and a smallish number of academics; crucially, his views appealed to Mrs. Thatcher, who made him a

Companion of Honour in 1984. He never received the knighthood he would have liked, but the CH is second only to the OM in prestige.

REFERENCES

Bellamy, Edward. 1887. *Looking Backward: 2000–1887.* New York: Houghton Mifflin.

Beveridge, William. 1909. *Unemployment: A Problem of Industry.* London: Longmans, Green and Co.

Beveridge, William. 1942. "Social Insurance and Allied Services." Report of the Inter-Departmental Committee. London: His Majesty's Stationery Office.

Croly, Herbert. 1909. *The Promise of American Life.* New York: Macmillan.

Dewey, John. 1927. *The Public and Its Problems.* New York: Holt Publishers.

Hayek, F. A. 1944. *The Road to Serfdom.* Chicago: University of Chicago Press.

Hayek, F. A. 1952. *The Counter-Revolution of Science: Studies in the Abuse of Reason.* New York: Macmillian.

Hayek, F. A. 1960. *Constitution of Liberty.* London: Routledge and Kegan Paul.

Macmillan, Harold. 1938. *The Middle Way.* London: Macmillan & Co.

Mill, John Stuart. 1855 [2006]. Letter to Harriett Mill, January 15. In *Collected Works,* vol. 14. Ed. Francis E. Mineka and Dwight N. Lindley. Toronto: University of Toronto Press.

Popper, Karl. 1957. *The Poverty of Historicism.* London: Routledge.

Michael Strong

SOME IMPLICATIONS OF HAYEK'S COGNITIVE THEORY

ABSTRACT: *Hayek's oft-neglected cognitive theory, articulated in* The Sensory Order, *provides a foundation for a theory of innovation that integrates cognition, experience, and the importance of freedom for the creation of entirely new conceptual categories and fundamentally innovative entrepreneurial endeavors. For Hayek, one sees only what one is prepared to see; that is, we can notice sensory and other phenomena only after we have classified the data into often-implicit abstract categories that are mediated to us physiologically. Learning takes places by using received categories while innovation takes place by creating new categories or moving data from one category to another, which is often an attempt to resolve anomalies. The new perceptual awareness required for discovery leads, in turn, to new categorizing and new perceptual horizons. Such innovation often requires not just freedom of imagination, but freedom of action, for one has to be able to try out many different perceptual possibilities.*

The gist of Hayek's interpretation of the economy is often taken to be his short essay, "The Use of Knowledge in Society" (Hayek 1945), in which Hayek discusses the implications of the fact that crucial economic knowledge is diffused throughout a society. Because Hayek supports the price system as a means of disseminating information, neoclassical economists have generally understood Hayek to be pointing exclusively to the type of "knowledge" that may be transmitted through the economy by means of prices.

From this "arbitrage" interpretation of Hayek, further developed by Israel Kirzner (1978), one might summarize the primary Hayekian insight to be that because price information is distributed throughout a society in such a manner that central planners cannot have access to it, markets therefore need entrepreneurs to play the role of arbitrageurs to discover and profit from discrepancies in prices. This "knowledge as prices" interpretation of Hayek leads to the neglect and dismissal of Hayek's deeper insights regarding cognition and entrepreneurial discovery. For instance, Richard Posner (2005, 160) argues that "with central planning and other forms of utopian social engineering now so thoroughly discredited, it is unclear what if any significance Hayek's cognitive theory and the political-economic theory that he derived from it retain." Yet in truth, Hayek did not view entrepreneurial discovery as a mere effect of price arbitrage. Instead, he thought that it stems from novel perceptions of value. This theory of innovation builds on Hayek's cognitive theory.

Hayek's Cognitive Theory: Perception and Learning

Hayek sets out the most important elements of this theory in *The Sensory Order* (1952)—sometimes regarded as an obscure detour in Hayek's corpus, a peculiar interlude between his work in economics and in political theory. However, *The Sensory Order* reflects the continuity of Hayek's lifelong attempt to understand society from an epistemological point of view. It is a crucial stepping stone between Hayekian arguments that emphasize the arbitrage perspective of entrepreneurship, such as those presented in "The Use of Knowledge in Society" (Hayek 1945), and arguments in which creativity is central, such as the 1956 essay, "The Creative Powers of a Free Civilization," later included as the second chapter of Hayek's 1960 magnum opus, *The Constitution of Liberty*.

Most cognitive theorists and epistemologists attempt to explain how we know what we know. But one of the most striking facts about Western civilization is that we are constantly learning new things. Indeed, over time, we come to know dramatically new things. As a consequence, our perceptual and experiential reality is constantly changing at a dramatic pace, and yet we hardly realize it. The notion that innovation takes place exclusively through science and technology dramatically restricts our awareness of the innovations that are constantly taking place around us moment by moment.

Hayek's theory of the ongoing creation of new knowledge has three elements. First, our interpretations of the world are suffused with ignorance. Second, when we notice contradictions in our existing interpretations, we are led to new perceptions. Finally, these new perceptions empower us to create new products, services, enterprises, and institutions.

Hayek starts by arguing that perception is not the passive reception of sensory inputs. Instead, perceptual inputs are incorporated into cognitions that have been pre-formed by extant cognitive categories: "Every sensation, even the 'purest,' must therefore be regarded as an interpretation of an event in the light of the past experience of the individual or the species" (Hayek 1952, 166) for "it is only in so far as the nervous system has learnt thus to treat a particular stimulus as a member of a certain class of events, determined by the connexions which all the corresponding impulses possess with the same impulses representing other classes of events, that an event can be perceived at all, i.e., that it can obtain a distinct position in the system of sensory qualities" (ibid.)

This is hardly a surprising perspective, though it may have been when Hayek originally wrote it. Artificial Intelligence (AI) researchers in the intervening years have abundantly shown that, in order for "perception" to be operational—i.e., to result in useful action of any kind—a mind requires an interpretive schema. For instance, computer-vision expert Richard Szeliski (2011, 7) writes:

> If someone comes to me and asks for a good edge detector, my first question is usually to ask *why*? What kind of problem are they trying to solve and why do they believe that edge detection is an important component? If they are trying to locate faces, I usually point out that most successful face detectors use a combination of skin color detection and simple blob features; they do not rely on edge detection. If they are trying to match door and window edges in a building for the purpose of 3D reconstruction, I tell them that edges are a fine idea but it is better to tune the edge detector for long edges and link them together into straight lines with common vanishing points before matching.

In the present state of the art, different recognition tasks rely on different algorithms that identify different elements as salient. A "visual field" that consists merely of undifferentiated data cannot guide action.

Indeed, one of the greatest challenges of AI is to create artificial minds that can determine perceptual salience across a robust variety of contexts and situations—something that human minds do remarkably well. For instance, in order to perceive a cubic block in order to manipulate it, a robotic mind needs to include an algorithm that assesses the perceptual patterns that mark the boundary perimeter of the block. Such an algorithm translates an undifferentiated mass of information into specific, separable "objects." The attributes, however, do not exist in the data intrinsically but are determined by the nature of the algorithm. Different algorithms would produce different object boundaries, different behavioral capabilities, and different perceptual realities.

This fact is sometimes difficult for us to grasp because we so utterly take for granted our own perceptual algorithms, which determine the salience (for us) of experiential attributes. But an AI researcher cannot take such algorithms for granted. It turns out to be quite difficult to find a complete general-purpose perceptual algorithm that has the flexibility of the human mind. For robotic minds, different perceptual algorithms (even when using evolved software) result in different perceptual capabilities and, consequently, different behavioral capabilities.

In Hayek's cognitive theory, just as robotic minds today are engaged in an ongoing process of development in order to improve performance, so too the human mind is engaged in an ongoing process of development in order to improve performance. Although human beings with normal capabilities can see and manipulate cubes well enough, there are an unlimited range of perceptual phenomena that are not yet perceived and thus on which we cannot yet act. Just as we may observe a robotic toy with simple sensors blindly bumping up against walls before turning around only to bump up against a different wall, so too, from the Hayekian perspective on cognition, human beings at any particular point of development are merely agents that bump up blindly against obstacles that will appear perceptually obvious to them from a later stage of development.

Useful perceptions depend, first of all, on interpretive schema drawn from past experience, which suggests that new experiences can always inspire new perceptions.

> Every sensory experience of an event in the external world is . . . likely to possess "attributes" (or to be in a manner distinguished from other sensory events) to which no similar attributes of the external events correspond.

These "attributes" are the significance which the organism has learnt to assign to a class of events on the basis of the past associations of events of this class with certain other classes of events. (Hayek 1952, 166)

Advances in perception are driven by learning, which leads to changes in cognition. Thus, while for a physicist, the scratchy lines in a cloud-chamber photograph clearly represent the paths of specific subatomic particles, for the rest of us they are merely scratchy lines. The physicist has *learned* to assign a particular pattern with the event she categorizes as, for example, "the trail of a neutron." Learning to read cloud-chamber photographs is a matter of learning to categorize certain classes of events (the lines in a new cloud-chamber photograph) on the basis of past associations of events of this class (previous neutron trails) with certain other classes of events (the physicist's conceptual understanding of the characteristics of neutrons and the consequent anticipated characteristics of their trails on cloud-chamber photographs).

Progressing via Inconsistencies

Hayek identifies a cognitive process that results in learning in the sense of developing novel cognitive schema that allow people to perceive phenomena that had not previously been perceived:

> While there can . . . be nothing in our mind which is not the result of past linkages (even though, perhaps, acquired not by the individual but by the species), the experience that the classification based on the past linkages does not always work, i.e., does not always lead to valid predictions, forces us to revise that classification. In the course of this process of reclassification we not only establish new relations between the data within a fixed framework of reference, i.e., between the elements of given classes: but since the framework consists of the relations determining the classes, we are led to adjust that framework itself. (Hayek 1952, 168–69)

Experience is essential to such a learning process.

> The reclassification, or breaking up of the classes formed by the implicit relations which manifest themselves in our discrimination of sensory qualities, and the replacement of these classes by new classes defined by explicit relations, will occur whenever the expectations resulting from the existing classifications are disappointed, or when beliefs so far held are disproved by new experiences. The immediate effects of such conflicting experiences will be to introduce inconsistent elements into the model of

the external world; and such inconsistencies can be eliminated only if what formerly were treated as elements of the same class are now treated as elements of different classes. (Ibid., 169)

The impetus for intellectual and perceptual development is provided when we recognize contradictions among thoughts or between perceptual expectations and perceptual experiences. If an experiment that is supposed to result in typical neutron trails repeatedly results in anomalies, the physicist may be driven to reconsider her perception, the experimental apparatus or setup, or, ultimately her theories of physical reality.

Thus, the manner in which we perceive reality changes by means of revised perceptual algorithms; in order to avoid contradictions (either among existing beliefs or between expectations and reality), we may develop a more consistent cognitive framework that results in new perceptions that had not previously been possible. Previously inaccessible (because invisible) aspects of reality thereby become accessible to our perceptual apparatus. The process of continually perceiving new phenomena is the result of an ongoing individual and/or social process of creating ever more logically consistent understandings of reality.

According to Hayek, when we acknowledge inconsistencies our brain is physically re-wired to create new perceptions and concepts to reconcile those inconsistencies. This physiological process is hypothetically correlated with changes in our perception of reality.

It thus parallels the process of scientific innovation. It has become a commonplace among philosophers of science that interpretative frames define which data are perceived and how the data are interpreted. While this insight was new when Hayek wrote *The Sensory Order* in the late 1940s, it is old hat today. Insofar as most academic debates take place within extended intellectual communities in which shared perceptual universes are mostly assumed but interpretations of data may vary wildly, much of the energy involved in analyzing scientific and academic disputation has focused on the manner in which differing interpretive frameworks lead to differing assessments of the importance of various types of evidence. Less attention has been focused on novel perceptions of reality and how we come to experience them. Less attention still has been focused on the ways in which a deferential attitude toward existing expertise, in any field, *ipso facto* reduces novel perceptual possibilities.

Science advances one funeral at a time. For example, progress in physics is driven by the combination of experimental evidence and the demand for conceptual consistency. As physicists discover inconsistencies between theory and data, or among conceptual frameworks, they are motivated to synthesize the inconsistencies into a new overarching conceptual framework (this motivates the ongoing search for a Unified Theory in physics). Thus, scientific revolutions are often characterized by dramatic changes in perception.

Before the Copernican revolution people perceived a crystalline sphere with points of light surrounding a stable earth; afterwards, they perceived themselves as small creatures on a tiny planet spinning through a vast universe with billions of stars incomprehensibly far away. Hayek's cognitive theory implies that different theoretical frameworks will lead to physiologically novel neural structures, which change how stimuli are processed by the brain. Thus, until Galileo began the process of perceiving distant material objects at great distances, medieval observers of "the heavens" actually perceived crystalline spheres above. Our perception of the Milky Way would have been inconceivable for Dante.

Hayek is clear that the increasingly consistent development of science constitutes a paradigmatic case of the phenomenon that he is describing:

> Science thus tends necessarily towards an ultimate state in which all knowledge is embodied in the definitions of the objects with which it is concerned: and in which all true statements about these objects are analytical or tautological and could not be disproved by any experience. The observation that any object did not behave as it should could then only mean that it was not an object of the kind it was thought to be. (Hayek 1952, 171)

On the other hand, it is possible for tautological conceptual understandings to interpret the world in such a way that new perceptions are screened out.

Lest this seem implausible, note that throughout much of the eighteenth century, scientifically educated individuals routinely observed phlogiston escaping from combusting substances, leaving a de-phlogisticated substance behind. Burning typically involved smoke escaping from a body (the phlogiston) resulting in a reduction of physical size as a small bit of ash remained (clearly a substance had left the combusted body). Insofar as "that which was left during combustion" was defined to be phlogiston, even after it was discovered that some metals weighed more after burning, scientists sought alternative hypotheses regarding the weight gain rather than questioning the obvious existence of phlogiston. Only when Lavoisier provided a complete alternative account of combustion (which required a new, hypothetical, invisible substance, later known as "oxygen,"), which was eventually adopted because of its greater overall explanatory power, did a few scientists begin to stop perceiving the escape of phlogiston during combustion. If the phlogiston scientists had been able to define scientific expertise and control scientific advance— say, by silencing advocates of the oxygen theory—oxygen and modern chemistry might never have come into being.

The fact that we don't know what we don't know has been a paradox from the time of Socrates. It has not been adequately appreciated that, for Socrates, that paradox was the impetus for developing new understandings. Hayek adds a plausible empirical model for how we gain such understandings: Our brains are rewired to create new concepts when we acknowledge inconsistencies in our perceptions and then create new concepts to reconcile these inconsistencies. (The "Socratic method," properly understood, is a matter of bringing inconsistencies to light and therefore enabling Hayekian creativity [Whitehead 1929, ch. 3; Strong 1996, ch. 2]). Lavoisier's "discovery of oxygen" is shorthand for a gradual but dramatic change in a conceptual framework and scientific paradigm, driven by inconsistencies in the phlogiston story, which led to changes in how reality was perceived.

Freedom to Experiment

Hayek's argument for freedom of action is analogous to John Stuart Mill's argument for freedom of thought and expression. Mill's argument is based on the notion that we can discover new truths only if we are completely unconstrained in expressing our thoughts. This doctrine was tremendously appealing to intellectuals, who, in the twentieth century, largely succeeded in transforming the legal landscape so that they could say, write, and read whatever they pleased.

But Hayek went a step further than Mill: He realized that, just as constraints on freedom of expression limit our search for the truth, constraints on freedom of action do so as well. In fact, limiting freedom of action can lead to long-term reductions in human well-being insofar as innovation is necessarily based on the cognitive rewiring that takes place from encountering specific new situations.

Experiential freedom is important in economic life because only by having new experiences do some people encounter situations that challenge their existing categories in such a way that they are driven to create new interpretations. In contrast, price arbitrage, which can be done by a computer, cannot visualize new relationships among the factors of production, cannot visualize new factors of production, and cannot visualize new ways to satisfy consumer preferences.

Successful entrepreneurs often see the world differently than do others. When Fred Smith proposed the idea for FedEx in a paper at Yale, he perceived a world in which the increasing demand for prompt delivery, combined with the declining cost of computation and air transport, would result in a fundamental change in logistics. Those who did not perceive this possibility perceived the U.S. Postal Service, which shipped parcels by truck and rail, as the only realistic parcel-delivery service. Nothing about envisioning FedEx required sophisticated technical knowledge, though the vision later drove technical innovations. It required the ability to perceive the salience of features of the late 1960s business and technological environment that, to others, were effectively invisible.

An entrepreneur in the act of visualizing a new project re-interprets ordinary objects based on their perceived role in the system to be created prospectively by the new enterprise. When Smith interpreted an airplane as a link in an overnight parcel-transport chain, he had "learned to give identical symbols," i.e. an airplane, "different values according as they appear in combination with different other symbols" (Hayek 1952, 169). That is, he envisioned the challenges and opportunities of linking air-transport to ground-transport systems on an integrated, real-time basis.

Experiential freedom is important because it is impossible to know in advance who in particular will have been prepared by his prior experiences to perceive a new possibility. For example, Steve Jobs obtained the idea for the mouse and the graphic user interface on a personal computer while touring the Xerox PARC research lab in Palo Alto in the late 1970s. Dozens of other people had seen what he saw, but Jobs was the first one to infer from it elements of the personal computer. In "The Creative Powers of a Free Civilization" Hayek (1956, 282–83) argues that freedom of action in even trivial matters is crucial to the creation of new ways of life:

The manner in which we have learnt to order our day, to dress, to eat, and arrange our houses, to speak, write, and use the countless tools and implements of civilization, no less than the "know-how" used in production and trade, all furnish us constantly with the foundations on which our own contributions to the process of civilization must be based. And it is in the new use and improvement of whatever the facilities of civilization offer to us that the new ideas arise which are ultimately handled in the intellectual sphere. . . . Thus, the importance of freedom does not depend on the elevated character of the activities that it makes possible. Freedom of action, even action in humble things, is as important as freedom of thought and freedom of belief.

This view of social change is consistent with Hayek's cognitive theory. Freedom of action allows for new experiences that might then provide an impetus for fundamental changes in our intellectual and perceptual capacities. We need to actually do things in order to discover what does and does not work. For Hayek, this is not merely a matter of pragmatic effectiveness; it is a fundamental impetus to epistemological advance. Boundaries to action radically diminish creative possibility. Moreover, "action" should not be limited merely to the opportunity to engage in typical Millian civil liberties, such as taking drugs or viewing pornography. Action must include the opportunity to create entirely new institutions, both individually and collectively.

Hayek argued that any one of billions of minute changes in how we live might dramatically change our intellectual, perceptual, or experiential capacities. Indeed, he thought that the creative powers of a free civilization can transform even the motivating ends of life:

> It is one of the essential characteristics of a free society that its goals are open, that new ends of conscious effort can spring up, first with a few individuals or a small minority, to become in time the ends of all or most. . . . We must recognize that even what we regard as good or beautiful is changeable. (Hayek 1956, 284)

Seeing the Unseen

According to Hayek, we have a tendency toward intellectual homeostasis because our perceptual categories screen out novel perspectives. Nevertheless, a commitment to intellectual consistency and coherence can lead us to recognize gaps in the consistency of our thoughts and thus lead to new insights and discoveries. Since it is generally not clear in advance where, when, and how innovation will occur, legal constraints on freedom may have the unintended effect of undermining the possibility of creative advance:

> It is worth a moment's reflection as to what would happen if only what was agreed upon to be the best knowledge of society were to be used in any action. If all attempts that seemed wasteful in the light of the now generally accepted knowledge were prohibited and only such questions asked, or such experiments tried, as seemed significant in the light of ruling opinion, mankind might then well reach a point where its knowledge allowed it adequately to predict the consequences of all conventional actions and where no disappointment or failure would occur. Man would seem to have subjected his surroundings to his reason because nothing of which he could not predict the results would be done. We might conceive of a civilization thus coming to a standstill, not because the possibilities of further growth had been exhausted, but because man had succeeded in so completely subjecting all his actions and his immediate surroundings to his existing state of knowledge that no occasion would arise for new knowledge to appear. (Hayek 1956, 284)

Hayek thus argues that we should allow non-experts, who have not internalized the existing categories, the freedom to engage in diverse activities, for they might discover new phenomena that remain invisible to members of the intellectual status quo. This means, too, that competing organizations, rather than legal monopolies, are likely to permit a greater diversity of perceptions. If the U.S. Postal Service had been able to prevent the creation of FedEx, or if IBM had had a legal monopoly that permitted it to prevent the creation of Apple, the long sequences of new perceptions that allowed for the creation of these innovative companies would not have taken place.

It is worth noting that economic regulation tends to eliminate Type I errors, in which permitted products and services cause direct harm, but to ignore Type II errors, in which incorrectly banned products and services cause indirect harm (i.e., by withholding potential benefits) (Friedman 1979). For example, some economists (e.g., Gieringer and Peltzman 1973) hypothesize that tens of thousands have died because safe medications were delayed by the FDA's approval process. Type I errors are more visible than Type II errors. In addition, it is often easier to gather information about the magnitude of Type I errors: If a drug has a trial history in which a particular negative reaction takes place with a given probability, one can assess the probable harm that will take place if the drug is made available to an entire population. Quantifying the benefits of something whose discovery has been prevented is, of course, impossible.

Here, as in all of human life, the first step toward wisdom may be to recognize the limits of our knowledge. Yet the more we know, the harder it may become to acknowledge that we remain ignorant, for this ignorance remains outside of our perceptual categories and therefore constitutes the realm of unknown unknowns.

REFERENCES

Gieringer, Dale H., and Sam Peltzman. 1973. "The Benefits and Costs of New Drug Regulation." In *Regulating New Drugs*, ed. Richard L. Landau. Chicago: University of Chicago Press.

Hayek, F. A. 1945. "The Use of Knowledge in Society." *American Economic Review* 35(4): 519–30.

Hayek, F. A. 1952 [1976]. *The Sensory Order: An Inquiry into the Foundations of Theoretical Psychology*. Chicago: University of Chicago.

Hayek, F. A. 1956. "The Creative Powers of a Free Civilization." In *Essays on Individuality*, ed. Felix Morley.

Strong, Michael. 1996. *The Habit of Thought: From Socratic Seminars to Socratic Practice*. Chapel Hill, N.C.: New View.

Szeliski, Richard. 2011. *Computer Vision: Algorithms and Applications*. Dordrecht, Netherlands: Springer.

Whitehead, Alfred North. 1929. *The Function of Reason*. Princeton: Princeton University Press.

Karen I. Vaughn

HAYEK, EQUILIBRIUM, AND THE ROLE
OF INSTITUTIONS IN ECONOMIC ORDER

ABSTRACT: *In the 1930s, socialist economists used the assumptions of equilibrium theory to argue that a central planner could coordinate supply and demand from above. This argument led Hayek, over the years, to try to explain the limitations of equilibrium theory and, conversely, to explain how capitalism functioned without the assumptions of equilibrium being met. In a changing world of agents who are ignorant of the future, how is a functioning market "order" possible? One answer can be found in Hayek's argument that evolved rules make people's future behavior more predictable and, more to the point, that they contain previously accumulated knowledge that provides the building blocks for future economic growth. Hayek's evolutionary theory was flawed, however, in failing to explain how people can know which rules are responsible for their success or failure so that they persist in using those rules and pass them forward in time. However, markets provide immediate feedback about success and failure through profits and losses. An evolutionary explanation of the economy would have permitted Hayek to dispense with the metaphor of general equilibrium, which was increasingly irrelevant to his understanding of economic order.*

In 1981, on the occasion of the fiftieth anniversary of his first lectures at the London School of Economics—lectures that eventually were published as *Prices and Production*—Hayek delivered a talk at the LSE entitled "The Flow of Goods and Services." Once again, as he had done in 1931, Hayek addressed the relationship between the signals given by the price system and the rate and nature of capital investments, but with a significant difference. In 1931, Hayek had regarded equilibrium theory to be the only scientific underpinning of economic explanation. By 1981, he was ready to jettison the equilibrium framework for a new metaphor to explain economic phenomena.

In 1931, Hayek (1931, 34–35) wrote that "if we want to explain economic phenomena at all, we have no means available but to build on the foundations given by the concept of a tendency towards an equilibrium. For it is this concept alone which permits us to explain fundamental phenomena like the determination of prices or incomes, an understanding of which is essential to any explanation of fluctuations of production." He went on to say that that we must "start with a situation which is already sufficiently explained by the general body of economic theory" (ibid.), that is, a situation in which all resources are fully employed.

Despite Hayek's emphasis on a structure of production that could be distorted by inappropriate price signals, his theory of crisis and recovery was in fact a comparative-statics exercise in showing the consequences of a disturbance in one equilibrium state that was resolved in another such state (Moss and Vaughn 1986). Equilibrium theorizing was central to his attempts to explain capital investment and macroeconomic phenomena. In this sense, Hayek's theoretical tools were very much in the spirit of the age. Sir John Hicks (1967) called Hayek's "Austrian" trade-cycle theory "non-English," but it shared with Hicks and most other English economists a theoretical common ground.

In 1931, Hayek regarded equilibrium as the scientific tool that was needed to explain economic order and disorder. By 1981, however, it is pretty clear that he had changed his mind; he does not mention equilibrium in the conventional sense in "The Flow of Goods and Services." He starts with the observation that "all production takes time" and is fraught with uncertainty about future outcomes—an observation that was not prominent in his earlier work—but then goes on to introduce familiar themes. Producers must choose among "various time-consuming possibilities of transformation . . . those for which the time-rate of increase of what we invest is largest." Prices guide the "lengthening" and "widening" of production. The structure of produc-tion is thus "a multi-dimensional affair in which at any one moment men work for the output of a wide range of future dates, and the output of any one date is correspondingly the effect of the application of resources during a wide range of earlier dates" (Hayek 1981, 334).

From there, however, both the analysis and the language of the paper become very unfamiliar indeed. Instead of a comparative-statics analysis of movement from one equilibrium state to another, Hayek (1981, 335) uses the analogy of running water to describe production processes: Production consists of "several parallel streams of maturing products." The production process should be conceived as "a continuous stream or flow which at its mouth yields a continuous output, emerging after having passed through various transformations since the first resources had been applied" (ibid.). In fact, production is a "complex river system" in some kind of "synchronized state" where finished products will emerge at different times. Further, the flow continually changes, since "it was the flows of the past which prepared the channels for the present stream" (ibid., 336). The stream will "swell or shrink" and its rate of flow will vary due to changes in final demand, but the stream maintains a certain steadiness through the constant adjustments of actors following price signals (ibid., 337). He then gets to the heart of his argument, which is worth quoting in full:

> It is tempting to describe as an "equilibrium" an ideal state of affairs in which the intentions of all participants precisely match and each will find a partner willing to enter into the intended transaction. But for all capitalistic production there must exist a considerable interval of time between the beginning of a process and its various later stages. The achievement of an equilibrium is strictly impossible. Indeed, in a literal sense, *a stream can never be in equilibrium*, because it is disequilibrium which keeps it flowing and determines its directions. Even an apparent momentary state of balance . . . may be *inherently* unrepeatable, irrespective of any change in the external data, because some of the constituents of the stream will be the results of past conditions which have changed long ago; or, to put it differently, part of the so-called "data" will always be an effect of earlier adaptations to different data which no longer exist. The stream is maintained by constant adaptation to passing local conditions—the use of passing chances which have no systematic connections with the rest of the structure. (Ibid., 338–39)

In the rest of the essay, he emphasizes the complexity of the stream in contrast to Keynes's more simplistic notion of demand, which Hayek compares to "sucking on a pipe" to get an increase in output. He reiterates the importance of changes in relative prices to actions that maintain the stream and points out that the economic order "can never continue in an unchanged state but can be preserved only by constant change" (ibid., 338).

The analogy of production to a system of rivers is intriguing and suggestive of the continuous market process that Hayek is trying to explain, but it is not particularly easy for the reader to follow. And while it does address many themes that Hayek introduced in his earlier economic writings, such as the ongoing nature of economic activity and the need for many small adjustments to change to maintain order, it does so in an entirely unfamiliar way. To economists trained to think in terms of equilibrium theory, thinking of output as a structure of production was difficult enough. To then compare it to streamlets and rivers and to declare that equilibrium is impossible is to speak in an alien language. Clearly, Hayek was attempting to lay out a new approach to understanding market order as an orderly process of continual change, but the exposition was too terse. For it to have had an impact, he would have had to flesh out the sketch he provides in the paper by writing a treatise on non-equilibrium economics. At the age of 82, that was he unlikely to happen, especially since he was at the time planning his final book, *The Fatal Conceit*.[1] By 1981, then, all we can say is that Hayek seems to have given up on equilibrium theorizing as an explanation of economic order without giving a full account of his alternative.

What made Hayek abandon his earlier attempts to embed trade-cycle and capital theory in the language of equilibrium, thus setting out to present the problem of economic order within the context of a completely new paradigm? Does Hayek's work contain an alternative to equilibrium as the basis of economic explanation?

I will argue that Hayek's disenchantment with conventional equilibrium theorizing began in the 1930s as a consequence of his participation in the socialist-calculation debate. The issues raised during the debate led to his exploration of the relationship between knowledge and equilibrium, as well as to his work on the importance of rules for social order found in his political and philosophical writings. Finally, I will argue that his study of systems theory in the 1950s and 1960s, in combination with his insights about the importance of social institutions, provide the basis for a reconstruction of a non-equilibrium explanation of economic order.

Equilibrium and Knowledge

Hayek's beginning disenchantment with the contemporary use of equilibrium theory was evident as early as 1937 in his seminal essay, "Economics and Knowledge," and increased as he questioned the assumption and implications of conventional economics in subsequent essays during the next three decades.

"Economics and Knowledge," is in fact an essay as much about the meaning of equilibrium in economic affairs as it was about the nature of economic knowledge. The essay was largely a reaction to the debate over the economics of socialism in which Hayek had recently become embroiled.[2] In this debate, the advocates of central planning used the tools of perfect competition and general-equilibrium theory to try to show that efficient resource allocation was possible under central planning. Prior to the debate, Hayek had been comfortable using equilibrium theorizing to do comparative statics. However, his opponents' claim that equilibrium theory demonstrates that central planners could find alternate means of arriving at economic prices without markets caused him to think more deeply about the nature of equilibrium.

Hayek begins "Economics and Knowledge" by investigating some of the limitations of equilibrium when applied to human action. Human action is not best understood as instantaneous choice: It requires planning over time, which means that, in order to act, we must base expectations about the future on knowledge of the present and past. However, since such knowledge is limited and the future is uncertain, how can equilibrium be useful for economic explanation?

Hayek's answer is to distinguish between the equilibrium of an individual and that of a group. Equilibrium may be useful to understanding a person's action if it is understood as part of an ongoing process: a state of affairs in which someone can carry out a plan without alteration. All that is necessary for an individual to be "in equilibrium" in this sense is that his subjective beliefs about the nature of the physical world conform to the facts. However, in an economy in which many people interact, the actions of one person constitute the environment of another. Interpersonal equilibrium, then, must reflect a coordination of plans among everyone such that their plans do not require revision in the course of their execution.

In this time-infused sense of equilibrium, the central question of economics should be how people come to know enough so that their plans can be coordinated with unknown others. To Hayek, this is essentially an empirical question that requires us to focus on the way in which knowledge is acquired and communicated.

> My main contention will be that the tautologies, of which formal equilibrium analysis in economics essentially consists, can be turned into propositions which tell us anything about causation in the real world only in so far as we are able to fill those formal propositions with definite statements about how knowledge is acquired and communicated. . . . The empirical element in economic theory . . . consists of propositions about the acquisition of knowledge. (Hayek 1937, 33)

"Economics and Knowledge" is remembered mostly for Hayek's theses about the nature of human knowledge: that it consists of beliefs and expectations (Hayek 1937, 49), that people learn from experience (ibid., 46), and that knowledge is fragmented and reflects a "division of knowledge" (ibid., 50). Yet his discussion of knowledge cannot be separated from his restatement of the nature of equilibrium. Together, they constitute a reformulation of the economic problem: "How can the combination of fragments of knowledge existing in different minds bring about results which, if they were to be brought about deliberately, would require a knowledge on the part of the directing mind which no single person can possess?" (ibid., 54). This reformulation would eventually prove subversive to conventional economics. Equilibrium theory is still, in 1937, the basis for Hayek's reasoning, but it is a very different kind of equilibrium in that it states the problem to be solved with no assurance that the theory is useful in offering a solution.

Prices and the Competitive Process

Almost a decade passed before Hayek once again addressed the issues he raised in "Economics and Knowledge." His primary research focus during the rest of the decade was still business-cycle theory and its underlying theory of capital, culminating in the publication of *The Pure Theory of Capital* in 1941.[3] He had planned to write a second volume about the dynamics of capital, but the advent of World War II disrupted his research agenda. Instead, troubled by the intensifying enthusiasm for planning brought about by the war effort, he published *The Road to*

Serfdom in 1944, a work pointing out the connection between political and economic freedom. After the war, though—perhaps stimulated by the experience with war-time price controls and the new enthusiasm for "planning the peace"—he again took up his exploration of knowledge, equilibrium, and prices, producing in quick succession two essays: "The Use of Knowledge in Society" (1945) and "The Meaning of Competition" (1946). Both essays can be viewed as attempts to answer the question Hayek had asked in "Economics and Knowledge": How can economic coordination come about despite dispersed, fragmented human knowledge?

Hayek reiterates that solving for equilibrium prices based on given knowledge is not the economic problem society faces; that instead, to explain economic order, one must explain how dispersed knowledge is communicated. His answer is that prices do the job. In one of his most well-known examples, Hayek explains that if the collapse of a tin mine in Bolivia reduces the supply of tin, the new scarcity will be reflected in higher market prices, causing buyers thousands of miles away who are ignorant of the mine collapse to economize on the use of tin. Prices communicate useful information to consumers in a coded form that allows them to adjust to change in an intelligent way. But the new information communicated by the price system flows from change, while equilibrium prices reflect history.

There is little discussion of equilibrium in "The Use of Knowledge in Society." Indeed, Hayek emphasizes that the natural condition of economic life is change; the greatest challenge people face is adjustment to change. "It is, perhaps, worth stressing that economic problems arise always and only in consequence of change. As long as things continue as before, or at least as they were expected to, there arise no new problems requiring a decision, no need to form a new plan" (Hayek 1945, 82). But change is ubiquitous. Even a relatively stable and orderly economy is maintained only because people can continuously adjust to small changes. Indeed,

> the continuous flow of goods and services is maintained by constant deliberate adjustments, by new dispositions made everyday in the light of circumstances not known the day before, by B stepping in at once when A fails to deliver. (Ibid., 83)

In such a world, one might wonder what relevance general equilibrium can have to understanding economic phenomena.

If "The Use of Knowledge in Society" was an attempt to put the price system in the context of changing circumstances, "The Meaning of Competition" was an all-out assault on the assumptions of the perfectly competitive model, especially the assumption of perfect knowledge. Competition is a dynamic process, yet the model of perfect competition "assumes the situation to exist which a true explanation ought to account for as the effect of the competitive process" (Hayek 1946, 94). For example, widely shared knowledge comes about because of competition; it does not exist prior to it. Also, very few markets consist of homogeneous products. Economics should explain why prices of heterogeneous goods are nevertheless constrained by the prices of the next-best alternative. The problem with perfect competition is not only that it starts by assuming what it should be trying to demonstrate, but that "the neglect of the time element makes the theoretical picture of perfect competition so entirely remote from all that is relevant to an understanding of the process of competition" (ibid., 102).

Despite his criticism of perfect competition, however, Hayek did not yet give up on equilibrium theorizing. He simply claimed that "the tautological method which is appropriate and indispensable for the analysis of individual action seems . . . to have been illegitimately extended to problems in which we have to deal with a social process in which the decisions of many individuals influence one another and necessarily succeed one another in time" (Hayek 1946, 93). Still, by confining the "tautological method" to individual action alone, and then by going on to discuss a process of continual change and adjustment to that change, it does seem as if, even at this early date, Hayek saw little use for equilibrium theorizing in explaining economic order. Certainly his insistence on continual change seems—if not to rule out comparative statics—to make comparative-statics analysis rather less important than he would have believed in 1921.

What kind of theory, then, can explain the economy as an orderly process? Hayek's answer will come not from his explicit economic essays, but from his evolutionary theory of social and political institutions.

At the end of "The Use of Knowledge in Society," Hayek hints at his later interest in evolutionary social theory when he embeds the price system in a larger context of communication media. He writes:

> We make constant use of formulas, symbols, and rules whose meaning we do not understand and through the use of which we avail ourselves of the

assistance of knowledge which individually we do not possess. We have developed these practices and institutions by building upon habits and institutions which have proved successful in their own sphere and which have in turn become the foundation of the civilization we have built up . . . the price system is just one of those formations which man has learned to use (though he is still very far from having learned to make the best use of it) after he had stumbled upon it without understanding it. . . . Man has been able to develop that division of labor on which our civilization is based because he happened to stumble upon a method which made it possible. (Hayek 1945, 88–89)

Obviously, by 1945, Hayek had already began thinking of society, and the market order in particular, as a system of rules and institutions that were the unintended byproducts of human action. The price system is a very important part of that system, but it is not the only important component of what Hayek would later call the "spontaneous" social order. However, instead of proceeding to work on a more comprehensive theory of how the price system functions in conjunction with other market institutions, Hayek turned his attention to the legal institutions within which economic activity takes place.

The Role of Institutions

Given the attitude of the economics profession in the 1940s, it is not at all surprising that Hayek would focus on political institutions rather than the role of market institutions in maintaining economic order. At the time of the calculation debate, one issue that was not well articulated, but that ultimately separated the two sides, was the relevance of institutional structure to the efficiency of an economic system. It was not well articulated because the socialist economists, along with most of their peers, assumed that there was no unique relationship between the institutions of capitalism and its ability to operate efficiently. The socialists argued that prices that accurately reflected individual preferences and relative scarcities could be generated by an institutional structure that differed significantly from that of capitalism: In particular, private property was not necessary to generate correct prices. In opposition to Ludwig von Mises, Oskar Lange, for instance, argued that central planners could establish prices based on feedback from firm managers about shortages and surpluses. The firm managers could be instructed to behave as if they were profit maximizers despite the fact that they were not also resource owners.

While the "incentive problem" was eventually recognized even by market socialists (Lange 1962) and was incorporated into models of incentive-compatible systems and property-rights economics, this was not the only example of insensitivity to institutional structure during the debate. Socialist theorists also wanted to make firms more consistent with planning goals by changing the size and structure of firms, changing the way managers were evaluated and chosen, and changing the way communication would take place among firms that relied on each other's products.

When Hayek initially challenged these proposals, he focused on the question of who had the relevant knowledge to make the best decisions. This led him to conclude that decision making had to be decentralized for the market to take advantage of local and tacit knowledge. He also argued that the managers would be remunerated based on the way in which their decisions were evaluated: Someone whose business decisions were to be evaluated after the fact by a remote overseer would be more likely to make decisions that would seem justifiable to a third party, rather than taking the actions he believed would be most likely to result in successful outcomes.

These arguments addressed the question of how people come to recognize and evaluate alternatives and how they make decisions within different institutional structures. But they were either brushed aside as empirically unimportant or dismissed out of hand as being outside the province of economics. Both Joseph Schumpeter (1942), an economist who did not hold out high hopes for socialism, and E.M.F. Durbin (1949), an avowed socialist, regarded such considerations as matters of sociology, not economics. Economics, clearly, was confined to solutions to maximization problems. It was for this reason that the profession could come to the consensus that socialism was possible, although perhaps fraught with practical difficulties. To say that socialism was possible in this sense meant only that a mathematical solution could be achieved given some initial conditions. The only way economists arrived at such a judgment was to give no weight to institutional structures and their effect on knowledge and actions.[4]

It is no wonder that Hayek believed he was giving up economics when he turned his attention to developing a theory of spontaneous social order and the evolution of social institutions. Economics had become so narrow that Hayek's understanding of the market order did not qualify as part of the discipline. Yet a case can be made that the evolutionary social theory that Hayek developed in his philosophical writings provides a template for a more complete theory of economic order.

Spontaneous Order and the Evolution of Rules

Starting with *The Road to Serfdom* and culminating in the *The Fatal Conceit*, Hayek spent almost five decades attempting to articulate a complete refutation of socialism. The linchpin of his argument was his theory of spontaneous social order, the order that emerges "as a result of human action but not of human design" (Hayek 1967, 96). For our purposes, the most important feature of a spontaneous order is that it is a product of the rules followed by individual participants. The kind of order that emerges is directly related to the kind of rules that people follow (ibid, 67; Hayek 1973, 43). While for economic theory, rule-following seems inconsistent with optimizing behavior and must be explained as a rational means of reducing uncertainty, Hayek thought that we are "as much a rule following animal as a purpose-seeking one" (Hayek 1973, 11).[5]

Rules are necessary to the generation of a spontaneous order for two reasons: They provide some level of predictability in an uncertain world and they reflect accumulated social wisdom that may or may not be recognized by the agents who follow those rules. While the need for predictability became conventional wisdom in economic theory, seeing rules as the repository of social learning was, and remains, controversial.

The first time Hayek mentions the importance of rules for predictability is in *The Road to Serfdom*, where he compares formal law to "a kind of instrument of production, helping people to predict the behavior of those with whom they must collaborate" (Hayek 1944, 73). Since he had already argued that the coordination of plans is complicated by the fact that one person's actions constitute the data for another person's plans, the idea that some actions are more easily predicted when people follow common rules is a logical step to explaining economic order.

The notion that social rules contain accumulated wisdom appears later, in *The Constitution of Liberty* (1960), where Hayek once again compares rules to "instruments of production"—in this case, to tools whose design evolves as they are improved upon and modified to fulfill new uses. A modern tool might look nothing like its ancient predecessor, yet it will incorporate the accumulated knowledge of all those who modified it in light of new circumstances over the years.[6] Traditions and institutions, the rules of social order, are like tools "which the human race has evolved and which enable us to deal with our environment. These are the results of the experience of successive generations that are handed down. And once a more efficient tool is available, it will be used without our knowing why it is better, or even what the alternatives are" (Hayek 1960, 27). Note that by comparing rules to evolved tools or technologies, Hayek is using economic concepts to explain the rules of social order.

That social rules reflect accumulated of wisdom means that people do not have to solve all social problems anew in every generation, making progress possible.

> Every change in conditions will make necessary some change in the use of resources, in the direction and kind of human activities, *in habits and practices*. . . . Thus every change in a sense creates a "problem" for society, even though no single individual perceives it as such; and it is gradually "solved" by the establishment of a new over-all adjustment. (Hayek 1960, 28, emph. added)

Problem solving in this way leads to "successful adaptations of society that are constantly improved and on which depend the range of what we can achieve" (ibid., 34).

But how is successful problem solving accomplished? What is the evolutionary process that allows previous learning to be embedded in the traditions and institutions of society?

Hayek is sometimes criticized for allegedly failing to ground his evolutionary theory in individual actions, but a close reading of his text should lay that criticism to rest. He clearly argues that innovations in social rules occur because in an essentially rule-following society, some people are willing to bear the disapproval of others as they attempt to solve problems in a new way. The growth of human knowledge proceeds, he argues, "by the selection and imitation of successful habits" (Hayek 1960, 110). "The existence of individuals and groups simultaneously observing partially different rules provides the opportunity for the selection of the more effective ones (ibid., 63). Evolutionary advance does not depend exclusively on simple observation and imitation, however; it also proceeds through persuasion: "Advance consists in the few convincing the many," where "individuals act according to their own designs" (ibid., 110).

Critics have rightly pointed out difficulties with this account of the evolution of social rules: Primarily, what is the selection mechanism that distinguishes good rules from bad ones? While Hayek thought that good rules would lead to greater prosperity, giving societies following those rules an adaptive advantage over others, he was hazy on the details. In particular, one might wonder—given the loose connection between laws and social mores on the one hand and greater prosperity on the other— how individuals in a society would know which rules were the ones responsible for their greater wealth. In evolutionary biology, no organism needs to know why a behavior is adaptive. But human beings are more complicated. As Hayek points out, they can be persuaded to follow new leaders who themselves have limited understanding of the consequences of a change in rules. Indeed, Hayek worried that the rules of the great society would turn out to be an evolutionary lucky accident that could not persist in the face of mistaken understandings of its function. Hence, his greater project to show people which of their evolved rules were conducive to human well-being.

Whatever shortcomings Hayek's evolutionary theory may have had when applied to social mores or political rules, however, when applied to the economy, the most serious objections can be overcome. It is a mystery, then, why Hayek did not generalize his social theory to encompass a theory of evolutionary economics.

Systems Theory and Equilibrium

While after 1950, Hayek became known mostly for his social and political theory, during the 1950s and 60s the problem of how to explain the economic order was never far from his thoughts. In 1952 he published *The Counter-Revolution of Science*, a work that was to have been part of a larger project to "explore the origins and expose the errors" of the "intrusion of the preconceptions of the pure scientist and the engineer" into social theory (Caldwell 2004, 240). Subtitled "Studies in the Abuse of Reason," it explored the difference between the social and the natural sciences, labeled as "scientism" the economists' uncritical adoption of methods of the natural sciences, and contrasted scientism to the appropriate method for studying social phenomena. Noting the subjective nature of the facts of the social sciences—that such facts reflect the meaning that we attach to the artifacts we create and to our actions, not any physical properties—he argued that social scientists were tasked with explaining phenomena by starting with people's concepts and trying to understand the structure that emerges from their conceptually guided interactions. It is only because these interactions produce unpredicted results that social science exists.

Prediction is unattainable in the social sciences because "the number of variables" that determine social outcomes is too large for the human mind to "master and manipulate." Instead, social scientists can only hope to explain the "principle on which a phenomenon is produced" (Hayek 1952b, 43). The example he gives is "the general theory of prices as represented, e.g., by the Walrasian or Paretian system of equations. These systems show merely the principle of coherence between the prices of the various types of commodities of which the system is composed since without knowledge of the numerical values of all the system's constants which in fact, cannot be known, we cannot predict the precise results that any particular change will have" (ibid.). So despite his earlier misgivings about the misuse of equilibrium concepts, Hayek still saw a general equilibrium as the scientific foundation of economic theory as of 1952.

Even as, over the next two decades, Hayek refined his understanding of the nature of social order, he continued to consider general-equilibrium theory to be the best model for explaining the coherence of an economic system, despite its diminishing relevance to his social and economic theory. In "Degrees of Explanation" (1952c) for example, he argues that as science tries to understand more and more complex phenomena, explanation of the principle may become the rule rather than the exception. Rather than differentiating natural from social science, then, we should rather distinguish between simple and complex sciences, articulating the different methodologies required for them. For simple sciences, such as physics and chemistry,[7] models can be specified and prediction is possible, while for complex sciences all that may be possible is to explain the principle leading to an observed phenomenon. Significantly, the two examples he gives of a complex science are biology and economics.

Hayek's 1964 paper, "The Theory of Complex Phenomena"—which was greatly influenced by his wide reading in the emerging field of systems theory,[8] as it was then called (the precursor to the modern theory of complex, adaptive systems)—reiterated that for complex systems, explanation was limited to explaining the principle by which a situation arose. Thus, for complex systems, one could predict only the patterns of outcomes, not specific events. To illustrate his point, Hayek takes evolutionary biology as the prime example of a complex system, where the exact outcome of evolution depends upon relationships between an overwhelming number of variables, the exact relationship among which could never be fully specified. Similarly, theories of social structures are so complex that they cannot be predictive in the conventional sense. One can, however, explain particular patterns of actions and rule out impossible futures (Hayek 1964, 32). There appears to be a chain of increasing complexity found in nature, ranging from the simplest inanimate systems to the more complex biological systems to the most complex of all, human social systems.

While Hayek regarded social systems to be prime examples of complex phenomena, he nevertheless still chose to illustrate his point by referring to general equilibrium as an example of complexity in social science. General equilibrium, he reiterated, describes a particular pattern of price relationships more or less observed in the real world. Its primary value is not to predict future outcomes but to provide a general description of a particular kind of order (Hayek 1964, 32). However, in this paper, he adds an important consideration. While still arguing that the complexity of a system is a function of the number of variables that it contains, he points out that complex systems demonstrate "emergent properties" (ibid., 26) that cannot be simply reduced to an account of their individual parts.

According to recent theories of complex, adaptive systems (of which evolutionary biology is a prominent example), complexity is defined not only by the number of variables, but also by the non-linear nature of the interaction among the variables (Holland 1996). Further, the outcomes of their interactions are non-reversible and hence they demonstrate path-dependence. Even more relevant, they lead to emergent properties that result from simpler interactions, but cannot be fully explained by them. That is, simpler systems become building blocks for more complex systems as, for instance, cells form organs and organs form bodies. The more complex system is composed of less complex ones, but is not reducible to them. These characteristics of complex, adaptive systems provide an excellent fit with the nature of the market order that Hayek described. Each of us pursues our own interests by interacting with others. We act in time, acquire knowledge of time and place, and hence must adapt to change. Non-reversibility and path dependence are natural implications of a growing and changing market order. The institutional structure is the unintended product of our attempts to routinize solutions to economic problems.

While Hayek understood the implications of complexity for biological systems, however, he never explicitly extended the analysis to economic systems. In fact, general-equilibrium theory, as it then was conceived, was emphatically not an example of a complex system. That he nevertheless clung to general equilibrium as a theory of market coherence suggests that at this stage of his intellectual journey he had no other way of describing an orderly market process.

Competition as a Discovery Procedure

In 1968, Hayek delivered a talk that arguably represents a major turning point in his thinking about economic order. "Competition as a Discovery Procedure" is noteworthy for a number of reasons. In it he once again emphasized that competition in markets is necessary to generate the knowledge that is assumed by economic theory, but he adds yet another characteristic of human knowledge that would be inaccessible to central planners. He argues that the "always unique combinations of individual knowledge and skills, which the market enables them to use, will not merely, or even in the first instance, be such knowledge of facts as they could list and communicate if some authority asked them to do so" (Hayek 1968, 182). Instead, it consists in "a capacity to find out particular circumstances, which becomes effective only if possessors . . . are informed by the market which kinds of things or services are wanted, and how urgently they are wanted" (ibid.). Market competition does not simply communicate knowledge—it is the impetus for generating new knowledge. And this new knowledge, which is the product of market discovery, is the source of economic growth. Societies that rely on competition are more successful than those that don't and they prevail in competition with non-markets societies (ibid., 180).

Once again, Hayek returns to the question of the use of equilibrium, and now he seems ready to dislodge it from its place of preeminence. Equilibrium is an "unfortunate term" that implies of the end of economic competition, because everything of relevance has already been learned. Instead, "at least for economic policy," Hayek prefers the concept of an "order" because it "has the advantage that we can meaningfully speak about an order being approached to various degrees, and that order can be preserved throughout a process of change. While an economic equilibrium never really exists, there is some justification for asserting that the kind of order of which our theory describes an ideal type, is approached in a high degree" (Hayek 1968, 184). In other words, in contrast to general-equilibrium theory, a useful model of economic activity requires some way of explaining degrees of order and orderly change. As he argued in 1937, orderly change implies that the plans of economic actors can "mostly" be realized, a situation he attributes to the "negative feedback" of the price system (ibid., 184).

Once again, the price system takes center stage in Hayek's explanation of economic order, but is it sufficient to generate the results he hopes to achieve? A theory of economic order that begins with uncertainty and continual change through learning in the marketplace perhaps needs something besides the price system to explain how the plans of individuals who interact with each other (where the actions of one constitute the data of others) can result in plans being "mostly realized." Learning and the growth of knowledge seem to imply that prices will be constantly changing, but how can constantly changing prices provide enough information to permit estimates of future relative scarcities? If constantly changing prices are the only sources of market information, how could anyone make any plans at all? To craft a satisfying answer to this question that is consistent with Hayek's thought, we must once again return to his theory of social institutions.

Rules and the Game of Catallaxy

In *The Mirage of Social Justice* (1976), the second volume of *Law, Legislation and Liberty*, Hayek finally brings economics directly into his social theory and, this time, economic growth and development play a central role. A society is a spontaneous order, a recognizable pattern of actions that emerges because people within that society follow common abstract rules. What most people refer to as an "economy"—and what Hayek prefers to call a "catallaxy,"[9] to emphasize the centrality of exchange as opposed to maximizing behavior—is "a special kind of spontaneous order produced by the market through people acting within the rules of the law of property, tort and contract" (Hayek 1978, 109). Laws of property, tort, and contract support a set of exchange relationships that contribute to the cooperative meshing of plans among a wide, interdependent network of economic actors. Trades can take place because people have a right to trade their property, promises must be kept, and reneging on legal agreements is punished.

One important consequence of people interacting—cooperating and competing with one another—within this set of exchange relationships is that the wealth of the participants continually grows. Wealth grows because people can innovate with their own property and trade it in the marketplace. They choose to exploit their innovations because the returns to their efforts accrue to them.

Hayek (1976, 108) calls this the game of catallaxy. Unlike the implications of the term "economy," in a catallaxy there is no single, unified hierarchy of values that can be maximized subject to constraints. Each person acts according to his own values to better his condition, subject to the actions of other people with whom he trades. There is no final "outcome" to such a system: Wealth continues to grow because individual gains and losses can be measured via the price system and its derivative, cost accounting. "It is by conveying information in coded form that the competitive efforts of the market game secure the utilization of widely dispersed knowledge" (ibid., 117).

The code Hayek refers to here is, of course, the price system once again. However, he also notes that the price system has its limits. Even with prices, given the limitations of human knowledge, there will be a "constant stream of disappointments" as circumstances change or as new market strategies fail to meet expectations. Moreover, Hayek implies that if change is too rapid, actors will find it difficult to use the price system effectively to formulate reasonable plans. Change is constant but, Hayek suggests in several places, people can cope effectively with it only if it is not too rapid or too extreme.

In a well-functioning market order, current prices must always "provide some indication" of what future prices will be if people are to plan effectively. Thus, for the "negative feedback" of the market to bring about more plan coordination, three conditions must be met: There must be a "fairly constant framework of known facts," "only a few of them change," and "the price mechanism operates as a medium of communicating knowledge which brings it about that the facts which become known to some, through the effect of their actions on prices, are made to influence the decisions of others" (Hayek 1976, 125). The implication is that for people to use the price system effectively, there must be large areas of stability that enable them to deal with changes at the margin. But if this is the case, the price system alone is insufficient to bring about economic order. The price system enables people to make rational decisions about resource use in response to changing circumstances, but to be effective it must be the case that changing circumstances represent the tip of the iceberg of human experience. The submerged part of the iceberg must be a stable set of actions and relationships that can be taken for granted by the economic actor. In other words, rational action requires both a price system for conveying information about change, and a set of market institutions that provide a background of stability.

Recall Hayek's claim that we are as much rule-followers as purpose-seekers. By this he means that we develop routines and practices, both personal and shared, that are repeated in what we perceive to be similar circumstances. Repeated routines are manifest in consumption patterns, methods of producing products, networks of individuals with whom one does business, methods of organizing firms and divisions within firms, particular inputs a business uses in production, particular brands of commodities people consume, the customs and rituals by which trade takes place, and the specific locations where people interact. These, it seems to me, are the "fairly constant known facts" that Hayek claims are necessary for the price system to function. Indeed, the routines and institutions that characterize action in the catallaxy are actually the instantiation of useful market knowledge, the "knowledge of time and place" that Hayek referred to early on. That is, rules and routines in the catallaxy are not aids to how people learn and plan; they are a large part of *what* people learn through market interaction and *what* they plan to do as a consequence.

While Hayek overtly focused on the price system as the means of achieving economic coordination, in fact, prices will only do their work if the complex of market institutions within which action takes place is relatively stable. The coordination problem is solved by *both* the price system and the complex of rules, practices, and routines that characterize the market order. Moreover, the market order evolves over time as people find better "solutions" to their problems.

Human Action and the Evolution of Catallactic Routines

I claimed earlier that Hayek's theory of the evolution of social rules is better suited to understanding the evolution of market rules and institutions than it is to social rules. The crux of my argument is that purposeful human beings have a mechanism (prices) by which to judge the value of market rules and institutions, but that they don't have as obvious a mechanism to judge the benefits of social and political rules and institutions.

Innovations in the rules of social order may survive for reasons that have little to do with long-run benefit. Political innovations in particular can have important long-term consequences that are impossible for individuals (including politicians or experts) to understand or judge. Hence, the often disastrous unintended consequences of well-meaning laws and regulations. As a result, the ultimate adaptiveness of a law or custom emerges only over time as civilizations rise and fall.

In markets, however, there is an immediate means of judging consequences to changes in rules and routines: Profit and loss provide people with criteria by which to measure both direct benefits to themselves and indirect benefit to others. "Monetary calculation," as Ludwig von Mises (1949, 29) called it, permits people to evaluate the consequences of their market activities more quickly and accurately than they can evaluate chains of consequences from political rules (Vaughn 1994). The feedback of the marketplace permits people to engage in actions that lead to long-term growth and development, which is why the West was able to achieve a rapid increase in wealth over the course of just a few hundred years.

Innovation is risky and costly, but a price system allows the innovator to judge relatively quickly whether or not her new creation—whether it be a new product, a new method of marketing, or a new production technique—is worth the expense. For the innovation to be successful, she must offer a product that others will regard as a better means of achieving their goals than is offered by their current routine purchases. Success is signaled by profits; hence the product will continue to be offered for sale. Profits imply that others are adjusting their routines to take into account the new product, causing price adjustments to ripple through the system. In addition, other producers may try to imitate the successful entrepreneur, offering their own versions of the new product in a flurry of rivalrous competition. In this way, the innovation will spread through the catallaxy and lead to many people to establish new consumption and production routines. If the innovation was not a success, the entrepreneur suffers monetary losses, ceases production of the new good, and the experiment dies without offspring.

There are two important points here. First, whether or not the new product (or new technology) becomes established is determined by a set of individuals, aided by relative prices, who evaluate it according to how the product improves their own welfare. For most market goods, the judgments of consumers are sufficient to determine the "fitness" of the good. Second, innovations build upon each other. What evolves in the marketplace is a set of institutions, products, and practices that were once attempts to solve some perceived problem, but then become the "background of known facts" that Hayek claims is necessary for the price system to work. The system is obviously "path-dependent" since knowledge is not unlearned. The base of knowledge grows as people learn better ways to solve their problems, and it becomes instantiated in institutions.

Profit and loss constitutes a selection mechanism for adaptive change. Plans can be coordinated because of the existence of market institutions that serve as points of reference—or as Ludwig Lachmann (1971) called them, "points of orientation." Further, an evolving catallaxy can exhibit degrees of order. Competing firms provide redundancy in the system so that some disruptions can occur in the institutional structure without it degenerating into chaos. But the disappointment of many expectations is a necessary part of the evolution of the order.

*   *   *

Given Hayek's intimate familiarity with biological evolution, it is surprising that he did not cast his economic analysis in an evolutionary frame. In "The Flow of Goods and Services" he was groping for a new metaphor to explain the essence of orderly change, yet "rivers and streams" does not adequately capture the growth of wealth that is an integral part of his understanding of the market order. On the other hand, the evolved social order—the outlines of which he took such pains to explore in *Law, Legislation and Liberty* and, finally, in *The Fatal Conceit* —captures all of the attributes of the market process that Hayek described in his various essays on knowledge and the market process.

That Hayek did not write a treatise on the evolutionary market order that was implicit in his other works is understandable, given that his primary purpose was to provide the definitive refutation of socialism. Yet one can still regret that his scholarly life came to an end before he could give a fully satisfying account of the workings of the catallaxy.

Nevertheless, in this area, as in so many others, Hayek was ahead of his time. Hayek probably would have welcomed the emergence of evolutionary economics in the 1980s and the growing field of complexity theory that blossomed in the 1990s. More to the point, a full integration of an evolutionary theory of the catallaxy would have enhanced his defense of the liberal order that he found so important to human flourishing.

It is perhaps time for others to follow Hayek's lead and to reformulate a defense of the liberal order that jettisons the equilibrium theory that was so ill suited to explain the nature of the catallaxy that Hayek saw as the ultimate product of political freedom. Contemporary economic policy suffers too much from the belief that equilibrium is the norm and that deviations from it require political remedy. In a world of continual change, equilibrium is a chimera. The real question is how we have learned to cope so well with the limitations reality imposes on us. A reformulation of economics in Hayekian terms would go a long way to answering this fundamental question.

NOTES

1. "The Flow of Goods and Services" might have received more attention had it been included in his final work, as Hayek originally intended (Caldwell 2004, 318), but it never made it into the final edition. The upshot is that the essay remains more of a curiosity than a contribution to Hayek's economic theory.
2. Specifically through the publication of *Collectivist Economic Planning* in 1935, a volume to which he contributed a concluding essay criticizing the economics of central planning as it was then understood. For an account of the debate, see Vaughn 1994, 49–55 and Kirzner 1988.
3. Late in life when Hayek reported that his attempt to improve upon Böhm-Bawerk's "oversimplified" theory of capital investment led to a result that became "so damned complicated it's almost impossible to follow it" (Hayek 1994, 141). Many of his readers would heartily agree with his assessment.
4. Hayek (1935, 238) alluded to the meaning of "possible" in one of his essays, where he drew the distinction between possible in the sense of being mathematically solvable and possible in the sense of being achievable under real-world conditions. Unfortunately, Hayek was misunderstood to mean that Mises had been incorrect: Socialism was possible, but suffered mere problems of implementation (Lange and Taylor 1938, 63)
5. That Hayek would hold such a view is unsurprising in light of the theory of the human brain he developed in *The Sensory Order* (1952a), where he described the brain as a kind of spontaneous order in which learning is characterized by the acquisition of layers of rules that are then available for interpreting and dealing with new situations. That is, rules are in large part the substance of what people learn; they are in essence causal relationships that become the stock of human

knowledge. When confronted with novel situations, we interpret them by making analogies with already acquired rules. Since no analogy is perfect, new ideas can thereby arise. In this picture of human action, purpose seeking can only occur within a context of learned rules. In his social and political writings, however, Hayek focused more on the social consequences of rule-following than on the nature of human action itself.

6. On thinks of flint-knapped stone axes evolving into the modern beautifully balanced stainless-steel versions found in every hardware store today. Nothing appears to unite the two other than some overlapping uses, yet the modern version achieved its current shape over a long series of small adaptations in form and material.

7. Obviously, simple does not mean easy. It simply refers to the ease by which initial conditions can be specified rendering prediction of outcomes possible.

8. To name those most prominent in Hayek's references, Hayek in various articles cites von Neuman on the theory of automata, Bertalanffy on complex biological systems, Lloyd Morgan on the nature of emergent properties, and Steven Toulmin on the ability of biology to rule out possible futures.

9. The term *catallactics*, as Hayek points out, was coined by Richard Whately (1832) as a better description of the study of markets than is economics. The term was introduced in the twentieth century by Hayek's mentor, Ludwig von Mises (1949, 232), who entitled part IV of *Human Action*, "Catallactics or Economics of the Market Society." Both Israel Kirzner (1960) and James Buchanan (1964) used the term to denote the science of exchange rather than of maximizing. As far as I know, however, Hayek was the first to use the term *catallaxy* as a substitute for the more common term *economy*.

REFERENCES

Buchanan, James M. 1964. "What Should Economists Do?" *Southern Economic Journal* 30: 213–22.

Caldwell, Bruce. 2004. *Hayek's Challenge*. Chicago: University of Chicago Press.

Durbin, E.M.F. 1949. *Problems of Economic Planning*. London: Routledge & Kegan Paul.

Hayek, F. A. 1931. *Prices and Production*. London: Routledge & Kegan Paul.

Hayek, F. A., ed. 1935. *Collectivist Economic Planning*. London: Routledge & Kegan Paul.

Hayek, F. A. 1937. "Economics and Knowledge." In Hayek 1948.

Hayek, F. A. 1941. *The Pure Theory of Capital*. Chicago: University of Chicago Press.

Hayek, F. A. 1944. *The Road to Serfdom*. Chicago: University of Chicago Press.

Hayek, F. A. 1945. "The Use of Knowledge in Society." In Hayek 1948.

Hayek, F. A. 1946. "The Meaning of Competition." In Hayek 1948.

Hayek, F. A. 1948. *Individualism and Economic Order*. Chicago: University of Chicago Press.

Hayek, F. A. 1952a [1963]. *The Sensory Order: An Inquiry into the Foundations of Theoretical Psychology*. Chicago: University of Chicago Press.

Hayek, F. A. 1952b. *The Counter-Revolution of Science: Studies in the Abuse of Reason*. New York: Macmillan.

Hayek, F. A. 1952c. "Degrees of Explanation." In Hayek 1967.

Hayek, F. A. 1960. *The Constitution of Liberty*. Chicago: University of Chicago Press.

Hayek, F. A. 1964. "The Theory of Complex Phenomena." In Hayek 1967.

Hayek, F. A. 1967. *Studies in Philosophy, Politics, and Economics.* Chicago: University of Chicago Press.

Hayek, F. A. 1968. "Competition as a Discovery Procedure." In Hayek 1978.

Hayek, F. A. 1973. *Rules and Order.* Vol. 1 of *Law, Legislation and Liberty.* Chicago: University of Chicago Press.

Hayek, F. A. 1976. *The Mirage of Social Justice.* Vol. 2 of *Law, Legislation and Liberty.* Chicago: University of Chicago Press.

Hayek, F. A. 1978. *New Studies in Philosophy, Politics, Economics, and the History of Ideas.* Chicago: University of Chicago Press.

Hayek, F. A. 1981 [2012]. "The Flow of Goods and Services." In *The Collected Works of F. A. Hayek,* vol. 8. Ed. H. Klausinger. Chicago: University of Chicago Press.

Hayek, F. A. 1988. *The Fatal Conceit: The Errors of Socialism.* Chicago: University of Chicago Press.

Hayek, F. A. 1994. *Hayek on Hayek: An Autobiographical Dialogue,* ed. Stephen Kresge and Leif Wenar. Chicago: University of Chicago Press.

Hicks, John R. 1967. *Critical Essays in Monetary Theory.* Oxford: Clarendon Press.

Holland, John. 1996. *Hidden Order: How Adaptation Builds Complexity.* New York: Basic Books.

Kirzner, Israel M. 1960. *The Economic Point of View.* Menlo Park, Calif.: Institute for Humane Studies.

Kirzner, Israel. 1998. "The Economic Calculation Debate: Lessons for Austrians." *Review of Austrian Economics* 2: 1–18.

Lange, Oskar. 1962. *Problems of Political Economy of Socialism.* New Delhi: People's.

Lange, Oskar, and Fred M. Taylor. 1938. *On the Economic Theory of Socialism.* New York: McGraw-Hill.

Lachmann, Ludwig von. 1971. *The Legacy of Max Weber.* Berkeley: Glendessary Press.

Mises, Ludwig von. 1949 [1963]. *Human Action: A Treatise on Economics.* New Haven: Yale University Press.

Moss, Laurence S., and Karen I. Vaughn. 1986. "Hayek's Ricardo Effect: A Second Look." *History of Political Economy* 18(4): 545–65.

Schumpeter, Joseph. 1942. *Capitalism, Socialism, and Democracy.* New York: Harper & Row.

Vaughn, Karen I. 1994. *Austrian Economics in America: The Migration of a Tradition.* Cambridge: Cambridge University Press.

Whately, Richard. 1832. "Introductory Lectures on Political Economy." Online Library of Liberty. http://www.econlib.org/library/Whately/whtPE.html.

Daniel Kuehn

HAYEK'S BUSINESS-CYCLE THEORY: HALF RIGHT

ABSTRACT: *The Great Recession has brought with it a renewed interest in Hayek's business-cycle theory, which holds that loose monetary policy generates an unsustainable boom characterized by a lengthening of the capital structure. Hayek's theory has received robust criticism for decades, although the criticisms have varied in quality. Various empirical disconfirmations pose the most serious challenge. The small empirical literature on the subject generally confirms Hayek's predictions about variations in the capital structure, but has not persuasively linked the capital structure to the business cycle. A better option, then, may be to abandon Hayek's business-cycle theory, preserve his capital theory, and graft it onto a Keynesian or monetarist understanding of the business cycle that is more consistent with modern macroeconomics.*

In standard histories (Chandler 1973) or accounts of the Keynesian Revolution (Gaibraith 1965), the policy recommendations given by the liquidationists appear to be nothing but incoherent barbarisms that were, for some inexplicable reason, believed. Such an interpretation gets the history of economic thought wrong. It also creates a climate of undue smugness among the present generation of economists.

—DeLong 1990, 34

Over the course of the last half-decade of depressed economic activity and subdued wage and price growth, nearly every economist's mind has been drawn at some point to the problems and personalities of the 1930s. Students of the Great Depression such as Ben Bernanke, Christina Romer, and Scott Sumner have risen to prominence, and Robert Skidelsky (2009) has heralded the "return of the master," John Maynard Keynes, as a source of guidance for economists (if not policy makers bent on austerity). But Keynes has not been the only posthumous beneficiary of the Great Recession. Although for decades most macroeconomists have considered Friedrich A. Hayek's work on the business cycle inconsequential, it has won a growing audience in recent years thanks to political movements like the Tea Party, promotion through social media, and the embrace of charismatic politicians such as Representative Ron Paul. This degree of publicity for Hayek's ideas is hardly new. In the 1980s, the endorsements of Ronald Reagan and Margaret Thatcher allowed Hayek to ride a fresh wave of conservative enthusiasm. Before that, *Reader's Digest* popularized the arguments of his book, *The Road to Serfdom* (1944), with an American public trying to make sense of the early days of the Cold War and the welfare state. However, this is the first time since the Great Depression that Hayek's business-cycle theory[1] (as opposed to his broader philosophical perspectives) has registered at all in the public imagination, raising the obvious question: Is there anything to the theory? The fact that most economists have dismissed it is not a trivial point, although it is possible that valuable Hayekian insights were overlooked in the rush to elaborate on advances made by Keynes in the *General Theory of Employment, Interest, and Money* (1936).

This article takes a critical stance toward Hayek's business-cycle theory, but one that is more nuanced than some of the blunt dismissals of Hayek in the 1930s and later years. I share J. Bradford DeLong's (1990, 33) view that "the advocates of the liquidationist [Austrian] point of view during the Great Depression were mistaken, but they were not crazy."

The paper will begin with a summary of Hayek's business-cycle theory and the causes of the "unsustainable boom" that Hayek thought would, after an inevitable "upper turning point," precede a bust. A brief discussion of the strengths and weaknesses of the major critiques of the theory will follow. The strongest critiques (Tullock 1987; Friedman 1993; Cowen 1997) are best thought of as empirical disconfirmations, which leads naturally into a review of the findings of a growing number of empirical investigations of Hayek's business-cycle theory, most of which have been conducted in the last decade. This empirical literature is still maturing in many ways, but it indicates that one of Hayek's major suppositions about changes in the capital structure over the business cycle was likely correct. After discussing the empirical literature, I present evidence that the changes in the capital structure over the business cycle are not closely tied to loose credit conditions (as predicted by Hayek). This new empirical evidence analyzes the tightness or looseness of monetary policy by comparing actual interest rates to an estimate of natural rates instead of looking at the absolute level of interest rates (as has been customary in much of the literature). I conclude with a discussion of a novel alternative interpretation of the evidence that finds a place for Hayek's capital theory, but only as an epiphenomenon in more traditional Keynesian explanations of the causes of the business cycle.

The Unsustainable Boom

To the uninitiated, Hayek's macroeconomic dynamics are evocative of a Rube Goldberg contraption, a complex assortment of sequential price movements and mechanisms that are supposed to produce the phenomenon of the business cycle. But it is also possible to reduce the theory to a few principal constituent parts without sacrificing any fundamental principles—an important contributor to its popular success in recent years. In its simplest form, Hayek's business-cycle theory can be thought of as a theory of two periods; the "unsustainable boom" and the "upper turning point," when the boom turns into a bust. Perhaps the best-known statement of the theory is Hayek's *Prices and Production* (1931), which was based on lectures delivered at the London School of Economics and focuses primarily on the generation of an unsustainable boom. Modern graphical popularizations have elaborated principally on this book, and the historical drama around the lectures adds to its allure. Hayek argues that the boom begins with a credit expansion that is not derived from voluntary savings decisions made by households and firms. Although Austrians often draw attention to the monetary policy of central banks as the source of this credit expansion, those who are skeptical of fractional-reserve banking are quick to add that it can also originate in the banking industry itself.[2]

Central banks engage in credit expansion for a reason, of course: New supplies of credit lower the interest rate, which encourages additional borrowing by investors in anticipation of future profits. All economists recognize that there are risks associated with this sort of expansionary monetary policy that have to be carefully modeled and managed, such as inflationary pressures or asset bubbles. Inspired by older monetary traditions, however, Hayek pointed out that even if these problems remain subdued, growth induced by credit expansion may be unsustainable because the investors who respond to the expansion of credit are fundamentally different from the initial set of investors in the credit market, before the policy change. The new investors are embarking on projects that were not feasible at the earlier, higher interest rates but are feasible after the central bank makes a credit injection that lowers rates. The character, and not just the volume, of investment are therefore affected. For Hayek, the most important difference in the investments made after a credit expansion is that they tend to be investments in relatively longer production processes, with a greater delay between the commencement of the production process and the ultimate sale of the good. This is often referred to as a "lengthening of the capital structure." Hayek reasoned that because production took place over an expanse of time, the optimal length of that production period would vary with the interest rate, either because credit was required for production to proceed (and a higher interest rate implied higher costs for longer processes than shorter processes), or because funds used for production had to compete with the return made possible by lending those funds at interest during the same amount of time.[3] Production processes that take a long time to earn returns have to take these carrying costs of capital into account when making investment decisions, and lower interest rates enable longer production periods than higher interest rates. Moreover, these changes to the capital structure under loose and tight credit conditions could be easily missed if capital is conceived as a more static factor of production that does not generate output over a period of time.

The lengthening of the capital structure is significant because it is not compatible with society's overall "time preference" in the absence of credit expansion. Hayek makes the familiar neoclassical assumption that the interest rate is determined in the market for loanable funds, and that the critical ingredient in the supply and demand of loans is time preference, or simply an agent's *patience*. Households and firms supply loanable funds to borrowers when the interest rate meets or exceeds the value they assign to delaying the expenditure of those funds. Likewise, borrowers demand loanable funds if the discounted benefits they expect to enjoy from the use of those funds meet or exceed the interest costs that they pay. When credit is injected into the loanable funds market independent of these decisions by market participants (say, by a central bank), the interest rate falls below its "natural" level. It is because the interest rate is artificially low that Austrians speak of artificial distortions in the capital structure.

Austrians cite the distortion of the capital structure as the primary reason why money is "non-neutral," or why it has an impact on real decisions as opposed to simply changing the nominal price level (Subrick 2010, 115). Fritz Machlup (1977, 23) wrote that "the fundamental thesis of Hayek's theory of the business cycle was that *monetary* factors *cause* the cycle but *real* phenomena *constitute* it." Hayek was not alone in asserting monetary non-neutrality, nor even in the minority. But most accounts of non-neutrality offer the prospect of an edifying monetary policy intervention (within the limits of human and institutional imperfections, of course). This is generally not the case for Austrians, who typically interpret central bankers (and in some cases, even private bankers operating under fractional-reserve arrangements) as merely contributing to the formation of another unsustainable boom.

The Upper Turning Point

The next step in Hayek's business-cycle theory was to explain exactly why the lengthening of the capital structure was unsustainable, or why an "upper turning point" would inevitably occur. An early, extended treatment of this question is provided by Hayek in *Profits, Interest, and Investment* (1939), although the question was revisited in subsequent articles as well.

According to Hayek, credit expansion changes spending behavior not only by lengthening production processes (so that proportionately fewer resources are used in early production stages), but by making production more capital-intensive in general (bidding resources away from consumer-goods producers). The resulting upward pressure on consumer-goods prices would have the effect of lowering workers' real wages. Lower real wages would, in turn, entice producers to shift capital away from capital-intensive and towards labor-intensive production. The changes in production techniques that would result from credit expansion therefore come to be reversed by the correction of the distortions in relative prices set in motion by those changes. This rebalancing process is known as the Ricardo Effect, after the early work on the relationship between capital-intensive production, consumer-goods prices, and labor demand by David Ricardo in the nineteenth century.

In the late 1930s and for many years afterward, the Ricardo Effect explanation of the "upper turning point" in *Profits, Interest, and Investment* (1939) proved to be far more contentious than the arguments about the lengthening of the capital structure in *Prices and Production* (1931). Nicholas Kaldor (1942) argued that the rise in the real wage that would end Hayek's boom hardly demonstrated the necessity of a crash. The rush toward capital-intensive production would be *tempered* by the increasing competitiveness of labor-intensive production until a new equilibrium was reached, but there was no reason to expect a crisis to result.[4] The ability of the Ricardo Effect to explain how the unsustainable boom turns into a bust has been further questioned by Mark Blaug (1968), Harald Hagemann and Hans-Michael Trautweinn (1998), and others.

Debates over the Ricardo Effect are of considerable interest in their own right, but this element of Hayek's theory is generally de-emphasized in modern renditions of his business-cycle theory. Modern expositors are typically content to note that the lengthening of the capital structure and the increased capital intensity of production are unsustainable because they are inconsistent with underlying time preferences.[5] Some fail to cite the behavior of market actors or any endogenous process at all in their account of the upper turning point. For example, in their defense of Austrian business-cycle theory against criticism from David Laidler (2003), Walter Block and William Barnett (2007, 47) say of the end of the unsustainable boom only that "eventually the rate of increase of price inflation, let alone the price inflation itself, must come to an end, either through the crackup boom associated with hyperinflation, or by the government's ceasing its unwarranted monetary policy," i.e., a policy that is not grounded in underlying time preferences.

Although other Austrians have elaborated on how a recession could be expected to play out, Hayek's business-cycle theory was composed only of the unsustainable boom and the distortion of the capital structure, which was said to lead inevitably to a bust. It was easy to see how this mechanism could cycle repeatedly, if the central bank or the banking sector in general responded to each crisis with more easy money, but the theory did not necessitate a repeated cycle. Gottfried Haberler (1986, 425–27), J. Bradford DeLong (1990), and Gene Callahan and Steven Horwitz (2010), among others, have noted that Hayek's theory need not necessarily describe all recessions. The question of how relevant the theory is to modern recessions and how much heed macroeconomists should pay it is thus in many ways an empirical one. Nevertheless, a wide variety of theoretical assaults on Hayek were mounted before any substantial empirical assessment got underway.

The Reaction to Hayek

Hayek's business-cycle theory failed to make a lasting impression on macroeconomics. Paul Samuelson (2009) called Hayek's work on these problems in the 1930s and early 1940s "a pebble thrown into the pool of economic science that seemingly left nary a ripple." This is not to say that Hayek's broader menu of ideas failed to have an impact on later macroeconomists, or that Hayek's theory was not a valuable contribution to the discussion of business cycles that occurred during the 1930s.[6] It is only to say that Hayek's specific explanation of how business cycles occur barely got off the ground as a research program during the Great Depression and has not subsequently been taken seriously by most macroeconomists. Hayek and his co-Nobel laureate, Gunnar Myrdal, are conspicuously the only ones cited by the prize committee for contributions to macroeconomic theory who typically fail to make an appearance in the principal macroeconomic textbooks written for graduate students.

To a large extent Hayek's lack of impact on macroeconomics is the result of the fierce initial criticisms he received in the 1930s in response to the series of lectures he delivered at the London School of Economics and his subsequent book, *Prices and Production* (1931). A well-known denunciation of Hayek's work at the time was John Maynard Keynes's 1931 characterization of *Prices and Production* as "an extraordinary example of how, starting with a mistake, a remorseless logician can end up in Bedlam" (Keynes 1931, 394).[7] Directly critical responses to his lectures were met with evasiveness from Hayek, which did not ingratiate him to his audience. Richard Kahn, a Cambridge economist and colleague of Keynes, recalled Hayek's lecture this way:

Usually a Marshall Society talk is followed by a lively and protracted barrage of discussions and questions. On this occasion there was complete silence. I felt that I had to break the ice. So I got up and asked, "Is it your view that if I went out tomorrow and bought a new overcoat, that would increase unemployment?" "Yes," said Hayek. "But," pointing to his triangles on the board, "it would take a very long mathematical argument to explain why." (Kahn quoted in Ebenstein 2003, 53)

The "triangles on the board" was a reference to a common diagrammatic exposition of the distortion of the capital structure, which has been expanded upon by Garrison (2000) and others. This dodge was especially ironic, considering that Austrian economics is usually associated with the rejection of mathematical formalization in economics, in favor of a more literary (and allegedly more intuitive) style (see, for example, the discussion of mathematics and Austrian economics in Boettke 1994, 605). In the early 1930s, the critics felt that Hayek had furnished them with neither the math nor the intuition for the theory he presented. After getting past their initial incredulity, more substantive critiques of Hayek began to trickle in, meeting varying degrees of success.

Interest Rates and Distortions

Hayek's early work in the United Kingdom was primarily concerned with the unsustainable boom, leaving detailed discussions of the upper turning point to later books and articles. Naturally some of the first criticisms were directed at this part of the theory. One of the most prominent detractors was Piero Sraffa, the Cambridge economist who was asked by Keynes (in his capacity as editor of the *Economic Journal*) to respond to Hayek. Sraffa (1932) pointed out that if the economy was not in equilibrium (as Hayek suggested it would not be), there could be no single natural rate of interest, so Hayek's concern with distortions caused by an interest rate pushed below the natural rate bordered on the unintelligible. Sraffa showed that given a certain basket of consumer goods as an index for consumer prices, you could calculate one natural rate, but with a different basket you would get a completely different natural rate, because each good has its own rate of interest.[8] Without any "correct" natural rate of interest it was hard to see how a unique capital structure could be considered *the* sustainable or natural capital structure.

Sraffa was right to dismiss the idealized version of the natural rate of interest used by Hayek, but the problems posed for Hayekian business-cycle theory by this point are relatively trivial. Joseph Conrad (1959) and Ludwig Lachmann (1956) showed that the solution to the puzzle was that multiple natural rates of interest could emerge if the economy was in equilibrium at a particular point in time, but not if it was in intertemporal equilibrium. Lachmann also pointed out that Sraffa ignored liquidity differences and differences in real costs (such as storage costs), which help to explain observed variability of own rates of interest. Robert Murphy (2010) agrees with the general thrust of Conrad (1959) and Lachmann's (1956) solution, but maintains that even intertemporally, the discussion of a "natural rate" is unintelligible. Although his was one of the more famous critiques of Hayekian business-cycle theory, Sraffa is better thought of as presenting an argument against casual discussions of a single natural rate than presenting a threat to the main contours of the theory.

A more substantial rebuttal to Hayek's concerns about a distorted capital structure is offered by Tullock (1987), who objects to the whole idea that firms care very much about interest rates in determining the volume of production. Hayek's theory requires that an artificially low interest rate increases the profitability of production processes that take longer, but in situations where interest costs are not even considered by firms, the whole theory falls apart. Tullock observes that

> the interest rate is of great significance in deciding whether or not to build a new factory, buy an expensive machine, etc., but of very little significance in deciding how much to produce in an existing factory. In my own experience as a member of the board of directors of a small company, we frequently discuss interest rates at great length when we are considering capital expenditures. I cannot recall the interest rate even being mentioned in any of our discussions of production matters. (Ibid., 75)

Tullock further noted that the reason that firms ignore interest rates in production decisions is that even highly capital-intensive production processes (which occur after all capital equipment has been acquired and installed) do not usually take a substantial amount of time to complete.

Tullock's experience with interest rates anticipates the finding of Akerlof, Dickens, and Perry (2000) that as long as inflation is modest, firms ignore it in their decision making. Although entrepreneurial responses to interest-rate variations (in Tullock's case) or low inflation (in Akerlof, Dickens, and Perry's case) need not be identical, the common conclusion of this and other behavioral research seems to be that such minor costs are discounted in the decision-making process relative to larger concerns. If low interest rates and inflation fail to drive distortionary production decisions, however, it is hard to see why a market correction would be inevitable or even necessary after low interests rates or inflation occur. Interest rates are critical for large capital expenditures, but the widely cited empirical work of Davis, Haltiwanger, and Schuh (1996) suggests that most job creation (and destruction) happens at large, mature establishments which are presumably primarily making capacity-utilization decisions rather than new capital-expenditure decisions.

Why Would Entrepreneurs Take the Low-Interest Bait?

A popular but ultimately unsatisfying critique of Hayek concerns the question of entrepreneurial expectations. If the average central banker is sharp enough to come up with the idea of lowering the interest rate to expand the economy, and the average Austrian economist is sharp enough to deduce the inevitable consequences of this policy, it seems appropriate to expect that the average entrepreneur should be able to foresee the unsustainability of the boom as well. So why are they fooled into building an unsustainable, distorted capital structure in the first place? Although John Hicks (1967) made this point early on, the criticism became particularly acute after the rational-expectations revolution, which made entrepreneurial expectations the centerpiece of investigations of the efficacy of both monetary and fiscal policy. The best-known modern version of this argument against Hayek is offered by Tyler Cowen (1997), who advocates building rational expectations assumptions into a "New Austrian" theory.

One approach to answering Hicks and Cowen is to point out that even rational entrepreneurs cannot afford to pass up a subsidy. Entrepreneurs face a sort of prisoner's dilemma. If a crash will ensue regardless, as a result of the actions of your peers, why suffer through the recession *and* miss out on the boom? This is a solid response, but a more straightforward problem with the expectations critique is simply that a purist view of rational expectations is entirely implausible. This is not a response restricted to Austrians or their heterodox counterparts on the left: It is a thoroughly mainstream viewpoint.[9]

It would be untenable to argue that human beings are *incapable* of forming fairly accurate expectations about the future. The best expectations formers naturally turn out to be some of the better entrepreneurs, whom Keynes credited with piercing through the "dark forces of time and ignorance that envelop our future" (Keynes 1936, 155). But it is equally untenable to suggest that people can never be fooled or that their expectations form instantaneously. A decade before the financial crisis and shortly after Cowen's book was published in 1997, J. Barkley Rosser (1999, 386) wrote in the pages of this journal just about everything that needs to be said in response to the expectations critique of Hayek: "It is profoundly ironic that just as some of the most influential advocates of rational expectations are moving in the direction of Mises and Hayek as well as Keynes, Cowen is rushing in the opposite direction and defending this movement by labeling it 'New.'"

The kernel of truth in the rational-expectations critique is that it is unacceptable at this stage in the game to leave expectations (regardless of their degree of "rationality") out of our macroeconomic models. Although Hayek was clearly aware of the importance of expectations in the 1930s (see, for example, Hayek 1937), this awareness does not inform his business-cycle theory as it is traditionally rendered.

Fitting the Data

If Cowen's expectations critique is weak, he offers a far more substantial case against the predictions of Hayekian business-cycle theory. Cowen (1997) points out that over the course of the business cycle, investment and consumption move together, a phenomenon he refers to as "co-movement." For at least two reasons, Hayek's theory predicts that investment and consumption should move in opposite directions during the business cycle, with investment rising in the boom and declining in the bust. First, *Prices and Production* assumes that the economy starts in a position of full employment before the unsustainable boom begins. Cowen notes that since the economy is operating at capacity, any increase in capital-goods production has to come at the expense of consumer-goods production. The second reason for the expected differential behavior of investment and consumption concerns the upper turning point, which accounts for the end of the boom with the Ricardian assumption that capital intensification occurs *at the expense* of labor income, and that this tension between capital and labor ends the boom.

Austrians have answered this criticism in at least two ways. Larry Sechrest (1998) offers what can be thought of as a demand-side response: that the growth in capital-intensive production raises the incomes of capital-goods producers, who then engage in more consumption. Roger Garrison (2000, 2004) provides a supply-side response by assuming that capital-intensive production processes are more productive than labor-intensive production processes, so the move to capital-intensive processes can accommodate a simultaneous increase in consumption and investment. Garrison's answer to Cowen is stronger than Sechrest's, as it provides a mechanism for a growing economic pie that affords both consumers and investors a bigger slice. However, it is not Hayek's answer.[10] Hayek clearly expected consumption and investment to move in opposite directions: "An increase in the demand for consumer goods will tend to decrease rather than increase the demand for investment goods" (Hayek 1939, 3). More important, if Garrison's correction of Hayek is accurate, it is not clear what needs to be rebalanced in a market correction (i.e., a recession). Recall that the upper turning point occurred precisely because of the expected tension between consumption and investment. If that tension is explained away by Garrison, then it would seem that the inevitable bust is explained away as well. A business-cycle theory without a bust is not a business-cycle theory at all; it is a growth theory.

Another telling critique of how well Hayek's theory fits the data is Milton Friedman's (1969 and 1993) "plucking model" of the business cycle. Friedman was interested in justifying a monetarist explanation of recessions and wanted to establish that recessions came from monetary mischief, not from booms coming to an end. He cited Mises (and by association, Hayek) as an example of a theorist of recessions that originate in booms. We would expect that if the conditions of the boom set the stage for the bust, then the depth of the bust would be proportional to the height of the prior boom, or at the very least the amplitude of the cycle should be random. A correlation between the depth of a recession and the height of a *subsequent* boom would strongly imply that recessions are the consequence of a shock that had nothing to do with the preceding growth period, and that the recovery was just a reversion of the economy back to its stable growth path. Friedman found that in a data series going back to the late nineteenth century, the depths of recessions correlated with the subsequent boom, not the prior boom. He called this the "plucking model" because it implied that recessions were caused by plucking the economy down from an otherwise steady growth path. In many ways, Friedman's simple empirical exercise offers the greatest blow to Hayek of all the criticisms discussed here. A theory of the unsustainable boom is of little use if busts are not caused by booms.[11]

The criticisms of Hayek's business-cycle theory I have covered are only a sampling of some important instances. Other notable detractors include Wagner (1999), DeLong (1990), Haberler (1986), Yeager (1986), and Hummel (1979). Roger Garrison is easily the most comprehensive respondent to these critics on behalf of Hayek. Generally speaking, Hayek's theory seems to be at its most robust against purely theoretical critiques. Sraffa's concerns merely obligate Austrians to avoid talking carelessly about natural rates of interest.[12] The long-standing criticism of Hayek's treatment of entrepreneurial expectations itself appears relatively retrograde in light of recent work on departures from rational expectations. More serious problems emerge with the critiques that bleed into questions of empirical verification (e.g., Tullock, Cowen on the co-movement of investment and consumption, and Friedman). Austrians have answered these authors, but their defenses of Hayek give the same impression to modern readers that the early attempts to salvage *Prices and Production* gave to Kaldor (1942, 359): that "when one attempted to fill these gaps, they became larger, instead of smaller." Since the empirically flavored criticisms seem to be the most cogent, a sensible next step is to take a closer look at the empirical literature on Hayekian business-cycle theory, to see if Hayek withstands even further scrutiny.

Empirical Evaluations of Hayekian Business-Cycle Theory

Efforts to defend Hayek's business-cycle theory empirically are often underappreciated by Austrians as well as their critics. This literature is not large, but it makes considerable progress in evaluating the validity of Hayek's theory.

One way to organize these studies is to distinguish between what could be called "reduced-form" and "structural" analyses. Reduced-form studies test for macroeconomic outcomes that are predicted by Hayekian business-cycle theory without investigating whether Hayek's theory of why those outcomes are predicted is true. In contrast, structural studies explicitly model the Hayekian mechanisms driving the business cycle (i.e., the lengthening of the capital structure) to test whether these mechanisms behave according to expectations.

A summary of twenty selected empirical evaluations of Hayekian business-cycle theory is provided in an online appendix (http://daniel pkuehn.wordpress.com/empirical-analyses-of-hayekian-business-cycle-theory/). The studies are divided into reduced-form and structural analyses. The variables used by the authors to characterize credit conditions, the capital structure, and the business cycle are each summarized in their own column.[13] A proper survey of this literature is beyond the scope of this article, but the following discussion should provide an organized guide to the typical approaches, and a sense of their strengths, weaknesses, and the most notable findings.

Reduced Form Analyses

Several of the studies can be characterized as reduced-form in the sense that they test whether headline macroeconomic variables such as GDP, investment, or the yield curve behave in a manner predicted by the theory, without trying to model the mechanism underlying this behavior. This approach is limited. Macroeconomic theories typically do not survive long in the marketplace of ideas if they fail to explain basic business-cycle facts, so unless they are carefully justified, reduced-form analyses are typically considered less helpful than "structural" analyses that do model causal mechanisms. Admittedly, the line separating a reduced-form analysis from a structural one is blurry, and the divisions imposed here are by no means immutable.[14]

Reduced-form investigations of Hayekian business-cycle theory naturally highlight the relationship between credit conditions and various macroeconomic aggregates such as output,[15] stock-market indices,[16] or the components of national income.[17] In the case of output measures and stock-market indices, the expectation is that expansionary credit conditions will generate a boom, followed by a bust. Since this line of approach does not attempt to demonstrate whether Austrian *processes* are important, these studies typically identify themselves with Austrian economics by motivating their analyses with a Hayekian theoretical discussion or by invoking Hayek to interpret the patterns in the data. Such an exercise is valuable for placing Austrian theories in the context of well-known macroeconomic regularities, but it is obviously limited in the degree of confirmation that it can offer.

Although the specifications of the reduced-form studies are all somewhat different, their results are comfortingly familiar. Reduced interest rates, increased loans, or larger term spreads are associated with growing investment and output, and for those studies comparing investment to consumption, investment accelerates more robustly than consumption (Mulligan 2005). These are fine results, but their only connection to Hayek is that Hayek (along with every other observant macroeconomist) expected to see these results. Carilli and Dempster (2008) and Hoffmann (2010) provide more intriguing evidence that in the United States and most East European economies, the economic growth associated with reduced interest rates is followed in later months by a decline in output. Of course they consider this suggestive of an unsustainable boom coming to an end. The problem is that *even if* monetary policy was unnecessarily expansionary in these cases, no one doubts that low interest rates encourage investment and that the withdrawal of those rates (perhaps as a result of the realization that policy was too easy) will put downward pressure on investment. There is no obvious reason to attribute this to Hayekian distortions. Additionally, the size of the relationship between interest rates and the lagged reduction in output is quite small in Carilli and Dempster 2008, despite its statistical significance.[18]

Callahan and Garrison (2003) and Schnabl and Hoffmann (2008) are distinctive in that their research interests (the dot-com bubble and bubbles in emerging markets) lead them to test for the impact of interest rates on stock-market indices. They both report the not particularly surprising finding that low interest rates are associated with asset-market booms. Although they cite Hayek and the credit-induced boom extensively, these studies depart most notably from the canonical version of the theory in their focus on the response of financial markets to credit injections, and in the lack of an attempt to estimate the lengthening of the capital structure that is the centerpiece of other investigations.

The reduced-form studies exhibit a range of variables chosen to capture the phenomenon of a credit injection. In addition to natural choices like the volume of commercial and industrial loans or the federal funds rate, two more creative (although differentially advisable) approaches have been tried. Bismans and Mougeot 2009, along with several of the structural analyses, use the "spread," or the difference between short- and long-term interest rates, as a measure of easy credit. This choice is grounded in the assumption that long-term interest rates represent the "natural rate" so that, in equilibrium, short-term rates would be equal to long-term rates. By this logic, the fact that short-term rates are normally lower than long-term rates indicates credit expansion. The problem is that this ignores the liquidity premium: Even in equilibrium we expect long-term rates to be higher than short-term rates because the future is less certain. Lenders require a premium to convince them to part with their liquid funds during progressively more uncertain future periods. Even to the extent that the natural rate of interest informs the level of long-term interest rates, changes in this term spread are as likely to reflect changing levels of uncertainty and liquidity preference as they are to indicate loose money.

On the other end of the spectrum, a much stronger variable for credit conditions is deployed by Carilli and Dempster 2008 and Hoffmann 2010. They use various estimates of the natural rate of interest, derived from the long-run growth rate of the economy, to determine the gap between actual interest rates and the natural interest rate. This is much more consistent with Hayek's understanding of the ultimate causes of the unsustainable boom and is preferable to using the term spread or even the actual interest rate.[19]

Structural Analyses

The overarching problem with even the stronger reduced-form articles is that they have no way of anchoring the relationship between credit conditions and the business cycle to Hayek's ideas about distortions of the capital structure. This effort has been undertaken by others using one of three general strategies.

First, some authors have classified industrial sectors into early and later stages of the production process. For example, extraction industries such as mining are classified as early production stages while retail and wholesale represent later stages. This is the approach taken by most structural analyses for the obvious reason that these data are readily available. Seven studies that use this approach are listed in the online appendix. The problem with assigning industrial sectors to Hayek's production stages is that official industrial classifications were not designed for this purpose. A firm's industry is defined by the sorts of products that it primarily produces for sale, not by the activities that are conducted by the firm. For example, a large manufacturing company is likely to provide its own human resources and management services internally, along with engineering services, transportation, and, in the heyday of the vertically integrated firm, perhaps even raw-material extraction. Each of these activities has its own industrial classification, but the value added from that activity could very well be counted as "manufacturing" if it is done internally.

Andrew Young (2011, 27) describes another problem with independently assigning industries to Hayekian production stages:

> Is "mining" an early stage? How long did it take to create the mining equipment? If some of the equipment was produced in, say, the "manufacturing" industry, is manufacturing an earlier stage? More disconcerting, if the "finance, insurance, and real estate" industry financed the mining industries purchase of equipment from manufacturing, is finance, insurance, and real estate the earliest stage of them all?

His point is that one industry's output is likely to contribute to multiple stages of the production process.

Most of these studies do find a capital structure that lengthens when credit is looser and shortens when credit is tighter. However, results derived from studies that make these arbitrary sectoral divisions are the most dubious of all attempts to model the capital structure, although they may be able to serve as a robustness check for more sophisticated approaches, to ensure that the results are not sensitive to how the capital structure is operationalized.

It is critical for the consumer of the empirical literature on Hayek's business-cycle theory to understand that these investigators are fighting a frustrating uphill battle simply to get intelligible results. The modern public statistical infrastructure is designed around the needs of Keynesian economists of the 1940s and 1950s. There is nothing nefarious about this; Indeed, most economists would agree that the budgets of the agencies that produce these economic statistics are resources well spent. But it does make modeling Hayekian concepts more difficult.

A second, stronger, approach utilizing readily available data is to track price or capacity-utilization changes for different stages of the production process. Examples of stage-of-process studies include Keeler 2001, which works with capacity utilization, and Lester and Wolff 2012, which looks at prices for crude-, intermediate-, and late-stage producer goods. Unlike industrial classifications, which define a *firm's* primary (although not necessarily their only) activity, stage-of-process classifications are associated with *goods*. For example, if a firm that is classified as being in the manufacturing industry purchases a raw material for $100, processes it into a semi-finished good that would sell on the market for $125, and then further processes and sells a finished product to a retailer for $150, those prices will be assigned to earlier and later stage-of-process price indices, even though all of them are associated with the activities of a manufacturing firm. Stage-of-process data are therefore much better at characterizing the capital structure as Hayek perceived it.

The evidence from stage-of-process studies is mixed. Keeler (2001), who uses capacity-utilization data, finds that a steeper yield curve (which he somewhat dubiously interprets to indicate loose monetary policy) is associated with higher capacity utilization in earlier stages of production than in later ones, consistent with Hayek's expectations. Lester and Wolff (2012) use price data for goods at each of these stages and conclude that there is no relationship between unanticipated changes in the federal funds rate and relative prices. They find that semi-finished and primary-production goods (the two intermediate stages) increase the most in response to an unexpected reduction in the interest rate, finished-good prices respond with a somewhat lower price increase, and crude-good prices register almost no increase. Hayekian theory suggests that crude prices should increase the most, due to increased investment in longer production processes.[20]

The most sophisticated empirical research on Hayekian business-cycle theory to date is offered by Andrew Young (2012), who develops a measure of the length of the capital structure rather than relying on qualitative industrial or process classifications. He estimates the position of an industry in the capital structure with the total industry output requirement (TIOR), or the gross value of all other industries' output required by an industry to generate one dollar's worth of that industry's final good. Industries that fall relatively early in the capital structure will use fewer inputs to produce their (gross) output, and so they will have a lower measured TIOR. Using this method, Young (2012) calculates the TIOR for sixty-five industries, and determines that the aggregated length of the capital structure measured using his methods is pro-cyclical and closely correlated with the federal funds rate from 1998 to 2009, as Hayekian theory suggests.

One problem with this measure that Young (2012) points out is that it is not clear how much meaning can be ascribed to a given change in the TIOR. From 2008 to 2009, the aggregate TIOR fell from about 1.8 to a little over 1.7. Is this a large change or a small one? Does it matter for macroeconomic fluctuations? At this point, it is difficult to say.

If nothing else, the empirical work suggests that Kaldor (1942, 363) was quite wrong in dismissing the lengthening of the structure of production as "one of those blind alleys of economic speculation which appear very suggestive for a time, but whose significance evaporates as soon as one tries to fit the theoretical conclusions more closely to the observed phenomena." The theoretical discussion fits the best analyses of the observed phenomena quite well. Questions remain, however, about the strength of the Hayekian mechanisms or their significance for the business cycle.

Despite these intriguing findings, the empirical literature on Hayekian business-cycle theory is small and mostly restricted to Austrian venues (and therefore somewhat sheltered from non-Austrian peer review).[21] Much of it is also unpersuasive. However, a spate of papers on the subject by doctoral students offers hope that in the future a stronger empirical literature will be built on the foundation that is summarized above. Research by five of these doctoral students is reviewed below.

Empirical Doctoral Research

A common exercise in the literature on the scientific workforce is to evaluate the "pipeline" of researchers, to see if a sufficient supply of scientists is making its way through the academy to support a research agenda in the future. Although the number of students interested in Austrian economics is inevitably small, several doctoral students are currently doing empirical work on Hayekian business-cycle theory. Since only a handful of established Austrian economists do empirical business-cycle theory work, this suggests that the outlook for robust growth in this area is quite positive.

Cameron Weber (2009), a doctoral student at the New School for Social Research, develops an aggregate measure of the length of the capital structure, much like Young (2012), using a weighted sum of production stages that he assigns to various industrial sectors. This approach is similar to many other studies, but Weber's unique contribution is to look at changes in the capital structure over the long run, rather than over the business cycle. He finds, as Austrian capital theorists would suspect, that long-run growth in the United States has been associated with capital-structure lengthening. Other doctoral work is equally innovative in its approach to Hayek. Nicolas Cachanosky (2012), of Suffolk University, explores the differential impact of a credit expansion on the capital structure of tradable and non-tradable goods in a small open economy. Open-economy considerations are fundamental to assessing the ultimate impact of national economic policies and forces, but they have been relatively neglected by Hayekian business-cycle theorists. Cachanosky therefore offers a bridge between Austrian macroeconomics as it is practiced and a vibrant element of the mainstream literature. Robert Lester and Jonathan Wolff (2012), both doctoral students at the University of Notre Dame, are co-authors of the structural analysis using stage-of-process data discussed above, which is one of the few studies that fails to find evidence in favor of Hayek. Finally, Richard Whittle (2012), of the Manchester Metropolitan University Business School, adopts the stage-of-process measure approach to modeling the capital structure used by Keeler 2001 to test the behavior of the British capital structure in response to variations in credit conditions.

The Stance of Monetary Policy

Many authors of empirical studies of Hayekian business-cycle theory have assumed that a relatively low interest rate implies loose monetary policy. This is a sin of commission; monetary policy may be tight under low interest rates or loose under high interest rates, depending on the value of the natural rate of interest. Others are content with setting aside the question of the monetary policy stance entirely by restricting analysis to the behavior of the capital structure over the business cycle or in response to credit conditions regardless of whether they are "loose" or "tight." This is a sin of omission but surely a forgivable one, given the difficulties posed by even that restricted research question.

Ultimately, though, identifying the stance of monetary policy is critical for assessing the usefulness of Hayekian business-cycle theory, even if it is firmly established that the length of the capital structure is pro-cyclical.[22] Even a stripped-down version of Hayek's business-cycle theory, jettisoning all the Rube Goldberg mechanisms, has *at least* two steps:

(1) Loose credit conditions lead to an artificially lengthened capital structure.

(2) An artificially lengthened capital structure leads to the end of the boom.

Young (2012) and others offer credible evidence that the capital structure lengthens during the boom and shortens during the bust. But if the stance of monetary policy is not also pro-cyclical, it is doubtful whether the mechanisms described by Hayek are critical for macroeconomists to consider.[23]

The stance of monetary policy can be thought of as loose if the real federal funds rate is below the real natural rate of interest, and tight if it is above the real natural rate. Overall credit conditions will determine the length of the capital structure, which may fluctuate with time preference even when monetary policy is entirely neutral. But the stance of monetary policy—its relative tightness or looseness—is what is critical for generating an *unsustainable* lengthening of the capital structure. Determining the real value of federal funds rate is trivial, but identifying the "natural rate of interest" is not as straightforward. The best estimates available are provided by Laubach and Williams (2003, and periodically updated), who use data on inflation and output to determine the interest rate consistent with stable prices and the economy operating at its full potential. Figure 1, below,

Figure 1. The Monetary Policy Stance

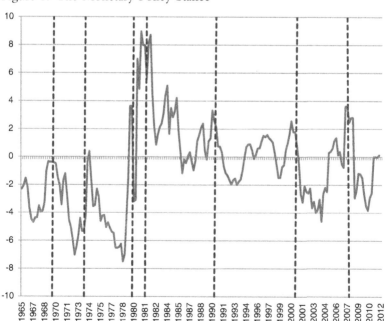

Source: Author's calculations from Laubach and Williams 2012, National Bureau of Economic Research 2012, and the Federal Reserve Bank of St. Louis FEDFUNDS data series.

subtracts this estimated natural rate from the real federal funds rate. If this difference is equal to zero, then the actual federal funds rate set by the Federal Reserve is equal to the best estimate of the natural rate of interest, and monetary policy is neutral. A positive value for the difference indicates tight monetary policy, while a negative value indicates loose monetary policy. Vertical lines are provided to indicate the start date of recessions, as determined by the National Bureau of Economic Research.

It is difficult to conclude from the estimates of the monetary stance in Figure I that Hayek's sequence—loose money, followed by the elongation of the capital structure, followed by an upper turning point, ending in recession—is the dominant experience for most of the postwar period. From 1965 until the late 1970s, monetary policy is persistently expansionary, through boom and bust alike. At the beginning of the 1969 and the 1973 recessions, money becomes tighter than it had been previously, which (given the error implicit in estimating the natural rate) may confirm Hayek's theory. However, the monetary stance never actually tightens between 1965 and 1980, nor does it even stay neutral for long. If Hayek is correct this should still be a period of unprecedented capital accumulation, malinvestments, and capital intensification, because the brief return of interest rates to their neutral position in the late 1960s and mid-1970s was immediately abandoned for continued loose monetary policy. This would imply a buildup of tension between the distorted capital structure and the true time preference of the population, leading to the endogenous emergence of a major recessionary episode. Although a large recession did occur in 1980, it is widely acknowledged that this downturn was deliberately (i.e., exogenously) caused by Paul Volcker at the Federal Reserve, and that it was not the result of any endogenous tendencies in the economy. Volcker orchestrated the recession to end the inflation of the 1970s, which is particularly awkward for Hayekians since the reduction of real wages by price inflation was supposed to be the source of the upper turning point and the end to the boom. After fifteen years of expansionary monetary policy, these endogenous forces were clearly not up to the task that Hayek had assigned to them: the task that Volcker accomplished.

The recessions of the 1960s and 1970s at least have the virtue of exhibiting the pro-cyclical (albeit persistently loose) monetary stance required by Hayek. Far less is available for Austrians to work with in the case of the 1981–82 and 1990–91 recessions, which were not preceded by any monetary loosening at all. Regardless of the actual level of the real interest rate, if this rate is not *below the natural rate*—if monetary policy is not expansionary—there can be no unsustainable boom that would be explained by Hayekian business-cycle theory. The capital structure may change in response to the real interest rate, but the unsustainability of these changes is contingent on loose monetary policy.

In the most recent recession, monetary policy returns to the natural rate of interest in late 2005, several years before the crisis. Laubach and Williams's estimates of the natural rate are admittedly imprecise, but estimates of the Taylor rule concur that monetary policy ceased being loose a few years before the financial crisis of 2008 (Taylor 2009). Hayekians who think that the capital structure lengthens and contracts with the price signals sent by monetary policy are confronted with an awkward question: Exactly what were entrepreneurs thinking between 2005 and 2008? The distortion in the price signal communicated by the interest rate had already been revealed. There was nothing preventing the capital structure from adjusting back to what was dictated by time preference in a recessionary event. But rather than being wracked by a rebalancing of the capital structure and the abandonment of unprofitable investments in 2006, the global economy was shaken by panic over a particular class of financial assets in 2008. These are two quite different stories about the onset of the Great Recession.

If Hayek offered a reasonable characterization of the business cycle we would expect to see a loose monetary stance before recessions that returns to its natural rate *and is maintained at the natural rate* during recessions. This does not appear to characterize the recessions of the postwar period, including the Great Recession. Many empirical analyses of Hayek's theory have established that some plausible proxy for the length of the capital structure moves with the interest rate in the way that Hayek predicted. However, it is critical to distinguish between a change in the interest rate itself and a change in the stance of monetary policy (loose or tight). Low interest rates do not indicate loose monetary policy if they are consistent with low time preferences. Hayek's theory requires a loose monetary stance to generate the business cycle and an unsustainable boom, not just *any* instance of low interest rates.

An Alternative Interpretation of the Significance of Hayekian Theory

To illustrate the importance of the link between the central bank's departure from the natural rate of interest and the validity of Hayekian business-cycle theory, consider a hypothetical case where Hayek is exactly right about the behavior of the capital structure, but the relationship between the interest rate and the business cycle is more Keynesian.

Keynesians contend that the interest rate is not the reward for parting with savings *per se*; it is the reward for parting with (and is the price paid for) liquidity. Parting with only a small amount of liquidity, for example in a demand deposit that can be drawn on at any time, pays only a small amount of interest. Parting with more liquidity by tying up assets for longer periods of time will pay higher levels of interest. This is known as the liquidity-preference theory of the interest rate.

A Keynesian view of the interest rate would suggest that recessions occur when some negative shock to entrepreneurial expectations (perhaps a financial crisis) causes a flight to liquidity and to the security that the ownership of liquid assets provides. Demand for *both* capital and consumer goods is reduced relative to what it would be in the absence of the shock, because households and firms will sacrifice both consumption and investment to stay liquid. At the same time that the demand for liquidity increases, however, potential lenders require a higher interest rate to part with liquidity than they required before the shock. As a result, the monetary stance is *tighter* than it was before the shock: investors face higher interest rates than otherwise, and higher than the "natural rate" consistent with full employment.[24] In this hypothetical case, we would expect to observe that:

(1) During non-recessionary periods, a certain length of the capital structure would be maintained, consistent with time and liquidity preferences.

(2) When a recession hits, the flight to liquidity raises the interest rate above the natural rate of interest that is consistent with full employment and stable inflation (i.e., the monetary stance tightens).

(3) The tighter monetary stance makes the capital structure of the full employment economy unprofitable, and entrepreneurs are incentivized by the tighter monetary stance to *shorten* the capital structure.

In other words, we should observe the very pro-cyclicality in the length of the capital structure identified by Young (2012) and others— even if the capital structure plays no role in bringing on recessions. In this case, the "natural" length of the capital structure is the relatively elongated capital structure of the full-employment economy. The unnatural, distorted capital structure is the shorter capital structure of the recession, when the flight to liquidity drives interest rates higher. This suggests that a pro-cyclical capital structure is not, on its own, proof of Hayekian business-cycle theory: An entirely different business-cycle theory, combined with Hayek's understanding of capital theory, can account for the same data.

The most defensible attitude towards the critics of Hayekian business-cycle theory is therefore one of sympathy and affirmation. But these critics are often too quick to dismiss the whole project of Hayek's early work in macroeconomic theory (i.e., up to and including *The Pure Theory of Capital* in 1941).

Hayek's arguments about the capital structure were eminently logical and entirely consistent with mainstream economic analyses of relative prices. It is no wonder that the empirical literature seems to find evidence for longer capital structures during the boom. The critics need to be more open to these insights, and pivot their discussions away from the question of whether Hayek has adequately theorized the capital structure and toward the question of whether Hayek was attending to the right phase of the business cycle. Another way of putting this point is to say that the relative lengthiness of the capital structure in growth years, and the relative shortness of the capital structure in recessions, does not mean that it is *too long* during growth years and *just right* during the recession (as Hayek theorized). It may be the case that it is just right during growth years and too short during the recession.

The empirical literature reviewed above is frustrating insofar as it does nothing to clarify whether Hayek's interpretation of the capital structure is correct or whether the alternative interpretation that I have provided is correct. However, Keynesianism's ability to explain other facts of the Great Recession, such as the unusual behavior of inflation and interest rates,[25] suggests that my alternative interpretation may have merit, and that while Hayek had important insights into capital theory, most economists have correctly declared his business-cycle theory unconvincing.

Integrating a Hayekian capital theory with Keynesian macro-economics should be easier than one might suppose. Both Hayek and

Keynes ultimately derived their understanding of capital theory from William Stanley Jevons. Hayek inherited Jevons' view through the work of the Austrian economist Eugen Böhm-Bawerk, and Keynes inherited it through the English economist Alfred Marshall. Böhm-Bawerk and Hayek highlighted Jevons's emphasis on the fact that the production of goods is not instantaneous; it takes place over time. Keynes was also concerned with the fact that capital goods were used over time, but he drew attention to expectations about the stream of future returns that would be earned from a quantity of capital. We might say that Hayek thought about the "intensive" temporal structure of capital—how temporally intensive a given production process is—while Keynes thought about the "extensive" temporal structure of capital: the way that the returns to capital extend into future periods. Both emphasized the relationship between time and capital heterogeneity and the impediments they imposed to smooth macroeconomic adjustments. Keynes and Hayek were also both deeply concerned with entrepreneurial expectations.

The most substantial obstacles to integrating Hayekian capital theory and Keynesian macroeconomics is likely to be differences of opinion on the determination of the interest rate, with Keynesians insisting (particularly since entering a liquidity trap) on a role for liquidity preference. Aside from these technical difficulties, Keynesians and Hayekians simply conceive of interest rates in different ways. Both are dedicated to the idea that the interest rate communicates valuable price signals, but Keynesians worry about the interest rate acting as a limiting and even distortionary influence on investment during recessions. Hayek, in contrast, was concerned that interest rates will present the opposite problem by being pressed too low during booms. In addition to being two different economic theories, these are two fundamentally different mindsets that seem to resist reconciliation. For Hayek, the unsustainable boom and the concept of the capital structure appear to be inextricably linked, although there is no necessary reason for this.

*　　　　　　*　　　　　　*

For a long time, Hayek's business-cycle theory has been ignored by most economists. This diversion away from Hayek is not entirely unjustified, but a consequence has been that more has been lost from Hayek by the mainstream than is really necessary. It is not lost, however, in the community of Austrian economists and interested historians of economic thought that continue to debate Hayek's theory and have recently commenced testing it empirically. The limited empirical literature indicates that Hayek was right about the dilation of the capital structure in response to changing credit conditions, a finding that should be of interest to mainstream and Austrian economists alike.

Attempts to link findings on the capital structure to the business cycle have been considerably less satisfying, and have largely ignored (or improperly operationalized) Hayek's view that a loose monetary stance—not simply a low interest rate—is required to make a boom unsustainable. The relationship between loose money and subsequent busts in the post-war United States is quite weak, though. As Milton Friedman (1969 and 1993) pointed out many years ago, there is a much stronger link between busts that are independently caused by tight money (and not by a preceding boom).

In light of the weak evidence for Hayek's "unsustainable boom," it seems far more plausible that Keynesian (or monetarist) forces drive the business cycle, and that the capital structure—behaving in an otherwise purely Hayekian manner—lengthens and contracts as a consequence of the business cycle, rather than as its cause. As always, more research is required to confirm this interpretation, but in light of the repeated failure of Hayekian business-cycle theory to clear the hurdles it is presented with, the suggestions offered here seem to be worth the effort of further exploration.

NOTES

1. Hayek's ideas are occasionally referred to as "Austrian" throughout this article, but it is important to keep in mind that there were other Austrian commentators on the business cycle besides Hayek, principally Ludwig von Mises and Murray Rothbard, as well as various monetary disequilibrium theorists. These perspectives are in many ways comparable, but not always identical, to Hayek's—for example, Garrison 2004, 327 describes Mises's business-cycle theory in *Human Action* (1966) as "largely compatible with Hayek's formulation but not obviously so"—but they are not considered here. Most discussions of "Austrian business-cycle theory" do seem to have Hayek's business-cycle ideas in mind, but to avoid confusion I will refer here to Hayek's own theory, leaving a broader review of Austrian macroeconomics to other, more capable hands.

2. See Block and Garschina 1996 for a review of the difference between Hayek and certain other Austrians on the question of the culpability of the banking industry in general. Garrison 2000 even discusses the prospect of fiscal policy or transfers initiating the credit expansion, although this is not a typical approach.

3. In other words, the interest rate was either the cost of credit faced by the firm or it was the opportunity cost of funds already held by the firm. In both cases firms would be more willing to engage in longer production processes if the interest rate were lower than if it were higher.

4. Kaldor (1942, 376) sums up his argument in this way: "However hard we try, we cannot construct a case where as a result of a rise in the rate of profit the capital intensity falls and as a result of this fall in capital intensity, investment expenditure will be less than it was before. To argue in this way involves the same fallacy as saying that because a rise in demand for a commodity will cause a rise in its price, and the rise in price causes a restriction in demand (because less is bought at a higher price than a lower price), the increase in demand will lead to a reduction in the amount bought."

5. Garrison (2000, 72) describes the switch from boom to bust as a situation where "entrepreneurs encounter resource scarcities that are more constraining than was implied by the pattern of wages, prices, and interest rates that characterized the early phases of the boom." The capital structure is simply unsustainable because the price signals gave false information: He makes no reference to pressure to switch away from capital-intensive production through a Ricardo Effect.

6. For example, Lucas (1977) cites Hayek as a personal inspiration in thinking about business cycles as an equilibrium phenomenon. We have to trust Lucas to identify his own inspirations, but the parallel is not exact. Hayek is probably better thought of as offering a theory of how equilibrium forces generate a recession as a correction to a prior disequilibrium.

7. Keynes's discussion of Hayek's book is often characterized as something of a cheap shot, because it actually appeared in a response to Hayek's critical review of Keynes's own *Treatise on Money*. Context is helpful in assessing the accusation. While the use of this opportunity to review Hayek was certainly unorthodox, Keynes discussed *Prices and Production* at length precisely because Hayek inserted his own theories into the original review of Keynes's book, discussing Keynes as if he had been working with Hayek's theories and ideas. Keynes (1931, 388) cited and discussed *Prices and Production* in his reply to address this point, alleging that by starting down this road Hayek was "looking for trouble." One casualty of the preoccupation with the etiquette of Keynes's reply is that people often ignore how substantive his discussion of *Prices and Production* was. An important element of the reply was one of the earliest direct criticisms from Keynes of the naïve loanable-funds theory of the interest rate. This criticism would later form the heart of *The General Theory of Employment, Interest, and Money* (1936).

8. This is because each good trades for different amounts of future versions of itself: An interest rate is simply how much of itself a dollar will trade for at some time in the future.

9. It probably is not entirely fair to say that anyone ever really "believed" rational expectations. Rather, it was a modeling convention that helped to highlight the impact of rationality in expectations, even if that rationality was only partial. Indeed, Cowen (2000) indicates that this is his own view in his reply to Rosser 1999. Of course, this has not prevented some economists from continuing to make arguments that implicitly depend on a stronger version of rational expectations.

10. There are ways to patch up these inconsistencies between Hayek and Garrison. One could assume that Garrison's unsustainable growth comes through consuming existing capital equipment or neglecting capital maintenance. But

this poses further problems. On an empirical level, expenditures on capital maintenance are known to grow during booms. But aside from that, capital consumption and the neglect of capital maintenance would weaken economic growth. The prospect of stronger growth was the whole point of Garrison's argument. Salvaging Garrison's response to Cowen by invoking capital consumption or the neglect of capital maintenance robs Peter to pay Paul. Presumably other patches are available, but none of them offer the clarity or parsimony of Cowen's critique. A helpful reviewer of a draft of this paper suggested a possible resolution that would bolster Garrison's case by relying on the creation of new businesses and the simultaneous neglect of investment in complementary factors of production required for sustaining those new businesses in the future. This would increase total output, supporting high levels of both investment and consumption (Cowen's co-movement), without necessitating the neglect of capital maintenance, which is known to be pro-cyclical.

11. Garrison (2000, 222–24 and 235–43) has responded to Friedman as well. He claims that the plucking model does not disprove Hayek's business-cycle theory so much as it suggests that the capital structure remains undistorted by monetary fluctuations over the business cycle. This seems to me to be a distinction without a difference.

12. An obligation I will ignore in the interest of exposition below, with the only defense being that I am not constructing a formal model.

13. In many cases, multiple variables were used for these purposes. For example, Keeler 2001 uses both the slope of the yield curve and the money supply to characterize credit conditions.

14. For example, in the online appendix, Mulligan 2005 and Bismans and Mougeot 2009 are classified as "reduced form" even though they justify investigating differentials between capital- and consumer-goods expenditures and prices on Hayekian grounds. Although Hayekians place a special emphasis on these variables, they are not unique to the Hayekian model. In contrast, studies looking at different stages of production or production periods are designated as "structural" because they are investigating a uniquely Hayekian construct. These are, admittedly, judgment calls.

15. See Carilli and Dempster 2008, Bismans and Mougeot 2009, and Hoffmann 2010.

16. See Callahan and Garrison 2003 and Schnabl and Hoffmann 2008.

17. See Mulligan 2005 and Bismans and Mougeot 2009.

18. Young (2011) argues that reporting statistical significance without considering whether results are meaningfully large is a pervasive problem in the literature on Hayekian business-cycle theory. I tend to agree with him.

19. This point will be discussed in more detail in the next section.

20. Keeler's (2001) use of capacity utilization for the dependent variable is also not ideal. If investment in a production process increases, capacity utilization may stay exactly the same if utilization of the new production capacity increases at the same rate.

21. A notable exception is Young 2005, which was published in *Economic Letters*.

22. My view is that the evidence to date does indicate the likely pro-cyclicality of the length of capital structure, but that these results are still highly preliminary.

23. Despite the advances in econometrically operationalizing the capital structure, to my knowledge only Carilli and Dempster 2008, discussed above, explores whether the monetary policy stance conforms to Hayek's theory. But this paper

fails to consider the capital structure at all, and while some of its results are statistically significant, it does not suggest a meaningfully large effect of loose monetary policy on output.

24. Another critical factor keeping the market rate of interest above the natural rate in the Great Recession is the liquidity trap associated with the "zero lower bound." When interest rates are at or near zero, investors are indifferent between cash and bonds and the Federal Reserve cannot reduce interest rates further. The Federal Reserve's inability to affect interest rates using conventional monetary policy does not necessarily imply that unconventional means are unavailable. Neither the liquidity trap nor the question of unconventional monetary policy is directly relevant to the arguments made in this article, but these issues are critical for understanding interest-rate behavior in the specific case of the Great Recession.

25. See Krugman 2012 for details.

REFERENCES

Akerlof, George, William Dickens, and George Perry. 2000. "Near-Rational Wage and Price Setting and the Long-Run Phillips Curve." *Brookings Papers on Economic Activity* 2000(1): 1–44.

Bismans, Francis, and Christelle Mougeot. 2009. "Austrian Business-Cycle Theory: Empirical Evidence." *Review of Austrian Economics* 22(3): 241–57.

Blaug, Mark. 1968. *Economic Theory in Retrospect*. Homewood, Ill.: Richard D. Irwin.

Block, Walter, and William Barnett, II. 2007. "On Laidler Regarding the Austrian Business-Cycle Theory." *Review of Austrian Economics* 20: 43–61.

Block, Walter, and Kenneth Garschina. 1996. "Hayek, Business Cycles, and Fractional Reserve Banking: Continuing the De-Homogenization Process." *Review of Austrian Economics* 9(1): 77–94.

Boettke, Peter J. 1994. "Alternative Paths Forward for Austrian Economics." In idem, ed., *The Elgar Companion to Austrian Economics*. Cheltenham: Edward Elgar.

Cachanosky, Nicolas. 2012. "The Mises-Hayek Business-Cycle Theory, Fiat Currencies, and Open Economies." *Review of Austrian Economics*, doi. 10.1007/s11138-012-0188-2.

Callahan, Gene, and Roger Garrison. 2003. "Does Austrian Business-Cycle Theory Help Explain the Dot-Com Boom and Bust?" *Quarterly Journal of Austrian Economics* 6(2): 67–98.

Callahan, Gene, and Steven Horwitz. 2010. "The Role of Ideal Types in Austrian Business-Cycle Theory." In *What Is So Austrian about Austrian Economics?* Vol. 14 of *Advances in Austrian Economics*. Ed. Roger Koppl, Steve Horwitz, and Pierre Desrochers. Bingley, U.K.: Emerald.

Carilli, Anthony, and Gregory Dempster. 2008. "Is Austrian Business-Cycle Theory Still Relevant?" *Review of Austrian Economics* 21: 271–81.

Conrad, Joseph W. 1959. *An Introduction to the Theory of Interest*. Berkeley: University of California Press.

Cowen, Tyler. 1997. *Risk and Business Cycles*. London: Routledge.

Cowen, Tyler. 2000. "Risk and Business Cycles: Reply to Rosser." *Critical Review* 14(1): 89–94.

Davis, Steven J., John C. Haltiwanger, and Scott Schuh. 1996. *Job Creation and Destruction*. Cambridge, Mass.: MIT Press.

DeLong, J. Bradford. 1990. "'Liquidation Cycles': Old Fashioned Real Business-Cycle Theory and the Great Depression." National Bureau of Economic Research Working Paper No. 3546.

Ebenstein, Alan. 2003. *Friedrich Hayek: A Biography*. Chicago: University of Chicago Press.

Friedman, Milton. 1969. *The Optimum Quantity of Money, and Other Essays*. Chicago: Aldine.

Friedman, Milton. 1993. "The 'Plucking Model' of Business Fluctuations Revisited." *Economic Inquiry* 31(2): 171–77.

Garrison, Roger. 2000. *Time and Money: The Macroeconomics of Capital Structure*. London: Routledge.

Garrison, Roger. 2004. "Overconsumption and Forced Saving in the Mises-Hayek Theory of the Business Cycle." *History of Political Economy* 36(2): 323–49.

Haberler, Gottfried. 1986. "Reflections on Hayek's Business-Cycle Theory." *Cato Journal* 6(2): 421–35.

Hagemann, Harald, and Hans-Michael Trautwein. 1998. "Cantillon and Ricardo Effects: Hayek's Contributions to Business-Cycle Theory." *European Journal of the History of Economic Thought* 5(2): 292–316.

Hayek, F. A. 1931. *Prices and Production*. New York: Macmillan.

Hayek, F. A. 1937. "Economics and Knowledge." *Economica* New Series 4(13): 33–54.

Hayek, F. A. 1939 [1975]. *Profits, Interest, and Investment*. Clifton, N.J.: Augustus M. Kelly.

Hayek, F. A. 1941. *The Pure Theory of Capital*. Chicago: University of Chicago Press.

Hayek, F. A. 1944. *The Road to Serfdom*. Chicago: University of Chicago Press.

Hicks, John R. 1967. "The Hayek Story." In idem, *Critical Essays in Monetary Theory*. Oxford: Clarendon Press.

Hoffmann, Andreas. 2010. "An Overinvestment Cycle in Central and Eastern Europe?" *Metroeconomica* 61(4): 711–34.

Hummel, Jeffrey. 1979. "Problems with Austrian Business-Cycle Theory." *Reason Papers* 5: 41–53.

Kaldor, Nicholas. 1942. "Professor Hayek and the Concertina Effect." *Economica* New Series 9(36): 359–85.

Keeler, James. 2001. "Empirical Evidence of the Austrian Business-Cycle Theory." *Review of Austrian Economics* 14(4): 331–51.

Keynes, John Maynard. 1931. "The Pure Theory of Money: A Reply to Dr. Hayek." *Economica* (November): 387–97.

Keynes, John Maynard. 1936. *The General Theory of Employment, Interest, and Money*. London: Macmillan.

Krugman, Paul. 2012. *End this Depression Now!* New York: W.W. Norton.

Lachmann, Ludwig. 1956 [1978]. *Capital and Its Structure*. Kansas City, Kans.: Sheed Andrews & McMeel.

Laidler, David. 2003. "The Price Level, Relative Prices, and Economic Stability: Aspects of the Interwar Debate." Paper presented at the Bank for International Settlements Conference on Monetary Stability, Financial Stability and the Business Cycle, Basel, March 28–29.

Laubach, Thomas, and John Williams. 2003. "Measuring the Natural Rate of Interest." *Review of Economics and Statistics* 85(4): 1063–70.

Lester, Robert, and Jonathan Wolff. 2012. "The Empirical Relevance of the Mises-Hayek Theory of the Trade Cycle." Working paper, University of Notre Dame.

Lucas, Robert E. 1977. "Understanding Business Cycles." *Carnegie-Rochester Conference Series on Public Policy* 5(1): 7–29.

Machlup, Fritz. 1977. "Friedrich von Hayek's Contribution to Economics." In *Essays on Hayek*, ed. Fritz Machlup. London: Routledge.

Mises, Ludwig von. 1966. *Human Action: A Treatise on Economics*, 3d rev. ed. Chicago: Henry Regnery.

Mulligan, Robert. 2005. "The Austrian Business Cycle: A Vector Error-Correction Model with Commercial and Industrial Loans." *Journal of Private Enterprise* 22(1): 51–91.

Murphy, Robert. 2010. *Multiple Interest Rates and Austrian Business-Cycle Theory*. Paper presented at a 2010 Liberty Fund Conference. http://consultingbyrpm. com/uploads/Multiple%20Interest%20Rates%20and%20ABCT.pdf.

Rosser, Barkley. 1999. "Between Vienna and Cambridge: The Risky Business of New Austrian Business-Cycle Theory." *Critical Review* 13(3–4): 373–89.

Samuelson, Paul. 2009. "A Few Remembrances of Friedrich von Hayek (1899–1992)." *Journal of Economic Behavior and Organization* 69(1): 1–4.

Schnabl, Gunther, and Andreas Hoffmann. 2008. "Monetary Policy, Vagabonding Liquidity, and Bursting Bubbles in New and Emerging Markets—An Overinvestment View." *World Economy* 31: 1226–52.

Sechrest, Lawrence. 1998. "Book Review, *Risk and Business Cycles: New and Old Austrian Perspectives.* By Tyler Cowen. London: Routledge, 1997." *Quarterly Journal of Austrian Economics* 1(3): 73–79.

Skidelsky, Robert. 2009. *Keynes: The Return of the Master*. New York: PublicAffairs.

Sraffa, Piero. 1932. "Dr. Hayek on Money and Capital." *Economic Journal* 42(165): 42–53.

Subrick, J. Robert. 2010. "Money Is Non-Neutral." In *Handbook on Contemporary Austrian Economics*, ed. Peter Boettke. Northampton, Mass.: Edward Elgar.

Taylor, John. 2009. *Getting Off Track: How Government Actions and Interventions Caused, Prolonged, and Worsened the Financial Crisis*. Stanford: Hoover Institution Press.

Tullock, Gordon. 1987. "Why the Austrians Are Wrong about Depressions." *Review of Austrian Economics* 2: 73–78.

Wagner, Richard. 1999. "Austrian Cycle Theory: Saving the Wheat While Discarding the Chaff." *Review of Austrian Economics* 12: 65–80.

Weber, Cameron. 2009. "An Empirical Application of the Austrian School's 'Stages of Production.'" Working paper, New School for Social Research.

Whittle, Richard. 2012. "Austrian Business Cycles: From Theory to Empirics." Paper submitted to Research Institute for Business and Management Doctoral Symposium.

Yeager, Leland. 1986. "The Significance of Monetary Disequilibrium." *Cato Journal* 6(2): 369–420.

Young, Andrew. 2005. "Reallocating Labor to Initiate Changes in Capital Structures: Hayek Revisited." *Economics Letters* 89(3): 275–82.

Young, Andrew. 2011. "Illustrating the Importance of Austrian Business-Cycle Theory: A Reply to Murphy, Barnett, and Block: A Call for Quantitative Study." *Review of Austrian Economics* 24(1): 19–28.

Young, Andrew. 2012. "The Time Structure of Production in the U.S., 2002–2009." *Review of Austrian Economics* 25(2): 77–92.

Index

Printed in the United States
by Baker & Taylor Publisher Services